Scenario Based Strategy

To Iris

For your love, faith and active support
For making my dreams come true

Scenario Based Strategy

Navigate the Future

PAUL DE RUIJTER
With Henk Alkema

Routledge
Taylor & Francis Group

LONDON AND NEW YORK

First published 2014 by Gower Publishing

Published 2016 by Routledge
2 Park Square, Milton Park, Abingdon, Oxfordshire OX14 4RN
711 Third Avenue, New York, NY 10017, USA

First issued in paperback 2016

Routledge is an imprint of the Taylor & Francis Group, an informa business

British Library Cataloguing in Publication Data
A catalogue record for this book is available from the British Library.

The Library of Congress has cataloged the printed edition as follows:
Ruijter, Paul de.
  Scenario based strategy: navigate the future / by Paul de Ruijter.
    pages cm
  Includes bibliographical references and index.
  ISBN 978-1-4724-3717-4 (hardback) -- ISBN 978-1-4724-3718-1 (ebook) -- ISBN 978-1-4724-3719-8 (epub) 1. Strategic planning. 2. Business planning. I. Title.
  HD30.28.R847 2014
  658.4'012--dc23

                                                                          2013048247

ISBN 13: 978-1-138-24743-7 (pbk)
ISBN 13: 978-1-4724-3717-4 (hbk)

Contents

List of Figures

Preface

Why another book about strategy? My business and engineering studies at the University of Twente in Enschede were mainly about 'minding the shop' – a little less costs, a little more turnover. This was completely the opposite of the idea I had about strategy being proactive and creative, as the youngest son of an entrepreneur. When I was looking for a subject for my Master's thesis, I read an article by Arie de Geus, coordinator of Group Planning at Royal Dutch Shell. He described the way in which Shell was already thinking about the possibility of an oil crisis prior to 1973 and consequently was able to recognize many opportunities when the crisis actually happened. Being proactive, involving the outside world and responding to it; for me that was real strategy!

Inspired by the article by De Geus, I decided I wanted to work with him and Shell. In 1992 I rang his department, Group Planning, but I found out he had already retired. Thanks to his successor I was given the opportunity to work there for six months and I was allowed to write my Master's thesis on how Shell used scenarios to develop strategy. At that time 15 people at Shell had already been working for 18 months on a vision for the future, which resulted in two possible scenarios. These scenarios were presented to more than 1,000 employees in 67 workshops, so they could be used in strategy creation. As the 'new recruit' I was mainly responsible for hanging up flip-charts and typing out the reports, but even in my modest role I was immediately involved in the most difficult part of scenario planning: using scenarios to create a dynamic strategy.

And that is what this book is about: strategy; not military strategy, but organizational strategy. How do you put the future on the agenda of your organization? How do you make your organization deal with this uncertain future and with the outside world? How can your organization contribute to this world? And how do you do that collaboratively with your colleagues? In many organizations people are busy with their own plans, and overlook the significance of contributing to the future and to the outside world. From childhood I learnt I had to use my talents for society, that I had to subordinate my own plans for the greater good, in order to create value for society. In classic books on strategy creating strategy always starts with your own goal. To me this is self-indulgent. It can be done differently, as I learnt at Shell.

A second social obligation which is deeply rooted in my upbringing is personal responsibility. My father never talked about his 30 employees, but about the 30 households for which he felt responsible. It is important to think about the long term: because of your employees, but also because of those to whom you deliver products or services. To me strategy also includes the responsibility to think further ahead. The reality is that everyone in an organization can and should contribute to strategy creation; this also I learnt in 1992.

Feeling personally responsible for putting the outside world and the future on the agenda – that sounds like a heavy burden. At the same time it is liberating. By thinking about possible developments in the future before they happen you create space and opportunities. By being ahead of the problem you have alternative options besides sink or swim. This forward-looking approach is much more valuable than solving problems after they have happened or only taking action in response to crises, which is what many managers do. The world is continuously changing. The economic, technological and political winds keep changing direction. A good strategic thinker prepares his or her organization, so it is always 'ready to tack' – the words which are shouted on a sailing ship immediately prior to changing direction. Aimless drifting is replaced by goal-oriented navigating. Shell's strategy of thinking ahead about a possible oil crisis turned the first oil crisis in 1973 into an opportunity for the company instead of a problem: Shell was ready to tack. The organizations which subsequently followed Shell's example enjoyed the same experience. Thus Rabobank was already mentally prepared for a possible economic crisis before 2007 and therefore better equipped than other banks: it was also ready to tack.

To everyone who is not satisfied simply with control and solving problems after they have arrived, but who wants to make a positive contribution to thinking about the future, this book offers the instruments to turn this intention into practice. *Scenario Based Strategy: Navigate the Future* is written for all strategic thinkers at all levels of the organization: from marketing staff to researchers or human resource advisers. It can be used within commercial organizations, government or trade organizations. This book contains many examples which show how others have undertaken future explorations and how they used these explorations to create a dynamic strategy.

Strategic thinking is a competence which is passed on from generation to generation. I owe a debt of gratitude to those from whom I learned. First of all to my father, and then to the people at Shell who taught me, such as Jaap Leemhuis, Graham Galer and Kees van der Heijden. Later in my career I met Henk Alkema. Henk, who in 1971 created the now famous scenarios about which Pierre Wack and Arie de Geus subsequently wrote. I am proud that he wanted to share knowledge, insights and ideas with me during the long talks and discussions which helped to create this book. Many insights in this book have arisen from my practice. The challenging work for Rabobank has particularly helped to create these ideas. So, I would like to thank Philip Idenburg, Henk Vlessert, Daniël Erasmus, Wim Boonstra and Cees Onderwater, with whom I was allowed to bring all this knowledge into practice over the last ten years in several departments at Rabobank. The nautical and military analogies in this book are no coincidence: Martijn Schouten of shipbuilder IHC, and Sebastian Reyn and Captain Kees Turnhout of the Ministry of Defence showed me clearly how old strategic thinking actually is. It is a competence which deserves to be transferred to future generations. I hope this book will contribute to that.

Paul de Ruijter, Amstelveen 2014

Introduction

We need strategy. The world around us is changing constantly. The future is uncertain and great vision is required. What will the future bring? Where are we going? What is our business idea? This book is a manual for all those who want to apply strategy in organizations: business leaders, CEOs, strategists, planning staff, or others. It is intended for everyone who wants to put the future on the agenda, to look beyond mere profit and further than just the short term. It describes in practical terms the eight questions we must continuously discuss in order to pursue a future-proof strategy in a dynamic and uncertain world.

But what is strategy exactly? And what is an organization? To understand one another and get started, we need to be using the same definitions.

I.1 Strategy Versus Problem-solving

Why did Shell emerge from the first oil crisis even stronger than before, leaving its competitors behind? What made the Rabobank prepare for the credit crunch as early as 2003? The reason Shell and Rabobank were able to act proactively and to undertake actions *before* problems became urgent is because they were acting strategically instead of engaging in reactive problem-solving.

Strategy originated long before the modern age, with the very first kings and generals. Our word strategy is derived from the Greek words '*strategia*' (generalship or command) and '*strategos*' (general), which in turn stem from the Greek words for army ('*stratos*') and leader ('*agos*'). Strategy therefore originally applied only to warfare, and continued to do so until the nineteenth century. Carl von Clausewitz (17801831), a Prussian general and military theorist, was an influential thinker in the field of military strategy. In his book *On War*, published posthumously in 1832, he used the following definition of strategy: 'Tactics is the theory of the use of military forces in combat, strategy is the theory of the use of combats for the object of the War'.[1]

We can distinguish between operations, tactics and strategy. In the art of warfare, strategy referred to the way in which an army manoeuvred before and after the actual battle. Tactics meant the way in which this battle was fought, and operations referred to the actual combats. Military commanders from Alexander the Great to Eisenhower deployed huge armies within the context of their strategies, which focused on the acquisition or liberation of territory – a question of definition. And then, there are several ways of acting strategically. Some strategists are focused on beating the competitor: they

---

1   Clausewitz [1832] 1997: 75.

are playing a game of chess. Other strategists are involved in the Asian game of Go, trying to gain as much ground as possible.

One of the most famous Dutch naval heroes, Michiel de Ruyter, was a great strategist. To prepare for battles at sea, he thought through possible scenarios and trained his men by means of mock battles. This brought any flaws and possible misunderstandings to light before the real battles began, avoiding problems along the way.[2] De Ruyter thought ahead and instead of trying to defeat individual ships, in 1667 his best-known raid targeted the naval base of the English fleet in Chatham.

However, we can also apply the terms operations, tactics and strategy to the world outside the battlefield. People who think operationally only tend to think in terms of implementation. A tactical thinker, on the other hand, is already thinking a few steps ahead. For example, if you were playing chess you might sacrifice a pawn to get another piece closer to your opponent's King during the next move: a tactical move. Strategic thinkers think further than just a few moves ahead. While the military aspect of getting people or actions in a single line remains, we interpret strategy within organizations more in the sense of planning. *The Oxford English Dictionary* defines strategy as: 1 the art of planning and directing overall military operations and movements in a war or battle; 2 a plan of action designed to achieve a long-term or overall aim.

If you do not think strategically, you tend to stumble from one problem to another and can only take action when empirical research indicates that a problem exists. This often causes problems, because it can take weeks, months or sometimes even years before policy leads to action and action to results. After all, if you wanted to construct a new factory, it would be a good idea to start building it before you actually need it.

Strategic thinking is the opposite of problem-solving thinking and starts in the future, allowing possible problems to be resolved before they even occur (see Figure I.1). A strategic thinker does not wait until empirical data shows that there is a problem; he looks ahead. This enables him to act before the data even indicates that a problem exists. Good preparation can therefore transform possible future problems into challenges or

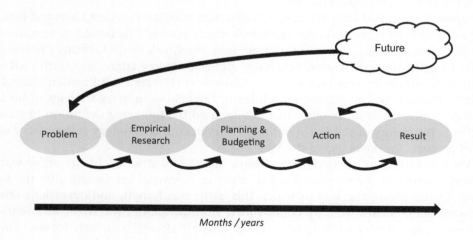

Figure I.1   Strategic thinking

---

2   Rietdijk and Van Winden 2003: 19.

even opportunities. A fundamental difference between problem-solving and thinking and acting strategically is that the first activity is powered by data and empirical facts: you are looking in the rear-view mirror, so to speak. The second activity, on the other hand, assumes a theoretical future for which no data (yet) exists. Whilst this future cannot be forecast, it can still be imagined. The strategic thinker looks through the front windscreen instead of glancing at the rear-view mirror, and makes sure he is always ready for change.

In my opinion, strategy in the broad sense involves the whole of the mission, vision, goals, plans and image of an organization in the long term, all in constant contact with the outside world. It therefore comprises more than strategy in the narrow sense: how to get from A to B. This is what I call a strategy plan or 'roadmap'.

I.2   What is an Organization?

Nowadays, military organizations still use scenarios for strategic thinking. In 2009, the Dutch Ministry of Defence initiated the Future Policy Survey project, in the scope of which it developed four scenarios for the future of the Netherlands' Armed Forces. The Multiple Futures Project of NATO is a similar exercise using the Allied Command Transformation (ACT) scenarios to cope with future uncertainties. This book, however, is not only applicable to military strategy, but also to organizational strategy. We should therefore establish exactly what constitutes an organization. The strategy books I read in the 1980s generally used the following definition: an organization is the whole of the resources and instruments which are used to achieve a specific goal. The people and resources serve the same single goal, such as making a profit. If you define an organization in this way, the strategy logically begins with the goal. For me, this is the traditional way of defining an organization. Only later did I realize that this was the Anglo-Saxon viewpoint which dominated strategic thinking at the time, and that most of these management books came from the US. Research by Fons Trompenaars and others has shown that the above-mentioned definition of an organization, also known as the *shareholder model*, is a highly American definition (see Figure I.2).[3]

In the projects I carried out for the Dutch government, companies and associations as well as in my father's company, I realized that you cannot always define an organization only as an entity of people and resources with a single goal. On the contrary: not only did my father's company have 30 employees each with their own goals and interests, it also had 30 families who depended on the organization. For example, one idea was to put the shares into a foundation, which would not only include the future shareholders (us children) but also the employees.

The way an organization was founded, its articles of association and the way the organization is governed tell us something about its focus. To use Rabobank as an example again, this bank was founded as a cooperative and therefore is obliged to always serve the customers' interests first. The judicial context of corporate governance is different in each country. In the Netherlands, it is embedded in laws which supervisory boards, although elected by the shareholders, do not only focus only on the shareholders'

---

3   Trompenaars and Hampden-Turner 1998.

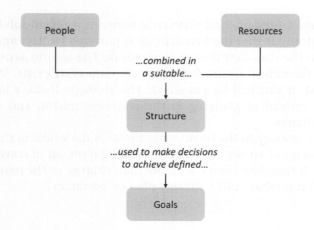

Figure I.2   Shareholder model

interests, but on the continuity of the organization as a whole – which means all stakeholders must be taken into consideration. On top of that, an employees' council secures the interests of the employees. In Germany, employees' representatives have a seat in the *Aufsichtsrat* or supervisory board, meaning that shareholders and employees are on an equal footing.

Once you grasp the extent of the web of mutual dependencies which often surrounds an organization, with stakeholders varying from government and employees to environment and even the management itself, you realize that the *shareholder model* is not always sufficient to describe the nature of an organization because the shareholder does not seem to be the dominant stakeholder in every organization. There appears to be an additional way of defining an organization: the organization as a *stakeholder model* (see Figure I.3). This is called the Rhineland model in analogy with the German organizational model in which employees sit on the board.

The stakeholder model considers organizations to be networks of relationships. Agreements are reached between the various parties, both members and non-members of the organization, and actions are undertaken to maintain the relationships. These relationships are formalized by contracts: an employment contract describes the relationship between the employer and the employee, and an order confirmation is the formal reflection of the relationship between the organization and its customer. There is an extensive network of relationships. Such organizations are often referred to as if they were people: 'Rabobank is thinking about the future', 'Shell has developed scenarios'. Although on paper these organizations only consist of contracts, a detailed strategic conversation develops in practice. This organization does not focus on a single goal, as is the case with the shareholder model, but on maintaining relationships in which each has its own goals.

In the stakeholder model, the organization is regarded as a social system and not, as it is often considered in strategic circles, as something mechanistic and autonomous like a machine or a computer. In this model, the organization is viewed as a so-called self-referential system: it exists only because we have agreed that it exists and these agreements are laid down in written documents. From a strictly legal point of view, organizations

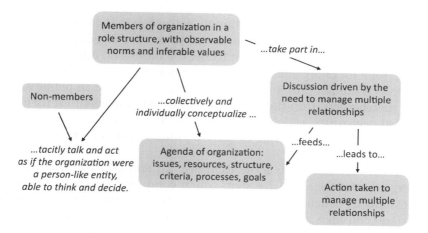

Figure I.3   Stakeholder model (after Peter Checkland)

therefore exist only by virtue of statutes, which we recognize as such by social consensus – just as bank notes represent no value other than the value we have all agreed upon. The statutes therefore form the essence of the organization; they are the written reflection of the relationships which a group of people has agreed upon among themselves. However, alongside legal agreements, an organization has many other written and unwritten agreements: its own ethics, its own 'soul'.

The important message which follows from this is that the way an organization sees itself determines how the organization will act. Just as there were in the 1980s, there are still various ways of looking at an organization. The way you look at an organization – as a *shareholder model* with the shareholder as the dominant stakeholder, a *stakeholder model* considering all stakeholders on an equal footing, or a combination of these – is a matter of choice. Is the organization a living community, or is it purely an instrument for achieving certain goals? Whilst it is not necessary to choose between the definitions, it is important to realize where you are coming from. Looking at the organization as a *shareholder model*, you might be slightly more inclined to prioritize short-term interests (of the shareholders or traders), while in a *stakeholder model* long-term considerations could be predominant.

In the shareholder model as well as in the stakeholder model both long- and short-term interests exist. Two variables determine which of these interests prevail: the first is the question whether you have share*holders* or share*traders*. In recent years we have witnessed a trend of shareholders becoming sharetraders, thus focusing less on the long term. The second variable is the degree of loyalty of stakeholders. Nowadays, not only shareholders but clients, employees and management tend to show less loyalty to an organization. Following from these observations, an important question arises: who is responsible for the collective interests of an organization and its stakeholders in the long run? Who 'owns' the long-term interests of the whole?

Sometimes it may be strategically useful to focus on interests other than those of the organization itself (*stakeholder model*); in The Netherlands, this is one part of the job of the supervisory board. At other times, in the interests of the continuity of the organization it will sometimes be necessary to focus on the organization itself and its own goals (*shareholder model*). It is important to realize that in the long term, shareholders and stakeholders have the same interest: that is, to create a bigger pie instead of merely dividing it. On the other hand, we cannot ignore the short-term interests of shareholders.

Of course, for a lot of organizations switching between the *shareholder model* and the *stakeholder model* is not relevant: many private organizations and all public organizations do not have shareholders, thus the *shareholder model* is not relevant for them. And stock exchange-listed companies, which do have shareholders and therefore do have a choice between the models, can still decide to place another stakeholder than the shareholder in the centre of attention.

Therefore, an organization is more than just 'an entity of people and resources'. I regard an organization as a social system which comprises a network of interpersonal relationships and in which the shareholder also benefits from long-term continuity.[4] Peter Checkland considers an organization as a network of relationships; the strategy of an organization comprises the desired end states, goals, vision, ideas, plans and mission of people in this network. This has fundamental consequences for the strategic thinker: seen in this light, strategy differs significantly from merely establishing the vision and the path to achieving it, as stated in most of the Anglo-Saxon literature.

According to Fons Trompenaars, strategy can also be considered as a conversation amongst the group of stakeholders in which mutual agreements are made. When shaping strategy, it is also beneficial to mobilize the collective intelligence; as long as they are well-organized, groups are smarter than the sum of the individuals. In the strategy process, you can tap into this collective intelligence by means of workshops, for example. The strategic thinker in you has to facilitate the strategic conversation: your task is to mobilize the knowledge which is already present in the people and thus enable the strategic process.

In a research conducted by Trompenaars, managers from different cultures were questions about the way they viewed organization. They could choose between two definitions of a business: the Anglo-Saxon definition (A) 'A business is the entity of people and resources with the goal of making profit' and Peter Checkland's Rhineland definition (B) 'A business is a network of relationships en is there to fulfil the needs of all stakeholders, including the shareholders'. The answers were revealing: 55 per cent of the Americans opted for definition A. The majority of the Dutch, German and French managers, on the other hand, chose definition B, with 56, 66 and 74 per cent respectively.[5]

I.3   The Need for a *Dynamic* Strategy

Strategy is often defined as a single plan for achieving 'the' goal of 'the' organization. This presupposes that the situation of both the organization and the environment is static. Single, linear plans are involved. However, if strategy is all the goals and plans taken together, if organizations are networks of people who each have their own aspirations and if we also find ourselves in a dynamic and unpredictable environment, a static

---

4   Although an organization is not regarded in this book as something with its own right to exist, but instead as a socially constructed system of relationships, for the sake of convenience this book will still regularly use the term 'organization' as if the organization were a person-like entity.

5   Turner and Trompenaars 1993.

organization and static strategy are not really useful. Many organizations therefore stopped using strategy all together: it did not work, because the plans were already out of date before the ink had a chance to dry.

Although planned economies – the entirely centrally managed economies which were mainly encountered in communist countries – disappeared from Europe at the macro level in 1989 with the fall of the Berlin Wall, today many countries and organizations still have their own planned economies and believe that their future can be shaped entirely as they wish. This static strategy formulation method focuses heavily on goal-setting, budgeting and bonuses: from May to October, people are busy calculating budgets right down to two decimal places. There is a fixed procedure for establishing the strategy; this is a linear process. The strategy is based on forecasts and only takes into account a single possible future, a single truth. There is a need for consistency and a single line in order to achieve 'the goal'. There is no place for uncertainty in the conventional strategy formulation process. For example, I once analyzed the multi-year plans of a medium-sized bank insurer. Everything had been calculated to two decimal places, but every year the forecasts were out by several tens of per cent. Whilst it is true that some elements in the future can be regarded as certainties, there are never enough of them to create a *single-line* forecast which takes the remaining uncertainties and possible changes into account to a sufficient extent.[6]

The need for forecasts partly arises from our need for budgets. We constantly enter into future obligations, despite the changeability of the environment, and thus take responsibility for some of the uncertainties of the future. For this reason, we would dearly like 'certainty about the future'. However, forecasts exist by virtue of the idea that tomorrow's world will be the same as the world of today. At some point, the forecasts will therefore be found wanting, precisely when they are most needed. The Amsterdam historian Geert Mak expressed this idea very well:

All forecasts, no matter how different they may be, have one thing in common: they project into the future what a society regards as the most modern elements at that time, both in the positive and the negative sense. The forecast future has no unexpected flaws, no imagination. It generally says more about the current time than the future, and without exception it demonstrates great self-assurance.

Geert Mak[7]

In addition, there is virtually zero chance of the future working out exactly as stated in the forecast: the chance of getting it wrong is far greater than the chance of getting the forecast completely right. Forecasts are therefore a dangerous surrogate for genuine thought in uncertain times. Even the forecasts by so-called 'experts' (for example about the macro economy) are consistently off the mark, not to mention the fact that the economic predictions of for example Moody's and other institutes often vary greatly.[8] Figure I.4 shows predictions of the oil price in the past, expressed most frequently in very precise straight line extrapolations of the past, and often very wrong.

---

6   Wack 1985a: 77.

7   Mak 2002: 437–8.

8   Rabobank 2009.

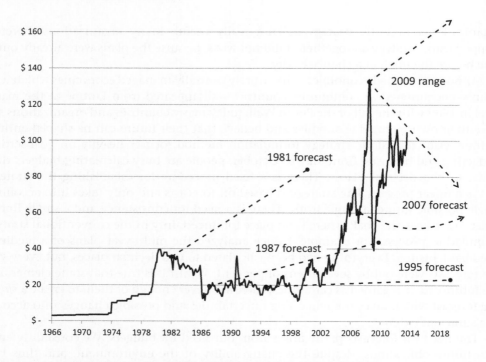

Figure I.4   Oil price forecasts and subsequent developments
Sources of data: Dow Jones & Company, US Energy Information Administration, International Energy Workshop

Fortunately, for those who are willing to look, other conversations which focus on the uncertain and changing future also take place in every organization, often between people in various positions. They discuss uncertainties and the possibility of multiple futures, and in these conversations people tend to hit the nail on the head more often. However, these conversations often occur around the coffee machine and tend to be poorly structured, informal and far removed from the formal planning cycle. You can also tackle strategy formulation differently and place the future on the agenda in a structured way: by bringing formalized and hypothesized certainties up for discussion you can embrace uncertainty instead of excluding it and make it part of your strategy. Whilst the uncertainty and changeability of the future are unavoidable, you can try to turn them to your advantage. After all, anyone can sail in good weather, but it is the bad weather which identifies the good sailors! It is liberating to view uncertainty and change as a challenge.

If you think about uncertainty in a structured and formalized way, strategy formulation is no longer a dull fixed procedure but instead becomes an iterative process and a pleasant conversation. This process is not only financially driven. In fact, it involves all the functions of the organization, from personnel policy to R&D and from production to marketing, and finance follows. There is room for intuition. This creates a social process which works on the basis of several possible future scenarios. This strategy formulation method is not a goal in itself but a tool which provides a broad spectrum of possible outcomes. The budget does not disappear from the picture completely: the options which appear successful on the basis of the scenarios may form a bridge between scenario planning and conditional budgets.

Recognizing uncertainty in the future environment of the organization and working with the multiple perspectives of the people within the organization forces you to develop a dynamic strategy. Thinking in this way, you do not work on the basis of an official view of the future, but take multiple future scenarios into account. Paradoxically, it is precisely the construction and use of multiple future scenarios which can provide something concrete to go on by stating uncertainties, identifying opportunities and threats, making conditions measurable, creating options for getting out or for upscaling, as the case may be. A dynamic strategy provides more control than a static budget (see Figure I.5).

Budget	Strategy
Single plan	Several outcomes
Procedure	Social process
Financially oriented	Involves all departments
Linear	Dynamic
Forecast: • One future • Implicit uncertainty	Scenarios: • Several futures • Explicit uncertainty
Consistency	Room for intuition

Figure I.5   A budget is not a strategy

However, scenarios do not replace budgeting: they are complementary to it. Therefore, it is very important to establish a connection between your strategy and the budgeting process. When you use scenarios for strategic planning, you have to make sure that they become part of the planning and control cycle. The link between scenarios on the one hand and planning and budgeting on the other is essential for your strategy to actually be executed. The success of the use of Shell scenarios lay not in the fact that Shell developed scenarios, but that the scenarios were included in the planning and budgeting cycle.

To make sure a strategy formulation process is dynamic, strategic conversations about a minimum of eight topics have to be involved: mission, trends, scenarios, options, vision and roadmap, and in addition, constant monitoring and action is involved – between the future and now, and between inside and outside. Some of the conversations are about what is happening inside the organization, and others are about events outside the organization. All these conversations intermingle and may take place at the same time. It is down to you to structure and formalize them. Figure I.6 below shows all the eight topics in coherence. In the rest of this book, this figure will constantly indicate where we are, both in terms of time (now or in the future) and place (inside or outside the organization).

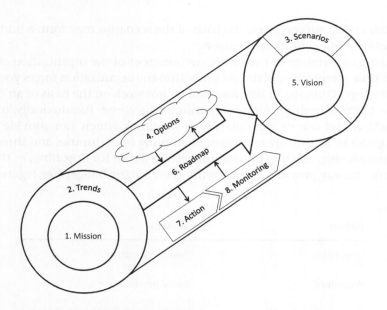

Figure I.6   Strategy in the broad sense

I.4   Eight Strategic Topics

Various definitions of strategy and organization have now been put forward. What should a person who feels responsible for an organization's strategy do? In order to pursue a dynamic strategy formulation process, it is the responsibility of the leadership to ensure that the following eight strategic topics are on the agenda within the organization and to structure and formalize these processes. It is also their task to ensure that these conversations lead to action. However, everybody inside and outside, from top to bottom can start or join the debate. You will find that all eight topics are constantly discussed in every organization, but often in an unstructured way and with no action being taken as a result. This leads to delays and miscommunication, and sometimes even to strategic blunders and frustration. In order to avoid this, the strategy formulation process can be facilitated, lending structure to the whole, initiating any missing conversations, keeping track of mutual relationships and the link with the implementation process. In addition, you can make (interim) results visible in an accessible way. In light of the constant changes and uncertainties in the environment, the strategy formulation process is an iterative one.

1. MISSION: WHAT IS THE REASON FOR THE ORGANIZATION'S EXISTENCE AND WHAT IS THE KEY TO ITS SUCCESS?

Sometimes an organization forgets the reason for its existence and loses sight of its 'calling': it goes adrift. This is the right time to bring up the conversation about the mission of the organization. Self-insight is essential in every organization, because the way an organization sees itself determines how it will act. Is the organization a machine which aims to make as much profit as possible? Or does the organization see itself as a community of people with complex relationships and multiple, sometimes even conflicting, goals? What is the mission of the organization and what are the associated core values? What is the success formula (the business idea)? The way the organization sees itself, its mission, its environment and its working methods greatly influences the conduct of the organization and whether it is able to keep all of its stakeholders happy, and therefore whether it is able to maintain relationships and be successful. If you are new to an organization, this is a logical conversation to begin with.

2. TRENDS: WHAT IS HAPPENING AROUND US?

If the organization is too self-centred, there is the risk that it might overlook developments outside the organization, just as the crew of a ship might overlook currents and wind conditions. At this point, it is sensible to focus the attention of the organization on the outside world. After all, if you want to be prepared for the future, you must be aware of the external environment. This involves drawing up an inventory of the developments, events and shifting trends over which the organization itself may not have any direct influence, but which could still affect the organization. Here, you can make use of empirical data from the past: trends and counter-trends. This conversation can involve both employees and other stakeholders, experts and outsiders: they all have valuable knowledge, expertise and powers of imagination. Exploring the environment involves drawing up an inventory which leaves no stone unturned: it is important to focus on the widest possible range of subjects and not only to concentrate on facts, but also on ideas, opinions and observations. Here, one could mention demographic, economic, environmental, political, technological and social developments. Driving forces and uncertainties with regard to these developments can then be mapped. As well as the contextual factors, the actions of relevant external parties such as clients, suppliers, competitors and legislators can also be mapped out. This provides greater insights into the outside world and leads to new and improved strategic questions.

3. SCENARIOS: IN WHICH SITUATIONS COULD WE END UP?

Even if the organization has a clear picture of what is happening in the outside world, it is often difficult to use this information in a structured way. Moreover, this information reveals nothing about what the *future* of the organization might bring. Which 'icebergs' remain in our path? Or in other words: in the future, which situations could we end up in? Merely coming up with a list of possible future developments and events is not sufficient. To get the most out of exploring the environment, it is best to combine these developments in a meaningful way, with the aid of modelling and scenario thinking, to form a number of sufficiently different, complex visions of the future: scenarios. This will lend significance to the information which has been found. Scenarios represent future environments in which the organization could end up, but over which it has no influence. The use of scenarios enables you to mobilize knowledge and powers of imagination within the organization. You can bring dreams and nightmares out into the open, addressing emotions as well as reason. The organization will then have the future on the agenda, together with a common language for discussing strategic issues in a structured way. Developing a number of different future scenarios is not a goal in itself. After all, a set of scenarios does not actually provide any concrete plans. Scenarios are tools for structuring information and making it meaningful, so that people in the organization can make increasingly well-considered decisions. For example, scenarios provide better insights into future risks and opportunities.

4. OPTIONS: IS OUR CURRENT COURSE FUTURE-PROOF AND, IF NOT, WHAT CAN WE DO TO MAKE IT SO?

In every organization, it is important to establish a connection between possible future circumstances and the course taken by the organization. If this connection is in danger of disappearing, it is down to you to breathe new life into it. Projection into future scenarios makes it possible to test whether the current organization and plans are future-proof and helps to come up with options which will allow the organization to flourish under any circumstances. In other words: what can the actual organization do in order to prepare for certain situations? In order to make this clear, all the options which are open to the organization will be mapped. These options will then be evaluated in the situations described in the scenarios. Which options are relevant and feasible in every scenario, and are therefore robust or future-proof? Which options are successful under certain circumstances (call options) and which would it be better to stop if certain developments occur (put options)? Existing activities can also be tested by comparing them with the scenarios which then act as stress tests (wind tunnels): what would be the consequences of these activities in the scenario situation? Do they turn out as they should, and do they contribute to achieving the vision or not?

5. VISION: WHERE DO WE WANT TO GO, WHO DO WE WANT TO BE?

The scenarios cover possible situations in which the organization might find itself and over which the organization has *no* influence. They only describe the external environment and do not comprise any actual plans or policies. Options are a long list of the action prospects and possibilities for action which are open to the organization for dealing with these situations. At the same time, it is important to know what the organization regards as the ideal situation. Organizations become more strategic when you create and conceptualize a vision. The vision is about where the organization wants to go and how everything should ideally look. By thinking about the desired end state as an organization (community, company, association etc.) together with all the stakeholders, a shared vision arises. The vision links the non-manageable future outside world and the manageable future inside world and thus provides direction. The desired end state is a hypothetical point of reference used to clarify future strategic choices.

6. ROADMAP: HOW DO WE GET THERE?

In order to take action, you need a step-by-step plan: a strategy in the narrow sense of the word, the path from A to B. This was often regarded as the core of strategy: creating and guiding the conversation about what I call the 'roadmap'. This may also be a multiple step-by-step plan or time schedule where you plot different routes, stating the circumstances under which you would choose each one. Creating a roadmap is a question of looking back from the desired end state and determining which steps the organization must take between the present and the future, under various circumstances, to achieve this ideal picture. The vision forms the starting point of this 'backcasting' process, the opposite of forecasting. The distance from the vision to the current situation is determined and backcasting is used to develop a roadmap, which also takes into account possible future developments as described in the scenarios. Ultimately, the roadmap describes in practical steps where the organization is now (the mission), where it wants to go in the future (vision) and which actions it must perform to get there. It outlines the route which may lead the organization from the current situation to the future and gives concrete shape to this route. Ideally, the roadmap will also describe the division of tasks: who will do what, when and how?

7. ACTION: FROM TALKING TO ACTING

As stated earlier, it is very important to link strategy on the one hand and tactics and operations on the other. It is not enough to work out a strategy: the organization must take action and continue to do so. Therefore, scenarios and strategy must be included in the planning and budgeting cycle.

There needs to be space within the organization for the power of imagination and the necessary creative energy and that these are formalized, structured and channelled, so that people become inspired and feel that they are part of the strategy. This action can be initiated by getting people to cooperate in workshops in which they create something together. When people are able to share their view of the path to the future and everyone can contribute, their enthusiasm with regard to the implementation of the roadmap will increase.

8. MONITORING: TO STAY ON COURSE

It is not enough for an organization to merely have a dynamic strategy. An essential activity is the continuous monitoring and measurement of developments inside and outside the organization. It is down to you to draw attention to the fact that time never stands still and the organization must therefore keep focusing on the changing inside and outside world, that scenarios need to be updated when necessary, options need to be exercised or activities need to stop. In brief, you must establish whether the organization is still on course and whether everyone is still where they should be. Tracking certain signals as indicators of change gives the organization an early idea of how the future is unfolding. The measured information serves as an input for the various strategic conversations. Dynamic strategy is an iterative and never-ending process!

1

Mission:
What is the reason
for the organization's
existence and what is the
key to its success?

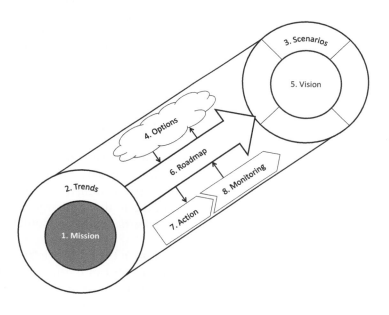

Self-insight and self-analysis are indispensable in every strategy. Because if you want to determine where you are heading, you ought to know your point of departure. After all, strategic decisions are about the future but they carry a past as well. The luggage aboard is equally important as the harbour and the course. A navigation system is useless if you do not know where you are and when it comes to navigation, it does make a difference whether you travel in a small speedboat, a cruise ship, a large tanker or even maybe a fleet of ships.

The sign at the gateway to the Oracle of Delphi said: 'Know thyself': an assignment from the god Apollo to visitors coming by to consult the Oracle. This was useful advice to the ancient Greeks but it still is very relevant to the modern strategist seeking to determine the route. I remember an ongoing discussion at Shell in 1992 about the question of whether Shell was an oil and gas company or an energy company. This discussion was crucial to Shell, because self-image determines direction. When the calls from society for wind and solar energy became ever louder, Shell had to decide how to react. When you consider yourself an oil and gas company, you do not want to be involved in wind and solar energy. But when you consider yourself an energy company, it makes perfect sense to invest in these new, sustainable technologies.[1] And self-image can change; something Shell knew first hand. In 1907 Royal Dutch Shell started as a collaboration between N.V. Koninklijke Nederlandse Petroleum Maatschappij (Royal Dutch) and Shell Transport and Trading, a company the founder started in 1833 trading shells – hence the name – but subsequently decided oil transport would be an interesting business. If Shell had stuck to their self-definition of being a transporter of shells, the company would have ceased to exist, but because it placed its identity in a broader perspective and changed its self-definition, it could become involved in oil transport and, together with Royal Dutch, grow into a multinational which is still here, almost two centuries later.

When you want people in your organization to think about the identity of the organization, two elements are essential: the mission and the formula for success. Both elements ('who are we and where are we now?') will be elaborated in this chapter, because they are fundamental as a starting point in the other strategic conversations.

1.1   What is our Mission?

WHAT IS THE ADDED VALUE OF OUR ORGANIZATION?

The use of the word 'goal' often creates confusion, because it is more indicative of what you want to achieve – long-term or short-term, in broad sense or narrow sense – than of what you do or who you are. Also 'mission' (derived from the Latin *mittere*, which means to send) is used in different contexts: from the military mission in Afganistan to the missonary work in Africa, and from *Mission Impossible* to the diplomatic missions of governments abroad.

However, in this chapter the word 'mission' is used in the sense of a 'greater cause', the reason for the existence of the organization. This greater cause can seldom be achieved within a set time, and is the starting point of all of the more concrete goals which an organization sets itself. In fact, the mission shows why the organization was established in the first place and the reason for its existence. The mission not only expresses the field of expertise of the organization, but also who or what the organization is by describing the core values or principles of the organization. While the field of expertise is still variable, the core values have deeper roots: in the case of Rabobank the core values are described as 'nearby, involved and leading', and in the mission statement of the Dutch police: 'to be vigilant and to serve'. Thus the mission is threefold and consists of its statutory goal, what the organization does, and why it does this (its higher purpose or core value). The mission forms the ethical foundation for the organization and exists as the value system underpinning each contract the organization enters into. In this way the mission gives meaning to relationships: with employees, with customers, with suppliers and with shareholders.

---

1   Later in this chapter we will return to this issue.

The mission has a major influence on the organization at a fundamental basis. The formulation of the mission can also have a major influence on its way of working. Take for example the mission of social housing corporations: to provide affordable housing to people who can't provide this themselves. However, there is a huge difference between 'affordable housing' defined in terms of just the rent or the total housing expenses. I experienced this in a strategy project involving a social housing corporation. With energy prices increasing, the total household expenses, including for those in social housing, increase even though the rent stays almost unchanged. The question as to whether social housing corporations should help their tenants, e.g. by insulating houses and apartments (for example, with double glazing), depends entirely on the formulation and the interpretation of their mission. Do they just provide housing with affordable rents? Or is it their mission to keep the total household expenses on an affordable level for the less fortunate?

THE MISSION OF SEVERAL SOCIAL HOUSING CORPORATIONS[2]

- *Wonen Zuidwest Friesland* 'Being dedicated to the customer Wonen Zuidwest Friesland provides housing services to everyone, in a pleasant and healthy living environment in South-west Friesland. The core of the mission is: housing services, dedicated to the customer, pleasant and healthy living environments for all.'
- *Rhenense Woningstichting (RWs)* 'As a social entrepreneur RWs is a professional supplier of good, affordable and appropriate housing in a pleasant living environment. RWs provides housing to everyone in the region and primarily to those who have difficulties in providing this for themselves. In addition, RWs aims to organize and/or facilitate good and appropriate service levels, with special attention on wellbeing and care. To realise this RWs works actively together with its stakeholders.'
- *Woningbouwvereniging Stadgenoot* 'Working with passion on quality for everyone, in a city to be cherished.'
- *Woningbouwcorporatie Vestia* 'Vestia is an entrepreneurial organization which implements good living for everyone and for vulnerable groups in particular, in a socially involved and creative way.'
- *Woningbouwvereniging Helpt Elkander* 'The motivation of Helpt Elkander is to offer affordable and attractive housing in a viable and sustainable living environment.'
- *Woningbouwvereniging Beter Wonen* 'Beter Wonen simply sees its name as its mission: improved living. Our organization is continuously working to contribute to an improved housing situation and living environment of its customers. We do this starting with involvement; in the broadest sense of the word. Only involvement in the whole spectrum of living eventually leads to real, intrinsically improved living!'
- *Woningcorporatie WoCom* 'Customized housing in a *livable* environment.'

---

2   As found on their websites, December 2010.

'Mission' and 'motto' are often confused. To distinguish one from another, consider the following definitions: a mission articulates why the organization exists, while a motto (derived from the Latin *movere* which means 'to move') summarizes the mission, e.g. by only mentioning the core values. The motto can be used to position the organization as a brand. Philips uses as its motto 'Innovation and You' (which replaced 'Sense and simplicity' in 2013 which replaced 'Let's make things better' in 2004) and the Foundation Children's Stamps has 'For children by children'.

WHY: THE IMPORTANCE OF SELF-KNOWLEDGE

Why is it important to have a conversation about the reason for an organization's existence? The answer is simple: who you are, determines what you do. This applies to both individuals and organizations: when you define yourself and place yourself in a certain group, this may lead you to overlook, consciously or unconsciously, competitors from outside this group. You only have an eye to what is inside your world. These are cases in which the mission and the formula for success are a dangerous obstacle; the unwritten law of the Hare and the Tortoise is a reminder that successful organizations become lazy. These companies are aware of changes in their environment, but prove unable to respond adequately because they are blinded by their mission and their adherence to an efficient process. This leads to 'active inertia' and to decline of the organization: the new, fresh thinking which created the success in the first place is now replaced with rigid defence of the status quo and with acting on autopilot. When changes in the outside world become apparent, the mission and the strategy which were successful at first now make the organization unable to meet these changes. The moment organizations which are apparently blooming find themselves victims to their own way of thinking and working, four things happen: the strategic framework becomes a blinder, processes become routine, relationships (with employees, customers, suppliers, distributor and shareholders) become ties and values become dogmas.[3]

But there is hope! History shows that a number of leading organizations, such as Shell and Rabobank, proved themselves able to react to changes in the outside world without giving up their mission. To avoid inflexibility you must first ask yourself what could possibly obstruct the organization, and focus attention on the existing strategic framework, processes, relationships and values, before you take any action to instigate change. It is often not necessary (and undesirable) to break completely with the past. In many cases the strategic framework, processes, relationships and values can be rearranged to face up to new challenges whilst showing respect for the heritage of the organization. So it is important that you make the organization know itself and at the same time understand how its mission and formula for success can work as a disadvantage.

All of this underlines the need to engage in a conversation about the mission of the organization and the explanation of that mission. The aim of such a conversation is not necessarily to change the mission, but to sense, check and internalize it. Does everyone know the mission? Is the mission still valid? Is it necessary to rephrase the underlying purpose? The mission needs to be alive in the heads and hearts of the people, otherwise it will not work: it will become an empty shell and the organization will be adrift and soulless.

---

3   Sull 1999.

Through conversations about the mission of the organization all stakeholders will understand fully what the mission means and be able to act accordingly. They are bound by common values. Arie de Geus describes the value of involvement of the whole organization in *The Living Company*. A common characteristic of long-living organizations was that the employees showed a strong sense of 'feeling at home in the organization' and identified themselves with its goals and successes. The fact that the employees saw themselves as a part of the bigger endeavour, working with others with a common loyalty to the mission, turned out to be essential for the survival of the organization in times of change.[4] Shared ideas and values give the organization a strong identity and a certain continuity which can keep it together in times of change.[5]

At the same time it is important to conserve the diversity of an organization. After all, different people will have different perspectives on the mission of the organization. Sometimes you need to pay attention to this diversity: you might open a conversation about the mission. At other times it can be more useful to have everyone rowing in the same direction, effectively to 'impose' the mission on the organization.When the organization is fighting to remain competitive, leadership and an unambiguous mission are needed. It is up to you to determine which moments require divergence and which convergence.

The mission can also play a role in the leadership of the organization. An executive can manage the company by focusing on milestones and targets, but also on the mission. In the case of the latter, a missionary organization, the values are guiding.[6] In a missionary organization we see common norms and values and a strong company culture. A simple example is the Disney Corporation which went as far as to create its own language: employees are *cast members*, customers are *guests* and jobs are *parts* in a *performance.*[7]

It is also valuable to connect the conversation about the mission with other strategic conversations, e.g. about the external environment, scenarios, options or vision – about which, more in the next chapters. Don't forget, the image of the organization can be as important as its identity, but how you are seen is sometimes much more influential than how you really are.

HOW DO YOU FIND OUT ABOUT THE MISSION?

I often ask people I meet if they know the mission of the organization they work for. Even top managers often confess that they don't have a clue, and have to look it up on their company's website. Each organization should have a greater cause. How the organization defines its mission determines what the organization does, and sometimes, a single word can make the difference, as seen in the example of the social housing corporations. The mission represents the reason for your existence and the core values of the organization; and it often appears in the communication to the most important stakeholders: e.g. employees (vacancies), customers (proposition) and financiers (annual reports). Any external party who decides to engage in the organization (as a provider, a client or an employee), effectively endorses the mission of the organization.

---

4   De Geus 1997: 13.

5   Collins 1995.

6   Mintzberg et al. 1998: 309.

7   Collins 1995.

When the organization does not have a written mission statement, the mission, or at least the basics thereof, can be found in the articles of association. As with contracts these are the formal, written account of relationships, the reason for the organization's existence and the mission of the organization. In that context, the mission is called the 'statutory objective'. Everyone who has ever founded a Limited company, a foundation or an association, knows from experience what it takes when it comes to the articles of association and other formalities. These articles are often quickly forgotten, but it is useful to revisit them. Legally the organization is obliged to keep itself to its articles of association and to limit its activities to those in line with the objects they describe! In the case of Rabobank, the articles of association specify the company's objective as 'to act on its members behalf'.[8]

So it is important that you check on your articles of association. Were the articles of association for Shell simply to state 'the company trades oil and gas', then it is not legal for Shell to become involved in anything else without a change in the articles of association. The *memorandum of association* of Shell states amongst other things that the company shall 'carry on business as a general commercial company and [to] carry on any trade or business whatsoever' and '[to] provide services of all descriptions'. Which makes trading in shells as appropriate as trading in oil and gas.[9]

TO BE VIGILANT AND TO SERVE: WORKING ON SECURITY AND TRUST IN THE HAAGLANDEN AREA

Haaglanden police force

Before the regionalization of the Dutch police in 1992–1993 the municipal police had the motto 'Vigilat ut quiescant' (He guards, in order that they can be at ease) while the state police had the motto 'Dutiful, and always ready'. In 2005 a new mission was developed for the 25 regional police forces and the Konklijke Landelijke Politiediensten (KLPD; corps national police services): 'To be vigilant and to serve; the police stands for the core values of the constitutional state'. This motto is abbreviated to 'To be vigilant and to serve', and displayed on police cars and uniforms.

Under the leadership of the new chief constable the Haaglanden police force wanted to create a refinement of the national mission by using the two core values of the corps of the Haaglanden area: Security and Trust. Security stands for preventing and fighting crime by maintaining public order, investigating and surveilling. Trust evokes the relationship of the police force with its citizens and its employees. The police force aims to serve the citizens, but it is only if trust is mutual between police and citizens, that the force can create a feeling of security. The values of security and trust are interdependent (see Figure 1.1).

Using these two values, which are important to the Haaglanden police force, the national mission was refined into a local mission, which could serve as a framework for different activities. This was expressed as: 'To be vigilant and to serve: ensuring Security and Trust

---

8   Rabobank 2008: 3.

9   Shell: 1.

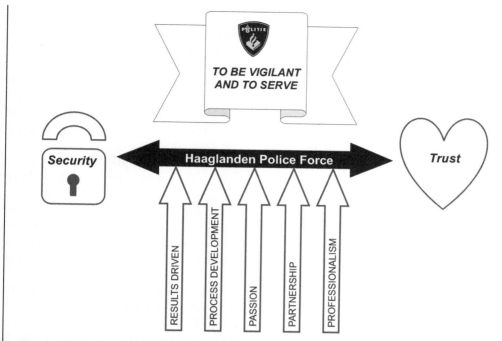

Figure 1.1   The mission of the Haaglanden police force

in the Haaglanden area'. Five instruments were identified to secure the values under this mission: results-driven, process development, passion, partnership and professionalizing. The police officers should be results-driven in the areas of trust and security; they should work with passion and show professional behaviour in order to ensure trust and security. Processes should run smoothly. And it was clear that the police could not do it alone: partnership with local governments, social housing corporations and citizens was needed!

1.2   What is Our Formula for Success?

When the mission of the organization is defined, it immediately generates new questions: who are the stakeholders for the organization? And what drives success in your mission? When you ask these questions, you are basically articulating the formula for success of the organization.

THE 'FORMULA FOR SUCCESS'

Searching for a simple formula of organizational success has been the corporate equivalent of the seach for the Holy Grail. Many strategists have researched the subject; Michael Porter and Hamel and Prahalad are amongst the most well-known. Hamel and Prahalad, who specialized in business strategy, introduced the concept of 'core competences' in 1990. These referred to specific, distinctive elements in an organization which derive from the collective knowledge and skills of this organization and which create an advantage for it. In 'The core competence of the corporation' (1990) Hamel and Prahalad describe their definition of core competences: a core competence is the result of collective learning in the organization, which (1) gives the customers an advantage, (2) is difficult to copy for competitors and (3) can be used in different products and markets.[10]

Michael Porter, Professor at Harvard Business School, is most well-known for his theories of competitive strategy. He created the concept of *competitive advantage*.[11] Competitive advantage can be achieved by asking a lower price for the same product than the competition (*cost leadership*), by delivering a better product than the competition (*differentiation*), or by serving a niche market.

Former Shell strategist and scenario specialist Kees van der Heijden has developed a concept to explain the success of certain organizations: the *Business Idea*, which we liken to the 'formula for success', builds on the ideas of Hamel and Prahalad and of Porter.[12]

Each organization has two goals: to pursue its vision and to create growth, whilst ensuring its survival by adapting to the continuously changing world outside. To be able to grow – yes, even to survive – in a changing world, the organization needs to continue to develop. Van der Heijden has joined the two goals – growth and survival – in the concept of 'formula for success'.

In order to survive as an organization you need to ensure that your formula for success is relevant and creates value, for both the customer and the organization. There are a number of things the organization does that define its nature; things which qualify you as the type of organization you want to be. To a supermarket selling groceries is not a competence which differentiates you when compared to competitors, but it is a qualifying factor which enables the company to be called a supermarket.

At the same time you need to make sure that your formula for success is not easy for your competitors to copy and that it is based on competences which distinguish your organization from others. Based on his experience as a strategist, Kees van der Heijden connected the core competences of Hamel and Prahalad on the one hand and the competitive advantage of Michael Porter on the other. He combined these two concepts to create his own concept of 'distinctive competences'.

The distinctive competences form the character of your organization; they consist of the resource which your organization has build up in the form of qualities, competences and knowledge, and they make your organization unique. In practice this translates as the technologies, processes or knowledge, ideally shielded by patents or copyright, which the company has developed over time.

Distinctive competences are usually latent. It can be difficult to see exactly what the real distinctive competences are or how they are expressed; in other words they often involve implicit (as opposed to explicit) knowledge. Over time, learning processes are condensed in procedures and behaviour. For a supermarket the distinctive competences might be the location and the knowledge employees have about the customers.

A formula for success shows how the organization, by developing itself, is able to grow and to survive. Whilst the concepts of Porter and of Hamel and Prahalad can be considered as a linear causal reason for success, Van der Heijden shows that the elements for success are in fact cyclical. After all, organizations are not static, but dynamic. The formula for

---

10   Prahalad and Hamel 1990: 79–102.

11   Porter 1985.

12   Van der Heijden 1996, 1997.

success should therefore be stated as a *positive feedback loop*: a causal model in which the elements reinforce each other and therefore create a snowball effect.[13] These elements can be very different by nature: they can include an element of competitive advantage, but equally an investment or a certain activity. The competences can involve production (e.g. better trained staff, developed technological know-how or a superior market share) but also relationships (reputation, brand name, access to distribution channels).[14] Some of those elements seem *tickets to ride*, criteria with which your organization has to comply, but it is the unique combination of factors which distinguishes your organization from your competitors.

In Van der Heijdens model of the formula for success (see Figure 1.2) we see a positive feedback loop in which the differentiating factors lead to creation of value and competitive advantage and therefore to success, growth and awareness for the market and changes in the market.The value which the organization creates is invested in resources and processes, and thus the organization develops and renews its core competences, which, in turn, reinforce the competitive advantage.

It does help if the organization is conscious of the formula for its success. In other words, what is essential and defines the basis of the success of the organization? And what is not? This kind of reflection allows an ever-clearer picture of the formula for success. Remember too that not only the hard, quantifyable aspects, but also, or even more importantly, the soft, human aspects are important.[15] The self-reinforcing character often derives from the simple fact that organizations which have a certain specialist skill are in demand because of this skill, which further increases their specialization, which increases their appeal, and so on. This process of learning over time gives the organization the ability to continue outshining the competition. For this very reason Arie de Geus

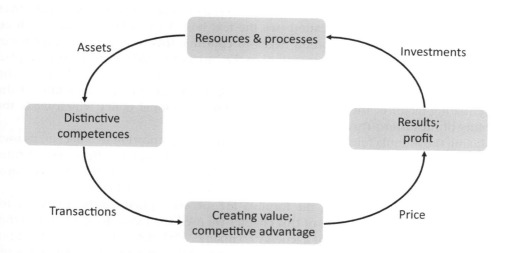

Figure 1.2   Formula for success (after Van der Heijden 1997)

---

13   Van der Heijden 1997: 14–15.

14   Van der Heijden 1997: 18.

15   Van der Heijden 2001.

observed that the ability to learn faster than your competitor is the only sustainable competitive advantage.[16]

Despite their implicit and latent nature, the distinctive competences often have an important share in the formula for success of the organization. Yet the organization's success story and the distinctive competences, just as with the mission, can be an obstacle when the formula for success has stopped working and is impeding the organization. When this happens, you need to change the formula for success. In this changing world every organization will need to abandon the habit of old formulas now and then, in order to stay successful. It is important to keep having the conversation: should we change our purpose? And if so, why? Or should the organization change the way it wants to fulfil its purpose? In an organization there are several concurrent perspectives: the continuous rediscovery of the formula for success (for example, by feedback from the environment), the continual adaptation to stay on course (the target does not change), or finally changing the course and setting a new target.[17]

What makes a formula for success essentially different from the more common 'business model' or a description of the core activities, is the fact that the formula answers both the questions 'What do we do?' as well as 'Who are we?'. Of course, the immediately apparent, concrete activities of the organization are important, but equally important are the competences which hide under the surface but nevertheless determine an important part of the identity of the organization. To a supermarket the most important part of the formula for success may be the wide range of products, but it may equally be the location. Although at first glance real estate does not seem to be the 'core business' of a supermarket, it may well be the basis of the distinctive competences of the shop: the fact that your supermarket is the 'shop around the corner', might be the core of your success. The formula for success: 'Who are we?', then determines what the organization does and what it is good at.

As a result of self-analysis, ABN Amro Trust developed new and important perspectives on several aspects of the organization (see the text box 'A formula for success with an unexpected core'). Your organization needs to continue investing in the competences which distinguish it from the competition. In the case of the ABN Amro Trust their plan to outsource their training programme might, in the first year, have resulted in extra profit. However, over the longer term these budget cuts would have undermined the differentiating factor of the organization; the strong personnel policy which made the reliability of ABN Amro Trust possible.

Making the formula for success explicit can help the organization to reflect on its own character and activities, and become aware of the elements which differentiate it from others. The formula for success becomes handy as a benchmark for strategic decisions; highlighting what the organization is, isn't, wants to be and should be.

On the other hand, making the formula for success explicit can be a catalyst for reinvention. In the introduction of this chapter we used the example of Shell; whether it was an 'oil and gas company' or a 'energy company'. Shell defined itself from the mid-1990s and then again at the start of the twenty-first century as a broad-spectrum 'energy company' and subsequently invested considerable amounts in wind and solar power. At the beginning of 2009 however, the company announced that it would decrease its

---

16   De Geus 1988: 2, 6.

17   The importance of adaptation for survival of organizations, see De Geus 1997.

A FORMULA FOR SUCCESS WITH AN UNEXPECTED CORE

ABN Amro Trust

In 1998 the trust division of ABN Amro Bank went looking for its formula for success. In the trust sector the most important values you can offer your customers are reliability and discretion: after all, customers trust you with their assets. Thus the mission of ABN Amro Trust was to manage the entrusted assets with complete assurance, and they were successful in the sector not as *cost leader*, but as *differentiator*. The premium to which ABN Amro Trust owed this differentiating role was the reliability of the organization.

In a series of workshops ABN Amro Trust started to look for the formula for success of the organization. At the time, the management team did not see the Human Resources (HR) department as part of the core business of ABN Amro Trust. One possible target for discussions about budget cuts was to outsource training from HR to the same (less expensive) external training institute which also provided staff training for the competition.

During the workshops it emerged that the formula for ABN Amro Trust's success was 'reliability'. Moving from this conclusion to the various aspects which made this reputation possible, the senior team discovered elements such as the solid image of the organization, the guidelines and norms which were followed and the brand name ABN Amro. All these elements were then connected in a positive feedback loop. And it then emerged that one of the most important pillars underpinning the reliability of ABN Amro Trust was precisely its internal HR management: the carefully selected and well-trained staff had a major share in living up to the reliable reputation. Only now was it clear just how much of a bad idea it would be to outsource this distinctive competence. HR, originally not seen as 'core business', was definitely part of the 'core' of the formula for success. The flat concept of core business could have led to completely wrong decisions.

investments in such sustainable energy sources, and would only engage in biomass as an alternative energy source, both for economic reasons and because it was closer to its existing core competences of Shell. Solar power requires knowledge of electricity and wind power requires expertise on mechanical engineering, while Shell's competences, as an oil and gas company, are more in the field of chemistry, process technology and geology. Wind and solar power might be a good idea, but not for Shell: other can do this much better.[18]

---

[18]   Several articles published between 1993 and 2009 in *Het Financieele Dagblad* give a picture of Shell's changing attitude concerning sustainable energy sources: from rejecting in 1993, via enthusiastic in 1996 and 1998, towards selective in 2009. See *Het Financieele Dagblad* 1993, 1996, 1998a, 1998b; Halberstadt 1998; Shiffers 2009.

HOW DO YOU DEVELOP A FORMULA FOR SUCCESS?

Of course, everyone has their own ideas about the formula for success of the organization. It is up to you to open those ideas up for discussion and create one common formula for success.

To establish a clear idea about the formula for success, it is important that you realize what has already been written before: the formula for success not only tells you what the organization *does*, but also what it *is*. So it is about the essence, the character of the organization. It is also important that you understand why it is useful to think about the formula for success of the organization and why you should be able to make this formula for success clear to the organization.

The formula for success can be about one single organization and about a group of organizations: a division with business units, a holding company with subsidiaries or an association with members. A useful comparison is to a fleet with its constituent vessels. The fleet represents a group of organizations, such as the GGD Nederland (an assocation of local Municipal Health Services) or Ahold (stock exchange-listed Dutch international retailer, *corporate level*). A ship represents one of the organizations, e.g. GGD Amsterdam or the branch of supermarket Albert Heijn (subsidiary of Ahold) at the Stadionweg in Amsterdam (*business level*). The fleet and the separate ships do not necessarily need to have the same formula for success. For that reason you need to imagine the level at which are you working: is it about a captain and a ship, or about an admiral and a fleet?

In the search for the formula for success there are several questions, such as:

- What is our contribution to this world, how do we create value?
- Who is our customer and what is the nature of the transaction between us and them?
- What is unique about the interaction of our organization with the customer?
- What makes us different from the competition?
- Which elements create this unique character?
- What resources are we using and how do we strengthen these?
- Why is it difficult or impossible for the competition to copy the special properties of our organization?

Although they seem trivial questions, the answers can be surprising and offer unexpected insights. Are the patients, the specialists or the referring GPs the actual customers of a hospital? Are you refuelling the customer of Shell, is it the gas station owner who buys the gas at Shell, or is it the government who issues licences for gas stations and oil exploitation? Behind the answers to those questions lie competences: they ensure that the organization can deliver what it is delivering, that the customers are happy with it and that the organization differentiates itself from the competition.

As soon as you have a list with elements which are important to the formula for success, you need to try to find out what the relationship is between these elements and thus to close the loop – of course, undertaken in dialogue with (the rest of) the organization. You'll often find a central variable which is seen as the most important element of the formula for success; from there you can determine what is needed to achieve this activity or property and which consequences this activity or property has. You can do this in a workshop by writing the separate elements on single post-it notes, and arranging and clustering them and connecting them to each other with arrows. These arrows indicate how the elements are connected with each other and if you include descriptive verbs such as 'lead to', 'increase', or 'reinforce' you can add a subsequent level of meaning by indicating the logic flow between them.[19] The resulting diagram is unlikely to show the answers. It is your job to come up with a model to correlate the elements from the list and their relationship. This model should be as simple as possible, but not too simple. It

MEDIUM-TERM PLAN 2012 AND THE FORMULA FOR SUCCESS

IHC Dredgers

In 2008 the outlook for IHC Dredgers, the division of IHC Merwede which builds dredgers, was good. Nevertheless there was uncertainty. To start with, there was the credit crisis. But the company also had to deal with more structural developments, for example, relating to developing markets. In this context in 2008 IHC Dredgers started making a *Medium-term Plan* to cover the period until 2012. In the first session they explored, amongst other things, the formula for success of IHC Dredgers. They wanted to get clear what the core of the activities were and where the competitive advantage of the organization lay. Important parts of the formula for success of IHC Dredgers turned out to be their knowledge of the dredging industry and their relations within it. Staff from IHC Dredgers regularly visits many of the largest dredging companies in the world. Product leadership also turned out to be a strong point. IHC Dredgers is internationally known for the quality of the dredgers it makes. These elements were combined with the company's aspirations, in terms of internationalization and market-led research and development. The separate elements were put together in a formula for success which illustrates these interdependencies (Figure 1.3).

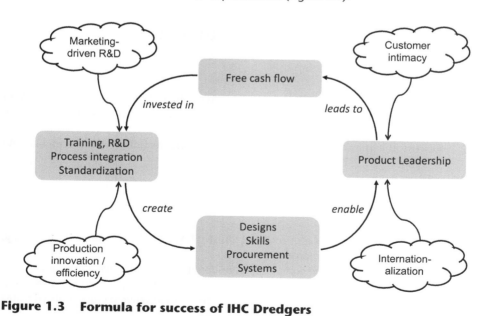

Figure 1.3   Formula for success of IHC Dredgers

---

19   See also Figure 1.2 Formula for success.

is important that the final version of the formula for success is discussed and approved by all who are involved.

A formula for success is the most powerful when it is not too complex, and yet not oversimplified. It is important that the 'systematic' character of the formula stays clearly visible: the model should be considered a whole instead of a collection of independent elements. The human brain can process up to seven concepts at the same time, so try to limit the number of elements in the formula for success to seven. You can do this for example by combining elements or replacing them with more abstract elements.[20]

You are looking for a formula for success that feels comfortable to the organization and is one everyone can recognize as their own. It is best to use the language of the organization to describe the formula for success. In certain organizations you'll find common expressions such 'we like to roll up our sleeves' or 'we are just a bunch of hobbyists'; it makes sense to use these exact words in the formula for success. These expressions, when you peel back the words to expose the meaning, can contain valuable information about the values which are important to the organization and show why they are used.

Once you have collectively established the formula for success, it is important to recognize that you cannot close your eyes to developments and competitors outside the group in which you have placed yourself. The degree of openness of your system defines the chances of survival of your company.[21] Each organization has to force itself to keep looking out of the window. Information which does not fit into your image of the world is often difficult to process. The chapters about trends and scenarios in the book offer tools to translate the signals from the outside world and to use them in designing your strategy. We'll show how this works in the next chapter.

CONCLUSIONS: MISSION

Mission

1.   Formulate the mission or the goal of the organization, if necessary look for them in the articles of association. What are the core purpose and the reason of existence for the organization?
2.   Discuss the mission within the organization and reconfirm or reformulate the mission.
3.   Stick to the mission once it has been formulated.

Formula for success

1.   Discuss what the formula for success consists of. What is the competitive advantage and why do customers come to you?
2.   Discuss which distinctive competences underpin the competitive advantage.
3.   Close the positive feedback loop by deciding where the organization should invest to continue developing its competences. Create an intuitive picture of the formula for success and use it as a guideline for action.

---

20   Van der Heijden 1996: 168.
21   De Geus 1997.

2 *Trends: What is happening around us?*

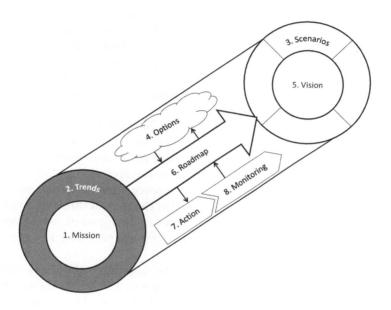

The helmsman stands behind the steering wheel and is focused on the compass. The captain is free to wander the ship; looking at the sea, the waves and the ships around them, sensing the wind and the rolling of the waves. Are there dark clouds on the horizon? Are the other ships overhauling them? Yet the analogy of the leader as captain is far from accurate. The environment in which an organization operates is far more complicated than the surroundings of a ship. The 'captain' of an organization, whether male or female, needs to pay attention to customers, competitors, politics, labour markets, financial markets and more. Scanning the environment and knowing where you are in a dynamic and constantly changing world is essential if you wish to stay afloat and on course.

Scanning the Environment

How much time in your organization is spent talking about internal matters? And how much time is spent sharing insights about what is happening out there in the real world? We encounter many organizations that can be characterized as internally focused; operating an internal world which seems completely disconnected from the world outside. Organizations which are surprised every time lightning hits them even though they were oblivious to the clouds looming and didn't seem to hear the thunder. And the few employees who do try to warn the others and who see the bigger picture are often ignored or labelled as difficult people. Of course, company employees see the news, read newspapers and magazines and chat with friends about politics, but as soon as they enter the workplace, it is back to work. No time or room for chit chat about the weather, politics or the economy. If you want to break this pattern, you have to put the outside world on the agenda and actually take the time to scan the environment, together.

It is important that you focus attention on the outside world. If you want to prepare your organization for the future, you must know what is happening in the business environment. Where are you now? What is the competition up to, what is happening in terms of legislation and regulations? And most importantly: what is happening in the world in which your clients operate? You need to explore trends and counter-trends, driving forces and events which are outside the direct control of the organization but still influence the organization.

The environment is unpredictable, but it can be explored. The organization needs to be sensitized to factual developments in the outside world. Empirical data and trends can be used, and these need to be seen by the inside team; structured charting of external developments keeps the organization sensitive to possible changes in the future. Facts about historical trends help to improve our appreciation of what might come. By combining empirical thinking about the past with theoretical thinking about the future, the interconnectedness of developments becomes more apparent. As do possible future scenarios about which you'll read more in the next chapter. The key message here is: outside-in.

However, beware. In this stage you cannot be normative about the trends. You are just exploring. Whether you like the trends you see or not, all of them need to be 'on the map'. In other words, trend-watching is not just about knowledge of trends. The process involved is just as important as the information gathered. Your colleagues need to be involved in the 'watching'. It encourages an external orientation and widens the perspective within the organization, and in that respect collective trend-watching is an intervention in the organization in its own right. These kinds of activities improve the awareness of discontinuities or incongruences. Learning more about what has happened in the past is as much about reinforcing the uncertainties of the future (if these kinds of things have happened before) as it is about planning ways to mitigate risk. Exploring the environment also results in developing new relations within the organization and with its stakeholders (who can be interviewed, or invited to brainstorming sessions), improves acceptance of strategies that follow, and it creates a common language that will help future decision-making!

2.1   What is 'Self', What is Environment?

Who is responsible for this kind of environmental scanning? The marketing department is responsible for scanning for consumer trends. The public affairs department is responsible for scanning the political and legal environment. The HR department looks at trends in the labour market. Of course all of these functions have their own discrete activities, but trend-watching isn't an easy task that happens automatically. There are tricks to the trade of trend-watching. To start, you need to know what you are looking for. I remember once participating in a project about the future of the rural areas surrounding the capital. There I heard for the first time about the 'de-cowing' and 'horsefication' trends. And ever since I cannot stop noticing that indeed there are less and less cows in the rural areas around Amsterdam, and more and more horses; the underlying trend is the reduction of agricultural use of the rural area and the increasing importance of recreational use. These are important trends if you are a farmer or a local city council. But I only noticed the trend once I knew it was there. And farmers and city councils will often need the growth figures before they can start to invest or make official policies: empirical data is needed before it is officially acknowledged as fact.

Developments in the environment need to be categorized or mapped out, named, described and numbered to decide whether or not they are relevant for your organization and before your organization can act upon them. Most organizations take years before they act on new trends. Take for instance the rise of the number of self-employed people in the Netherlands in the last decades: in 2011 728,000 people in the Netherlands were self-employed, but in 1996 it was not even 400,000.[1] This trend has been spotted in many countries and has been covered in newspapers and books for some time. But most organizations took it for granted. The trend in the labour market wasn't really appreciated and acted on by many until recently. Many banks, for instance, still segment the market into private and business clients. The self-employed don't fit into these categories. And many recruitment agencies are also running behind the trend. Most of them are still looking for employees to fill job vacancies when they get an assignment from an employer. It are only the innovative recruiters which are offering the self-employed their services to find new projects, not jobs. This change in the labour market is a risk for those who do not adapt, but an opportunity for those who do. So a simple trend such as an increase in the number of self-employed people can create tension between your organization and your environment. And it is not just the HR department that should see this. Marketing people in banks, directors of recruitment agencies and even line managers in any business can benefit from seeing this new pool of talent looking for projects. And they are seeing this. Is your organization connecting the dots? Do you know of any relevant trends that other people, inside or outside your organization, are seeing? And are these trends shared across the organization? All your colleagues are reading newspapers, talking to customers or checking out the competition. Each of them individually only sees a small part, but together they form an intelligence community of enormous power. Collectively you will be able to see the big picture.

CONTEXTUAL AND TRANSACTIONAL ENVIRONMENT

The Serenity prayer asks 'Lord, grant me the serenity to accept the things I cannot change, the courage to change the things I can, and the wisdom to know the difference'; a simple aspiration which is not so easily put into practice. To each organization it is important to differentiate between what the organization can influence and what the organization will have to cope with, because it cannot be influenced or changed by the organization. When scanning the environment it is therefore important to know what is 'inside' and what

---

1   Statistics Netherlands, www.cbs.nl

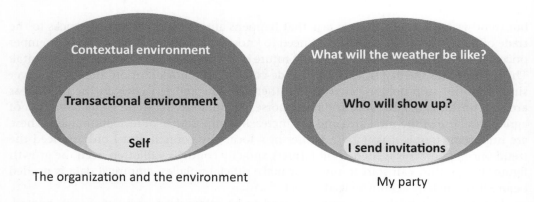

The organization and the environment   My party

Figure 2.1   Self, transactional environment and contextual environment

is 'outside'. To make this clear we distinguish between the changeable organization, the influenceable transactional environment and the contextual environment which, by this definition, cannot be changed. The contextual environment is defined as the factors and actors on which the organization itself has no influence, but which in return influence the organization. The contextual environment is outside the sphere of influence of the organization.

Let's take the example of planning a garden party (see Figure 2.1). I first need to decide who I will invite to the party. Whether these people actually show up is only partly under my influence; and this is what is called the transactional environment. The weather is totally out of my control, and this is called contextual environment.

In your organization context, the transactional environment consists of players and events in the direct environment of the organization on which the organization can have some influence. Just as the organization the transactional environment is influenced by the contextual environment. However, unlike the contextual environment, in the transactional environment there is a direct interdependence and direct interaction with the organization; the transactional environment belongs to the sphere of influence of the organization. Shareholders, investors, customers, competitors, partners, suppliers and unions are players you will find in the transactional environment. This sounds very simple, but if you are in a department within a ministry, or if you are running a business unit within a larger company, exactly where you draw the lines between self, transactional and contextual environment is complicated. To some, the ministers or CEO's are more like the weather and completely contextual: to others these people are more like a friend and therefore part of the transactional environment.

It is important to reflect together where you would put the players, events and developments in this model. The model then becomes a representation of how you see yourself in the world, and this is valuable in itself. It offers a map which can be used to explore your level of influence. My experience is that public institutions often overestimate what they can control. On the other hand, businesses tend to underestimate what they can do. One CEO of a large multinational once said: 'What can I do, I am only a multinational'. And sometimes it is only once the whole strategy project has been completed that you find out where your leverage lies. Maybe it is less, maybe it is more than you anticipated. To give you an example: the Dutch Ministry of Transport often presumes it is in charge of the nation's congestion problems. In reality, there isn't much this ministry can do once the Ministry of Housing, Spatial Planning and the Environment has planned all the houses to be built at a distance from where all the offices are planned. If on top of that the economy starts growing, there is not much the Ministry of Transport can do about congestion. Traffic jams are, to a large extent, contextual to them. The Ministry of Transport on the other hand influences housing, unknowingly: for people want to live close to good infrastructure. To the Ministry of Housing, Spatial Planning and the Environment traffic jams might be more transactional than they thought! When the Minister for Transport in the Netherlands realized this, and publicly stated that she could not be held responsible for the number of traffic jams, it came as a shock. However, it did help her accept the things she couldn't change and helped her to focus on the things she could.

So, with trend-watching, it matters whether you are the CEO or a member of a trend-watching team within a marketing department. In the latter case, you might notice a trend that the CEO is pushing a policy of acquiring more and bigger companies. Is that a contextual trend to you, such as the weather? Or can you influence it a little? Or is the CEO inside your zone of control? It certainly helped when the project team of a department within a large bank realized the CEO's behaviour was completely out of their control. They started to notice the trends in his behaviour and accepted it as they would the weather, but at the same time, understanding the pattern helped them to plan ahead, rather like having insider information.

FACTORS AND ACTORS

Trend-watching is a divergent activity; you should cast the net as wide as possible. To start, you don't need to limit yourself to the facts at hand: all ideas, opinions, observations and even hunches are welcome. We often use the DESTEP acronym to make sure we don't miss any of the Demographic, Economic, Societal, Technological, Ecological and Political developments. All of these factors can entail interesting and relevant trends.

Simple trends can be very powerful. The World Business Council for Sustainable Development (WBCSD) did a study of the facts and trends regarding the energy efficiency in buildings. They found out that up to 40 per cent of all energy consumption and related greenhouse gas emissions where caused by buildings.[2] This growth was spurred by the growth in the number of buildings in the world through urbanization combined with the increase of energy use per building. Just think of the increase in the number of buildings in the world that now have air conditioning. At the same time, counter-trends could be seen. The energy efficiency of heating systems, air conditioners and even elevators is going up. This report had a huge impact. It provided a strong warning to policy-makers and it was a sign of hope for everyone in the building industry. It put the issue of energy efficiency in buildings at the top of the agenda.

When scanning the world outside you should not only pay attention to the factors, but also to the actors. If politicians, customers, competitors and suppliers are relevant to you, what trends do you see there? Is there more or less competition? Are politicians likely to require greater compliance in your industry? Do you see consolidation under your suppliers, or do you see a growing number of new entrants?

---

2   *Energy Efficiency in Buildings, Facts & Trends*, World Business Council for Sustainable Development, 2008.

Actors usually belong to the transactional environment: you can influence them to a certain extent. For organizations analyzing actors can also be a way of *benchmarking*: what is the position of your competitors or your allies and how does your position relate to theirs? And this is also true in the public sector. For example in the interdepartmental project 'Future Policy Survey' the Dutch expenditure for the armed forces was placed in an international perspective and compared to that of allies and partners in Belgium, Canada and Denmark.[3]

Again, the *Facts & Trends* study of the WBCSD analyzed all the players in the building sector, and found architects, builders, designers, engineers, financiers, agents, subcontractors and regulators to name but a few. Among those players, there even was functional separation into mechanical, electrical and structural work, and managerial separation into planning, tendering and commissioning. They called this trend of ever-increasing numbers of specialized players 'fragmentation', a trend that helped the WBCSD to understand why the sector was incapable of collectively embracing sustainability: everybody could always blame another player for not taking the necessary action. And they called that phenomenon the circle of blame.

This demonstrates the importance of scanning the larger trends in the context and also looking at trends in what we call the actor space. Most companies already do the latter as part of business or competitive intelligence. These kinds of trends are often the easiest to find. Trends in market shares, benchmarking data of competitors, or number of new entrants are trends that you must be able to pick up from your marketing department. However, if you work in the public sector this data is often lacking and you may have to gather these trends yourself. This data, whatever the source, can be very valuable. Once you know that Ministries of Defence in other countries are spending more than you, this can be used. Or you can use it to show how efficient you already are. Or if you see that the population of the city next to yours is growing faster, you could frame that as losing market share. So don't just look at the broad factors to find your trends, also pay attention to the local actors around you.

2.2   Scanning the Environment: Things to Take into Account

WHAT ARE TRENDS AND WHAT DO THEY MEAN TO THE FUTURE

Trend-watching is hot. We all want to read about the newest and the latest. Trends are strongly associated with hip and cool, with fashion and music. But in this book we refer to developments in the environment of the organization. The scientific definition of a trend is the general direction in which something is moving. As mentioned earlier, there can be trends relating to all letters of the DESTEP acronym, trends regarding actors and internal trends. Trends are one layer deeper than single events. Only when you see multiple events in a certain direction can you talk about a trend. It is the pattern that counts. Single observations can be the start of recognizing a trend. One hot summer in the Netherlands is meaningless, until you start to notice more hurricanes in the US, floods in Bangladesh and rising temperatures over the years. Could this be the trend of climate change? The individual events might just have been the tip of the iceberg.

---

3   *Future Policy Survey, A New Foundation for the Netherlands' Armed Forces*, Ministry of Defence, 2010.

Underneath the surface of one hot summer lies a deeper pattern. But at the same time, you need to be very alert to the risks of trend-watching: is it a genuine trend or am I forcing my own worldview on the data? Am I interpreting my data to fit a trend of which I am already convinced?

History does not repeat itself and facts or data about the future do not exist yet. Although many people interpret trends as something of the future, trends only say something about the past. We cannot see the future. Our current observations are outdated almost as soon as we make them. All empirical data are about the past, by definition. We can use the trend we see in the data to extrapolate towards the future. The fact that something is moving in a certain direction often means that this direction is continued for a while. That is what we call momentum. But a trend is only a trend until it bends. Many trends can be extrapolated. Many organizations make a mistake here: they extrapolate data from the past and think they can predict the future exactly. Some developments can indeed be reasonably well predicted based on linear extrapolation of historical data. For instance, roughly the same number of people that are 18 today will be 28 in 10 years time. Yes, migration and deaths play a role, but there is a high degree of certainty to extrapolate this number: for many other trends, developments are seldom neither linear nor certain. Despite this, many organizations only prepare for a linear extrapolation of the past. If the economy is booming, businesses tend to plan for growth. If there is a crisis, businesses often assume this crisis will last and they downscale with the trend at that point in time. Organizations should prepare for situations in which the historic trends do not continue but bend. This preparation often defines the success or failure of the organization more than the preparation for well-known trends which will continue anyway.

Where even the demographics of a country are difficult to extrapolate, the progress of technology might be even more difficult. In the *Boston Post* of 1865 one could read about the telephone: 'Well informed people know it is impossible to transmit voice over waves and that were it possible to do so, it would be of no practical value.' And given the data about the telephone (which didn't exist before 1865) the statement was empirically completely justified based on the data. Up to 1865 it wasn't possible and there was no demand. The same happened with the introduction of the personal computer (PC). In 1977 Ken Olson, the president of Digitial Equiment Corporation (DEC), stated that there was no reason for an individual to have a computer at home. This was entirely understandable, since in those days computers were the size of several large refrigerators and would cost as much as a car. And yes, based on the data, there were zero PCs sold in the period between 1945 and 1976, so the most logical extrapolation of this trend was to predict that over the next 30 years it would remain zero. But we now know that almost everyone in the Western world has a computer, laptop, smart phone or tablet at home, each of them with a memory and the processing power larger than that of the biggest mainframe computer of that time. DEC, the metaphorical Goliath, used to be the number two computer company in the world. It lost out to Apple, a small David at the time. DEC extrapolated the all-time trend that the market for computers at home was zero. It did not notice that two other trends where decreasing exponentially – the size of computers was getting smaller and smaller, and their cost was decreasing.

Some trends develop exponentially. The linear extrapolation of a trend is a straight line, exponential growth is an ever-steeper curve. Technology often develops in this exponential manner. It was Gordon Moore, the co-founder of Intel, who described this

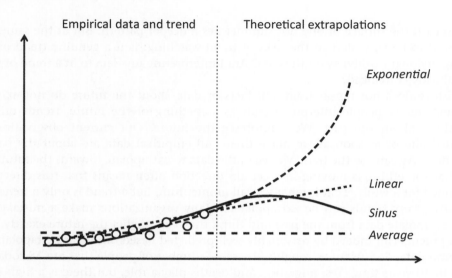

Figure 2.2   Several possible extrapolations of a series of observations

exponential growth in 1965. He noted that the number of components in integrated circuits had doubled every year. Looking back, computer chips have indeed continued to grow in number of transistors per chip in this way. Most people now know words like kilo, mega, giga and now even tera to describe exponential growth in numbers of bytes or pixels. When watching trends is important to notice the difference: do you see linear or exponential growth? It is easy to underestimate exponential curves (see Figure 2.2)!

In their famous book *The Limits to Growth*,[4] the Club of Rome pointed out that most trends will eventually bend. There are limits to growth. This will result in a wave-shaped sinus curve that goes up and down. And in nature most things are indeed S-shaped or cyclical. Again, trends in the data tell you something about the past. It is how we extrapolate this trend that brings us into the future. Most serious forecasters only use the straight line extrapolation. The hip trend-watchers hope to see exponential growth in every one or two cool observations they see, hoping that by repeating the message the hype will fulfil itself, which is indeed possible regarding trends in the social domain.

In the social domain, trends often cause acoustic feedback. Trends are popular topics to write about, and many conferences have trend-watchers as speakers. Once a trend is spotted, it gets repeated over and over again. Take for instance the trend of 'growing individualism' which has been noticed for decades now.[5] It really resonates with the audience. In the past we took care of each other, but because of 'growing individualism', nobody is taking care of each other anymore. But is this really true? Or is it a self-fulfilling prophecy, and is this trend an excuse for many to do the same? One could easily start to think: 'If nobody is taking care of each other anymore, the only thing I can do is to take care of myself'. But look at the rising number of people providing 'informal care'. Or the growth of communities on Facebook, or the open source communities developing

---

4   *The Limits to Growth*, Meadows et al. 1972.

5   This trend was already used by Leonard Sayles in *Individualism and Big Business*, 1963, and recycled by trend-watcher Alvin Toffler in *Future Shock*, 1971.

free software together. It is easy to be caught off guard with these self-evident trends that nobody cares to check. This can easily lead to hypes and blindness to counter-trends.

Most trend reports are one-sided. They report about globalization, and ignore the counter-trend of a growing anti-globalization movement. Because more often than not, one trend gives rise to another. Globalization evoked anti-globalization, fast food evoked a slow food movement and in every consolidating industry you are bound to see fragmentation and new start-ups at the same time. The counter-trends are most often the most interesting. People know most trends, but the counter-trends are often full of new insights, and at the same time, counter-trends are often the bases of real foresight. During the Rabobank project, one participant was complaining that he was unable to finish his part of the trend study. He couldn't decide which trend to report: globalization or anti-globalization. It wasn't until he was allowed to report both that the message sunk in: the future is uncertain, we see both trends at the same time, and we don't know which trend will prevail. And this was exactly the point; it is this explicit uncertainty and 'not knowing' that open our eyes to real new developments, both risks and opportunities!

The interplay between the trends generates uncertainty. We don't know, or better, we cannot know exactly in what the interplay will result. Rather than linear extrapolation it is better to be explicit about the range of uncertainty. Many banks, real estate investors and pension funds spend a lot of time trying to predict the future interest rate. It is difficult for most to accept that we simply don't know. Too many variables, like inflation, monetary growth, growth expectation, speculation, currency rates and even war play a role in determining which direction interest rates will go. And most organizations would be better off just to consider both an increasing and a decreasing interest rate, and focus on the possible risk and opportunities this will generate. The past will not help to predict the future, but it can help to realize the bandwidth that interest rates can take. And at the same time, also be aware that the future can be even more extreme.

ORGANIZATIONAL BLINDNESS

Trend-watching is a good way to put the outside world on the agenda. This doesn't happen by itself. Most meetings are about internal issues. Yesterday's problems and urgent issues tend to clutter our agendas. The important trends in the outside world are often outside the normal scope. Trend-watching helps to have a reason to focus collectively on what is happening in the world out there. And this is why, as an individual, you might spot important trends, but you simply lack a spot in the meeting agenda to address it. And if you do, and if it is a real new development, those who didn't spot it yet will tend to wave it off the agenda again.

Once you have made time to discuss trends, the next hurdle to cross is the induction problem. Imagine a turkey being fed every day at 8 o'clock in the morning. After 199 days like this, he will tend to predict that he will be fed again at 8 o'clock the 200th day. But if the 199th day happens to be the day before Christmas, he is in for a big surprise. The turkey would simply but wrongfully have induced that because something happened 199 times, it would be the same the 200th day. The same can be said about driving without filling up for gas. The fact that it works for the first 400 miles doesn't mean it will for the second 400 miles. On the contrary, some trends are less likely to continue the longer they last. So take a step back. Don't look back 199 days, look what happened to the other turkeys in the years before. Looking back further helps. Just as looking elsewhere. The fact that we did not have a long period with low interest rates in Europe doesn't mean that it can't happen. It happened in Japan. And many pension funds struggling with low interest rates today thought: it cannot happen here.

Create time to discuss trends, and make sure your team understands the induction problem. Discuss what is going on in the world. And be prepared to 'agree to disagree'. This requires an open culture. Not every trend is welcomed as much as others. Seeing new competitors that are truly better, or new technologies that would heavily impact the company are often left unreported. Remember the now infamous Iraq minister of Information saying during the second Gulf war: 'There are no American infidels in Baghdad, never', while you could see the tanks driving in behind him.

A practical way to get the trends listed is to literarily get them on the wall. Just plan time with your team to brainstorm and use post-it notes on a wall to capture as many as you can. These trends, once spotted, can then be clustered. However, important decisions are not based on trends which resulted from a quick brainstorm. You will be asked to 'proof' your trends. You will need to find data for things you are already seeing. Are tanks really entering Baghdad? Where? When? How many? What is your source? Just mentioning: 'it came from a brainstorming session' is seldom good enough. And this is the moment when the early warning signals, or weak signals, are swept off the table again.

Once you think you have come up with a new trend, getting the data to support it is often the hardest part because it's often the new trends that we are not yet counting. Because data requires capta; the data needs to be captured, hence the name capta.[6] We measure what we know, and we know what we measure. Brand new developments often have no name. Was there already a slow food or an anti-globalization movement before we gave them these names? It all starts with naming the trend, only then can the counting start. Take climate change for instance. We have been measuring the melting of our ice caps only recently, because in the past it wasn't an issue. And now that we measure it, it has become more of an issue, and therefore we measure even more. But that doesn't mean it wasn't there before we measured it, we simply didn't know.

So what is your organization measuring? What trends do you follow? Are you only tracking the data that the organization is already measuring, or are you also reading other sources, observing different developments in the outside world or talking with outsiders about the variables they are tracking? We often hear that 'we don't experience cyber crime in our organization'. Is that really true, or is no one looking?

Once you have spotted a trend, named it, and captured data to support it, the next issue is representation. How you present your trends is always highly suggestive. In 2005 we often heard of the trend of 'more terrorism'. And it makes a different impact whether a trend like this is presented as just that, two words; or as a list of all the incidents or a list of potential targets with your home town at the top (see Figures 2.3 to 2.7). Even starker are the actual images of the 9/11 event and its victims. These pictures have a strong emotional impact. Apparently objective data such as graphs and tables are suggestive. We all know: you have lies, damn lies and statistics. Most of the time you can always find a data set to prove your point, any point. Let's take terrorism again. Which data set do you

---

6   Checkland and Holwell 1998.

take? Global data? Local data? Do you take the number of incidents, or the number of victims? Where do you start your data set, and where do you stop? By selecting different start and end points, you can make curves go up or down, just as you like. And do you compare your selected data set with a reference, for example the number of deaths as a result of car accidents, in this case for example? The message is clear: reporting trends is very subjective. There is so much data out there you can almost always find data to prove your point, whatever it is. For the impact it greatly matters what you report and how you report it, and that is exactly the point. Trend-watching helps you set the agenda, and it can even be used to start people moving.

More terrorism Terrorism increases. After the attacks in New York, Madrid and London it is uncertain where and when we'll have another attack.	**More terrorism** • New York, 11 September 2001 • Madrid, 11 March 2004 • London, 7 July 2005 • Amsterdam, ?

Figure 2.3   More terrorism?   **Figure 2.4   More terrorism?**

Figure 2.5   More terrorism?

Credit: Reuters / Steven James Silva

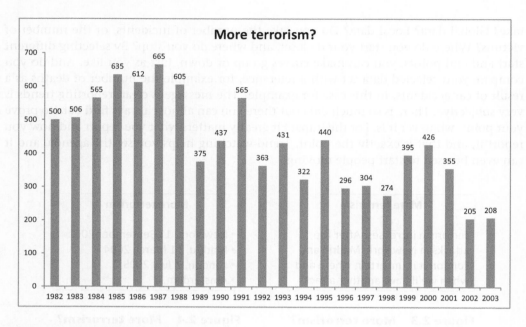

Figure 2.6   More terrorism?

Source of data: Patterns of Global Terrorism 2003, U.S. State Department

Car accidents USA

In 2002, alone:
• 6,316,000 car accidents
• 2.9 million injured
• 42,815 died

Figure 2.7   More terrorism?

Source of data: http://wiki.answers.com/Q/How_many_deaths_are_caused_by_car_accidents_a_year

SELECTIVE PERCEPTION

A well-known myth from anthropology illustrates how we are all seemingly blind. Anthropologists found a jungle person who had never been in a city. They took him to New York and let him see the city. When they later asked him what he noticed, he mentioned seeing a man who was transporting more bananas than anyone he knew. He didn't have a word for a truck, because he had never seen one. But transporting bananas was relevant, so he did see the truck with bananas. Many of the other 'important' aspects, like the Uggs women were wearing and the latest model of a Ford car just passing by, were unnoticed. It didn't fit his frame of reference. We can think 'how silly is he, that jungle person'. But we would completely miss tracks of wolves on the ground, or specific edible berries on hedges. We probably would only see dirt on the ground and lots of trees.

You only see what you know: this is called selective perception. And when it is collective, it is even worse. Take Ford and General Motors in the 1970s. They were watching each other closely, both companies were based in Detroit and making similar cars. They measured everything by reference to each other, being fierce competitors. But neither of them saw Honda as a competitor in those days. Honda made small cars, and was not considered a serious competitor. Honda's growth in sales was not mentioned in reports; Ford and General Motors were organizationally blind. Individuals saw Honda's in the street, but for the company as a whole they didn't exist, until Honda had become really big. The same happened to Dutch banks, which didn't see mortgage retailers as competitors until they already had 20 per cent market share. You will see this selective blindness everywhere. All organizations have blind spots, and it is up to you to shine a light.

If you want to create an experience for your team about this, show them a video of the Visual Cognition Lab of the University of Illinois. They have many examples of slow changes, or quick changes during a basketball game that will pass unnoticed. It will help your team to realize that we all have blind spots, and that we all need time to step back to see what is really happening around us.

PERSPECTIVISM, COGNITIVE DISSONANCE AND GROUPTHINK

Selective perception is not the only hindrance in clearly seeing what is happening around us. There are more complicating factors. One of them is perspectivism. No-one is able to see the whole. When watching we are all using our own 'mental model', as if we all wear personal spectacles. Our frames of reference are all different, and we look at things from different angles. This is called perspectivism, and is both a help and hindrance at the same time. Each of us sees only a part, but collectively we see a lot more. And this is the trick: by interviewing or through workshops, it is possible to broaden our collective perspective. This enables you to 'zoom out' as if every individual is bringing his or her piece of the puzzle. If you put the pieces of the puzzle together, you can literally start to see the bigger picture.

A second hindrance that you will need to overcome, however, is cognitive dissonance. Even if you have all the pieces of the puzzle on the table, there is always the urge to disqualify pieces that don't fit the presupposed puzzle in your mind. Pieces that don't fit will be ignored, normatively labelled as a 'wrong' piece of data, or even get manipulated. The piece will be redrawn, or 'corrected', to fit our own worldview. Especially if the trend you are looking at is against your organization's interest, or worse, against your organization's policy, it is easier to change the data than to accept the facts. This happens individually and collectively.

Suppose you want to organize a garden party in summer. On the morning of the event you see clouds looming over your garden. The easiest thing to do is to deny this fact and to think: 'the clouds will blow over, it's going to be a very nice day today, it's summer! It is not raining yet, and statistically, it hardly ever rains in summer!' The clouds, as a precursor for rain, do not fit your idea of a lovely garden party outside in the sun. This happens on an individual day-to-day level, but also on a company or even country-wide level. The credit crisis started in 2007. Halfway through 2008 the Netherlands Bureau for Economic Policy Analysis still forecasted a growing economy for the future, although individual companies saw their order books decreasing. The bureau had predicted earlier that the economy would grow, and the statistics they use did not indicate any trouble yet. It was not raining, yet!

Cognitive dissonance on a collective level is called groupthink. It is a natural phenomenon to force everybody in a group to think the same. For visioning and alignment (getting all the noses pointing in the same direction) groupthink is very useful. It provides focus and a 'true belief' that a group is heading in the right direction. But this groupthink can also make organizations blind, especially if there is a dominant leader or very strong peer pressure to think alike.

Perspectivism, cognitive dissonance and groupthink have a practical implication. It means that you cannot trend-watch alone. You are bound to miss things. And you will always need to check: am I really seeing what I am seeing, or am I just confirming what I already believe is happening? Be open to signals that don't fit. And it is essential to bring outsiders in. They operate outside the group, and can therefore break the groupthink. They can see and say things that insiders are not supposed to see or say.

For every group there is a tipping point, where the news can no longer be denied. And sometimes this can lead to a *paradigm shift*. Thomas Kuhn, the historian and philosopher of science, introduced this term in 1962 in his seminal work *The Structure of Scientific Revolutions*. He used the term paradigm shift to describe a fundamental change in worldview and connected basic assumptions as a result of a new (scientific) insight. Often these shifts in paradigm result in conflict. The group is clinging on to the old paradigm, and not only the new, opposing insights are being fought, the messenger is combated too. And some groups even kill the messenger! The most famous examples are of course Copernicus and Galileo Galilei, who saw so many problematical observations in the dominant worldview of those days, which placed the earth in the centre of what we now call our solar system. Their observations would make more sense in a different worldview, one where the sun was the centre. A paradigm shift means that you are rearranging the data you already have to give new meaning. This rearranging of data was shown by Kuhn with the picture in Figure 2.8 which can both be seen as a rabbit and as a duck, based on the same visual data.

These paradigm shifts are not limited to the scientific arena. The same thing happens in organizations, with the same risk of 'killing the messenger'. We saw it in the 'there is no need for individuals to have a computer in the home' statement in the days of centralized mainframes of Digital Equipment Corporation. And we see it today in the world of energy, where the predominant worldview is still that of centralized fossil energy

Figure 2.8   Duck or rabbit?

Source: Jastrow, J. (1899) 'The Mind's Eye', *Popular Science Monthly*, 54, 299–312

systems. But the world is already shifting to a decentralized sustainable energy world. We also see it in many organizations in which the dominant belief is that centralized, large-scale organization are always better than distributed, decentralized organizations. I call this the myth of economies of scale. But fighting those myths can be very difficult, and won't always make you friends. So make sure you know the existing paradigms. Know when you are finding conflicting views, and be prepared to be opposed.

GROUPTHINK, PERSPECTIVISM AND COGNITIVE DISSONANCE

Rabobank and the mortgage retailer[7]

Rabobank's competitive analyses used to focus on their big competitors, the four other Dutch banks who all, like Rabobank, provide mortgages to home buyers. This made the bank blind to a new category of players, the mortgage retailers.

Of course, none of us could miss the rise of mortgage retailers in The Netherlands in the 1990s. They were very visible in the streets and in the news. New brands appeared and radio commercials could be heard all over the country. It was impossible to miss it. But in the collective thinking of the bank, this remained a blind spot. The banking sector in those days was already highly concentrated, just five banks controlled over 70 per cent of the residential mortgage market. Those banks constantly tracked each other's moves. And all the statistics which were kept showed Rabobank vis-à-vis the other four banks.

However, from a consumer perspective there was another choice, the mortgage retailer and the insurance broker who also sold mortgages. But for years these small retailers were never seen as competitors for a simple reason: they were not banks! Just as Digital Equipment did not see a real competition from small companies that made PC's, Rabobank did not see mortgage retailers as competition until these mortgage retailers and other intermediaries gained a market share of 20 per cent.

7   De Ruijter 2007: 236.

The German philosopher Schopenhauer is alleged to have said that each new truth knows three phases. At first you are ignored or ridiculed, than you are vigorously opposed and finally your insights are seen as self-evident. This was the case for the home computer; most people in the computer industry in the 1980s would say today: 'We always knew that there would be a huge market for computers at home!' That's trend-watching for you. You are unlikely to be given the credit you feel you deserve for noticing the important trends. And if you are too blunt, you might even get fired for pointing out new developments which are in stark contrast to the official view. So it is not enough just to spot the trends, you must also be alert to the prevailing organizational perspective. Understanding the institutional frame of reference will help you find the blind spots and at the same time will make you aware of the potential resistance you will need to overcome to get the message through. A simple trick here is to use 'outsiders'. Outsiders are not infected with company blindness, and outsiders cannot be fired. They are allowed to say things that insiders can't. The outside view will help to stretch the corporate mindset, and allow for a view with a wider angle.

To spot all the trends, you will need to scan the horizon through 360°. Outsiders are needed to shine a light in all the blind spots. However, the wider the net, the more difficult it will be to separate the signal from the noise. It is easy to get overwhelmed once you start looking. And not just overwhelmed, sometimes it can be outright scary to see what is really happening out there. The world is filled with unhappy customers, better competitors, cheaper technologies, unfavourable legislative trends and growing tensions, conflicts and even wars that might hurt you. Luckily you will also spot trends like new political coalitions that work in your favour and new unmet needs that could result in opportunities. And you do not need to do it alone. You will find that many of your colleagues are very willing and eager to help you with the task of spotting all the trends and sifting out the signals from the noise. Here is how you do it in practice.

2.3   How do you Scan the Environment?

There are several ways to make everybody see the external environment. A practical way to scan the external environment is to map the uncertainties, the seen developments, trends and counter-trends. Choices which are made in scanning depend on the available time, manpower and budget. Extended research on the external environment will improve the quality of a dynamic strategy project. How do you know which developments are important? It is wise to formulate a number of questions which are sufficiently broad and do not exclude unexpected signals but which are also sufficiently specific to avoid the collection of irrelevant and superfluous data.[8] Next we describe four methods to scan the environment: desk research, interviews, workshops and observation.[9]

Using each of these four methods it is essential to keep in mind that scanning the environment requires no value judgement, it just involves making an inventory. Scanning the environment is not about truth-finding. The aim is to be inspired, so you will have an idea about the relationship of developments in the past, about possible trend breaks and about the bandwidth of future uncertainties. This inspiration will help you develop a broader and wider conceptual framework. The knowledge and facts of the past are slowly replaced by imagination and theoretical thinking about the future. Instead of making predictions you learn to cope with uncertainty and change. And it is not only the content of the scanning that is important, but the process too: thinking about the environment is a way to raise support for future-oriented decision-making, and a way to create a common language which helps you as a collective, as an organization, to think about the future.

What is your role in making the outside world visible for your organization? You don't need to generate the content of the scan yourself. Your task is to bring the outside world inside, in a structured way. It is important to be aware of the ruling paradigm in the organization, so you can encourage colleagues to look in the mirror. You should endeavour to show the city dweller who is visiting the wilderness the tracks of the wild bear!

---

8   Fink et al. 2007: 148.

9   Janssen et al. 2007.

1. READING: DESK RESEARCH

Desk research, researching backgrounds and facts, is a sensible starting point when you want to map the outside world. But what is it that you should be looking for when you undertake desk research? In fact, you are looking for signals about the future. DESTEP analysis is a tool to remind you which factors need attention. You do not need start from scratch, often an amount of research has already been done and interesting information may already be available: the Internet is filled with information and numerous books are written about trends and the future. There are several other sources that can be useful, such as market reports, reference books, annual reports, articles in newspapers and magazines, and reports. Other, less obvious sources can offer fascinating information too. If you suddenly find several articles about 'cheap loans' in *Cosmopolitan* magazine, this can be an interesting sign of an increasing interest in borrowing money. But when a popular magazine such as this publishes more articles about budgetting, a bank may interpret this as a sign of an increasing preference for saving money, at the expense of borrowing.

Desk research offers several advantages: you can do it at your office, you do not need other people and it focuses on facts. And desk research can be well planned. It helps to put things in a wider, more abstract perspective. Software can be used to support this way of scanning the environment. For example, you can scan RSS feeds using search words which are of interest to you.

TREND-WATCHERS: ADJIEDJ BAKAS

When doing desk research you can use the work of trend-watchers. They often have a unique way of seeing things and are able to connect several apparently independent events, thus discovering new trends. Adjiedj Bakas is a trend-watcher. 'Trends come – as is well known – in all shapes and forms. Next season's fashion is, as a trend, of a different kind of order to the question of how we will incorporate technology in our lives in twenty years. But all trends are linked, however conflicting they may initially appear', he says.[10] Bakas is perhaps the best-known trend-watcher in the Netherlands. He was born in 1963 in Surinam, the son of a school teacher and has lived and worked in the Netherlands since 1983. He is author of several leading books: *Megatrends Europe* (2006), *Living without Oil* (2009), *Beyond the Crisis* (2009), *World Megatrends* (2009), *The Future of Finance* (2009), *The Future of Work* (2009), *The Future of Faith* (2010), *The Future of Love* (2012), *The Future of Health* (2012), *The End of Privacy* (2012), *The Future of Food* (2012), *The State of Tomorrow* (2013) and *Plenty* (2013). If you do not have the time or means to scan for trends or counter-trends you can take one of his books as a starting point. He describes the future developments – from micro trend to macro trend – of a broad spectrum of subjects: from work to religion and from love to oil. When you select the trends from his books that are relevant for your organization, you can scan a large part of the outside world in a short time.

---

10   Bakas 2009: 13.

As a source of scanning the environment, desk research has some disadvantages. Published material is often outdated, and you may lag behind if you base your research solely on this material. It is important to know and identify the 'official', known developments, but the new trends are inspiring. The danger of desk research is that you have allowed yourself to be guided too heavily by data from the past – while our interest is the future, for which we have no data (data of the past should only be used as a tool).

When you use desk research you run the risk of losing yourself in time-consuming, theoretical studies which contain an enormous amount of expertise but for which you have only consulted a few people and opinions. By involving several people in your scan of the environment, you can create ownership in a broader group and raise support for the project. The content we generate is only one goal in scanning the environment. The intention is also to involve people in the process and to prepare them to broaden their view and to deal with uncertainty and change.

2. LISTENING: INTERVIEWS

Talking to people – whether we talk to the taxi driver or we take part in an interview (a more formalized form of conversation) – is a good way to gather information and to help you look at things from a whole new perspective whilst at the same time building and strengthening the relationship with those who are interviewed. This makes an interview a useful tool in the process of scanning the environment.

When you scan the environment, you should aim to talk to people who have different approaches and perspectives. People from all levels within the organization and from outside the organization can be interviewed. Interviewing is pre-eminently a appropriate method to bring the outside world inside. By interviewing external stakeholders, customers, suppliers and other outsiders you get an idea of how they see the world. They see another part of the world and have another world view than that of you or your organization. Furthermore you will build relationships, because you involve different people in the strategic conversation, and you develop a common language to talk about the future. The process is as equally important as the content.

It is also often useful to interview people who are completely out of the scope of the organization. You are looking for *remarkable people*, those who have a special view on the world; are experts in fields which are interesting for your organization and who have a relevant and refreshing perspective to add to your scanning. The interviews can thus provide new perspectives and offer insight in practice. Interviewing remarkable people is thus an effective antidote to phenomena such as selective perception, cognitive dissonance and groupthink, which we discussed earlier in this chapter. Usually 10 to 15 interviewees are sufficient to gain the relevant information; for political or process reasons it can be sensible to interview a wider number.

THE VALUABLE VIEW OF THE CUSTOMER

At the end of the twentieth century the world of IT had expanded tremendously. The number of available IT professionals fell short of the demand. Because of this lack of employees in the sector new IT personnel were even recruited in the car showroom: once they had signed their employment contract they could immediately choose their lease car. IT companies assumed that this trend would continue in the future: the growth of the sector and the shortage of personnel were both linear extrapolations.

In 1999 I undertook an assignment for an IT company. To scan their environment I interviewed both experts as well as customers. In 1999 many customers blew their IT budget because of the threat of the Millennium Bug. As a consequence they had less money to spend on IT in 2000 and their IT budget decreased. This observation was diametrically opposed to the expectations which were raised by IT experts in official reports. Thus we had a trend (seen by the experts) and a counter-trend (practised by the customers). The IT company was only aware of the counter-trend when customers were asked for their opinion – luckily just in time – before the market collapsed in 2000. This example shows how valuable it is to interview people with another perspective than that of the organization itself.

When conducting an interview – this can be done both live and digital or over the phone – there are a few things to bear in mind. It is important that the person you interview knows from the start what the aim of the process is and how the data from the interview (anonymous or not) will be used. It is important that they feel free to speak openly. The interviewer should be an effective listener; this helps to establish a relationship of trust with interlocutor (which is necessary for a good result). When the interviewer is from outside the organization, this often works to their advantage, provided they speak the 'language' of the organization. People who are being interviewed usually talk more openly to an unknown outsider; they will look beyond the normal range of their organization.

It is also important that the interview has an open character. A prepared questionaire is useful as long as it includes general, open questions which serve as a *trigger* and which give room to the person who is interviewed. At the same time it is important to keep an eye on the aim of the interview: it should be about external trends. Therefore it is useful to ask about possible worries and uncertainties and about hopes.[11] Other good questions for a external-oriented interview could include:

- Which relevant trends and developments do you see?
- What are the important uncertainties to you and of which issues are you uncertain of the outcome?
- What would a good/bad world look like from your perspective, and what indicators for this good/bad world do you see?

---

11   Van der Heijden 1996 (amongst other things gives more information about the best way to ask questions as an interviewer) and Janssen et al. 2007 (gives practical tips about interviewing and interview questions).

- Imagine you had been cryogenically frozen and you wake up after ten years. What would be the first thing you would like to know?[12]

When taking an interview you need to be aware that you hear selectively. When you take notes during the interview or record the interview, perhaps with an audio recorder, you should record, as accurately as possible, the actual words the interviewed person used and reproduce the perspective of the other person as faithfully as you can. If you are not sure that you understand what the other person is saying, you can have a second person listen to the recording: they might hear different things than you, because you both have a different reference framework. Interview reports which are written based on the interviews can serve as a raw material for trend workshops and brainstorming sessions.

FUTURE POLICY SURVEY, A NEW FOUNDATION FOR THE NETHERLANDS' ARMED FORCES: THE USE OF INTERVIEWS

Ministry of Defence, Ministry of the Interior and Kingdom Relations, Ministry of Foreign Affairs, Ministry of Finance, Ministry of Justice and Ministry of Development Cooperation

In 2008 and 2009 the interdepartmental project, Explorations, was carried out by the Ministry of Defence, Ministry of the Interior and Kingdom Relations, Ministry of Foreign Affairs, Ministry of Finance, Ministry of Justice and Ministry of Development Cooperation. The project was an exploration of the future of the armed forces, and several experts from inside and outside the organization were interviewed about developments in the field relevant to the Dutch armed forces.

The subject of this project implied that a large number of developments needed to be looked at and to be linked. The interviews helped considerably in achieving this. We interviewed people from the Ministry of Defence, but also outside experts with another reference frameworks and another angle. Ministers were also interviewed. Involving ministers served both as substance – they see a lot and can give valuable input – but also as a political purpose. By interviewing the ministers, who did not have the time to visit the workshops, we generated greater involvement in the process.

---

3. DISCUSS: WORKSHOPS AND BRAINSTORM SESSIONS

I use workshops most of the time because it is the most efficient method. Workshops and (digital) brainstorming sessions deliver a wealth of information about the external environment of the organization in a short period of time. Each participant brings their own angle to the table: all of them talk to other people, read literature and see things. For these reasons they offer a great deal of original knowledge: the work has already

---

12   The 'freezer' question was taken from Rietdijk and Van Winden 2003: 140.

been done and all you need to do is 'harvest' the knowledge. This is even more the case when external stakeholders are invited as well as employees: the broader the background of the participants, the wider their view. I often use the information which came from the desk research and the interviews as input. You may also invite one or more speakers to introduce the subject and challenge the participants to widen their view and think 'outside of the box'. Scanning the environment is an iterative process. After conducting one set of interviews and workshops you can write a report which is then used as input for the next round of interviews and workshops.

Depending on the scale of the strategy project and the budget available you can choose to use a single workshop, during which a whole or half day is dedicated to making an inventory of developments in the environment of the organization – or a series of workshops in which each workshop can be completely dedicated to a specific development. In one workshop you can generate a long list of many uncertainties, developments and trends in relatively little time – but note that value judgement should be excluded from this collection of trends, uncertainties and driving forces.

What's more, workshops offer the opportunity, perhaps even more so than other methods, to create solidarity, support and involvement amongst participants. More than once I have seen participants who are more commonly opponents become 'friends' during a workshop. By scanning the environment together they learned to focus not on their opposition, but on the common challenges in the outside world. The mutual context, the relatively safe process of scanning the environment and of working together in a positive atmosphere has ended many battles. Thus workshops not only offer a contribution to the content, but also to the process. They are an excellent way to involve people and to create support for a stronger external orientation. During the workshop the participants will also develop a common language to talk about what is happening in the world.

Workshops are therefore a useful tool to scan the environment, because of the information which can be collected and because of the opportunity to create support. But they require a lot of preparation and organization, a suitable location and perhaps someone to record the minutes. Of course, workshops can be held digitally, perhaps using the organization's intranet. There is one other prerequisite for a good workshop and that is an experienced facilitator who is capable of looking after the theme of the process.[13] He or she can make sure that the conversation is structured.

A single trend workshop is by definition generic and superficial. To improve the quality one must later check, investigate, and support the items which were mentioned in the workshops, e.g. by desk research and interviews. The result of this further research can be fed back in the next workshop.

4. WATCH: OBSERVATION

Observation of the natural behaviour of stakeholders can offer leads for trends and developments in the enviroment. Walking around and observing is the literal and original form of trend-watching. By visualizing the actual reality you can make a dull project vibrant and meaningful. Observations can range from a personal observation to log books or visual registration by camera, video or photo. If you are interested in

---

13   Designing and conducting workshops is a expertise in its own right. More about this in *Regeren is Vooruitzien* (Janssen 2007) and *Hartelijke Gefaciliteerd* (Noordik and Blijsie 2008).

mobile communication, for example, you could walk around town for an afternoon and observe how people use their mobile phones in practice. Of course it is then important to share your experience with others and to point out interesting observations to one another.

When you travel, you will also be open to all kinds of interesting phenomena. If you want to know more about mobile communication you may spend some time in Japan, or in Paris if you are interested in trends in haute couture. The particularity about travelling as an observation method is that on the one hand you will see phenomena in other countries more precisely because they are exaggerated or more developed than at home, whilst on the other hand when you return you will see more clearly what is going on in your own country. Your horizon literally becomes stretched. Travelling has the potential to enable a sharp focus. For this reason many think tanks and industry associations organize learning journeys for their members on a regular basis.

Whether observation is a practical research method depends on the subject of the scan. In 2001/2002 the Netherlands Food and Consumer Product Safety Authority and the Ministry of Justice ran a scenario project about acohol use amongst young people in order to check the enforceability of article 20 of the new Dutch Alcohol Licensing Act. For this project, field research was conducted by observing how café owners dealt with young people and by observing how parents at campgrounds dealt with alcohol use by their children. We also visited several shops where we asked the cashier about the policy of selling alcohol to young people.[14] In other cases observation will be much harder. For example when you are searching for macro trends, like globalization, or when the development you want to observe only appears abroad.

A disadvantage of observation as a tool for scanning the environment is that it is often impossible to get a representative image of reality: the outreach of your research is always limited. In many cases you may only gather fragments and snapshots: $N = 1$. The sample will need to be extended in order to make it representative for the whole population. One single observation is not statistically significant – with the exception of what Nassim Nicholas Taleb called *black swans*. If you assume that all swans are white, one single observation of a black swan is enough to nullify your assumption. A deviant observation can also lead you to a counter-trend; particularly when the observation runs completely counter to the current paradigm. In that case, a limited number of observation can already be important.

WHO WILL SCAN THE ENVIRONMENT?

So it is important to take your environment into account in your strategy; to take decisions not just based on your last month's turnover, but also on a wider and more fundamental view. As mentioned before, the choice of who you ask to participate in scanning the environment can vary. The process can be limited to your own organization, in dialogue with all employees, or just a small select group. Other stakeholders, experts or outsiders may also be involved to widen the perspective. The process can be undertaken by one person or a small group; alternatively you may use a broad network of all sorts of people.

---

14   For a more elaborate description of this project, see Janssen et al. 2007.

It is important to ask yourself several questions before you decide who should participate in scanning the environment. Who is the organization or group for whom you are designing the strategy? Who will execute the strategy you are about to design? Who are your stakeholders? Who exactly do you want to involve in the scanning and the strategy process? And when exactly?

THE *VIEWING FUTURES* NETWORK[15]

Scanning the environment can be done by a small group of people, or alternatively by a large cross-section of people in the organization with, when necessary, external experts added. When the conditions are good, groups can be much smarter than individuals. Rabobank chose to have a dialogue with a large group in a project about consumer scenarios which I conducted. In line with their cooperative character, around 1,600 people were involved in the strategy process and made partially responsible for the strategy, ranging from local bank employees to members of the Supervisory Board. The network which they formed together was called the Viewing Futures network, after the scenario project's name. Such a network is also called a Collaborative Learning and Innovation Network or COIN: a team of people, intrinsically motivated and with a common vision, who are enabled by the network to reach a common goal by sharing ideas, information and work.[16]

In 2002 the first workshop for *Viewing Futures* was organized. In the next 6 months around 20 other workshops followed. Employees from all kinds of different departments and echelons of Rabobank participated. Their enthusiasm made them true ambassadors of the process and the support for the project grew. Alongside workshops desk research was commissioned. Members of the *Viewing Futures* network talked with experts outside the organization, such as politicians, academics, financial experts and stakeholders; to people working at the European Union offices in Brussels and at the Netherlands Bureau for Economic Policy Analysis (CPB). Although many of the developments could have been identified using the Internet or in other easily accessible sources, this elaborate process served to create a sensitivity for the outside world and among Rabobank employees.

The network recorded mega trends in five fields: economic, political, social, technological and ecological. This resulted in several trend booklets, which described in total 42 mega trends and counter-trends over hundreds of pages. These were distributed within Rabobank in five thematic booklets and on a CD-ROM. The trend booklets were not only meant as a report of the process of scanning the environment, but also as a marketing tool – to raise the internal support for the project. The fact that as many as 100 Rabobank employees were involved in putting the booklets together helped control the cost of the project and injected more fun. In addition the employees who were involved felt greater 'ownership' towards the project.

---

15   For an elaborate description of the Viewing Futures project of Rabobank, see De Ruijter 2007.

16   Gloor in De Ruijter 2007: 244.

2.4   Clustering and Describing Developments

It is likely you will have collected a huge amount of raw data and material during the process of scanning the environment. By clustering the trends, forces, developments, opinions, insights and possible events, all of the separate pieces become more meaningful (Figure 2.9). Clustering also helps to provide insight into the underlying factors and driving forces behind the developments and their correlations. The goal of clustering is to establish a number of clusters of influence which are roughly similar or of a similar theme. At the same time you can check whether the clusters are logical and internally consistent. At this stage the information is compressed into the most important composite variables which shape the future.[17]

There are several ways to cluster. You can do it alone, but because of the value of the process it is a good idea to do this during a workshop. Participants then try to group every trend on the basis of content. Each cluster needs to have an appropriate and appealing name, preferably one that refers to a measurable external variable, such as 'social support', 'employment' and 'movement'. It is important that each variable can develop itself in several directions and therefore has a certain bandwidth. In the case of 'employment' the extremes could be 'high unemployment rate' and 'a shortage of personnel'. Ideally, you want to form a comprehensive number of clusters which, rather than representing events, represent patterns of events or general structures which are behind them.

Clusters can then be elaborated by focusing on the specific features of the cluster and by describing the features on which the developments within each cluster depend. What are the underlying factors and driving forces? Elaborating these can – once again – be

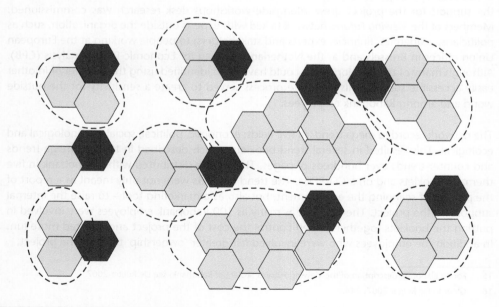

Figure 2.9   Clustering trends

---

17   Janssen et al. 2007.

done in different ways: in workshops (which have the advantage of doing it together) or as desk research (with the advantage that clusters can be supported by data).

The next question you should ask yourself when elaborating the clusters is how might the cluster develop on the basis of the factors and forces which influence it? The answer to this question can consist of two (plausible!) cluster extremes which showed the bandwidth of the cluster (as described above for 'employment') and therefore also the level of uncertainty.

AND THEN: DESCRIBING

Scanning the environment and indicating (possible) developments is only half the work. Large organizations often live in a paper world; they will not take trend-watching seriously until the results have been definitively written down. References are important, as is the source. Observed developments should be investigated and supported: decisions for the future are preferably based on facts and supported expectations rather than hunches. If you generate separate trend reports, these can be quoted as the rationale behind decisions: give people something to which they can refer and give the development a name, and they will tend to integrate this information quicker into their work. For example, the 'Facts and Trends' of the World Business Council for Sustainable Development (WBCSD) are described objectively and are much quoted. Recording accurately the information and insights which have become clear during scanning the environment is also an important source of feedback for the participants of the process and the wider organization. It helps to keep participants, both within and outside the organization, involved. Ideally the material should be available to all stakeholders.

When you appreciate important signals from the outside world, you and the organization will have a wealth of information at your disposal which can be of great use when designing a future-proof, dynamic strategy. Knowledge of the outside world is often unstructured. It is up to you to find a form and structure for the observed developments, uncertainties, driving forces, trends and countertrends, so the organization can deal in a useful way with all collected information and insights. Thinking in scenarios is one such appropriate method.

CONCLUSIONS: TRENDS

1. Decide on your domain of influence: what is the 'self' to the organization; what belongs to the transactional environment (actors) and what belongs to the contextual environment (factors)?
2. Map trends, developments and uncertainties, using desk research, interviews, workshops and observation.
3. Be aware of phenomena like selective perception, perspectivism, cognitive dissonance and groupthink. Try to look deeper and more critically; keep asking 'why?'.
4. Cluster the developments and uncertainties you have found and elaborate these clusters. Decide what the extremes of uncertainties in the future might be.
5. Generate a rigorous, well-structured, readable and attractive report of your findings and discuss this.

3 Scenarios:
In which situations could we end up?

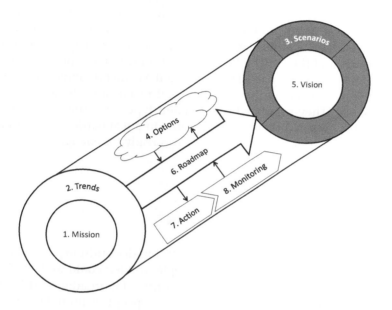

Imagine you are alone on a boat. There is a lack of wind and you have been drifting about for two days. It is hot. A boat in the distance. It is this nightmare which makes a good captain prepare by bringing water, fuel and lifejackets. Will there be icebergs on the way? Could the fleet be attacked from larboard or starboard, or will the coast be safe? Can we expect stormy weather, or will the sky stay clear? The question of what the future might bring keeps every captain awake at night and produces both dreams and nightmares.

When formulating a long-term strategy it is important to get an insight into what tomorrow's world might look like, even when historical trends are clear. This is why you use scenarios. By clustering and modelling historical trends and developments and assessing them you can, together with the rest of the organization, decide on which are the key uncertainties: what should keep the organization awake at night? That will provide insight into the connection between the empirical past (trends, data and statistics) and the theoretical future (shaped in the scenarios). The key uncertainties that you have in the present are the link between trends (past) and scenarios (future). This way, you can mobilize both knowledge and imagination, put the future on the agenda and create a common language to discuss strategic issues in a structured way.

Scenarios are images of the future constructed by combining possible developments in different ways. In this way, imaginary situations are created which you can explore. This has helped many organizations to pre-imagine situations in which the organization could end up in the future. This, in turn, has helped organizations to better anticipate them. Scenario thinking is a way of thinking which can be of use in many situations. Multinationals take advantage of it, as do individuals. After all, in our everyday personal life we continually use scenario thinking, consciously or unconsciously: 'If the weather is nice tomorrow, we will go the beach, but if it rains we will stay at home'.

Developing a number of different future scenarios is not a goal in itself. After all, a set of scenarios is not a long-term strategy or a concrete plan – yet. In times of turbulence, scenario thinking is a useful *instrument*: it prepares us for change. Scenarios help the organization to take better-considered decisions. Scenarios help to form a notion of future uncertainties and they offer a better insight on risks and opportunities.

In the seventeenth century the Dutch admiral Michiel de Ruyter was also aware of the benefits of scenarios: before he set out to sail to England, he and his fleet trained for several scenarios. They simulated the different types of battles their fleet could find themselves in. This prepared them for the future: in a real battle, they would be able to act faster and no time would be lost. The fleet was ready for change!

3.1   What are Scenarios?

THE EARLY HISTORY OF SCENARIO THINKING

The world is dynamic and uncertain. After each big discontinuity – think of 9/11, the credit crisis, the oil crisis, the Arab Spring – people wonder: could we have foreseen this? And at the beginning of every period of uncertainty – for an admiral this can be a war, for an entrepreneur the start-up of a new company – people want to know: what will the future look like?

Even before the start of our calendar, mankind concerned itself with the future. The Ancient Greeks consulted the Oracle of Delphi. In the centuries and millennia that followed, people kept trying to look into the future by consulting prophets or using rune stones, tarot cards or even patterns in coffee cups. Slowly, more scientific methods for predicting the future were developed, such as linear extrapolation. In the 1950s and 1960s, another scientific method to predict the future was developed: the Delphi method. In this method, a large number of experts is asked for their opinion on a subject about which no consensus exists. After every round of opinions, a summary of their forecasts is provided. This encourages the experts to revise their earlier opinions, and in this way a prediction of the future is tried to be reached. Nonetheless, the danger of groupthink is still present: even scientists can all be wrong.

The Second World War showed that future studies as a scientific discipline was still in its infancy. Then Herman Kahn, strategist at Rand Corporation and founder of the Hudson Institute think tank, developed the founding principles of what we now call the scenario methodology. The biggest revolution in his thinking was the fact that he no longer tried to predict a certain event exactly. Instead, he tried to uncover patterns and structures underneath events, the mechanics which drive developments: directly visible events are sometimes only the top of an iceberg, and patterns and structures lie beneath it. Kahn took the structures he discovered further to a logical path of hypothetical events that led to a certain end state. He tried to use the insight in the structures and the underlying influencing factors to make a certain extrapolation of these structures towards the future. He defined a scenario as a hypothetical chain of events, built up in an internally consistent way, with the purpose of drawing attention to causal processes and possible intervention points.[1] The essential difference between Kahn's method and the scenario method that is common nowadays is that Kahn still used only one single scenario or prediction as a starting point.

THE SHELL STORY

Scenario thinking as we know it became famous for its use by Ted Newland in Shell's planning department.[2] Newland used Kahn's scenario method to develop possible scenarios for Shell. They realized that for an organization it is not as important to have a clear view on *what will happen*, as on *the different things which could happen*. This was the turning point from a single view of the future, or a single prediction, to multiple views of the future or predictions, based on the same model of structures and influencing factors. Later, this approach became famous through articles of Pierre Wack and Arie de Geus.

Taking into account various possible futures based on one or more models enables an organization to decrease the reaction time needed when a new development actually occurs. This changed scenario thinking from a method to *predict* the future into a method to *explore* possible alternative futures and to *think through* what the organization could do in these possible situations. Eventually, the purpose of the scenario method is not to make better predictions, but to make sure the organization is better prepared for the future.

The first step was taken in 1971, even before the first oil crisis. At that time, Shell's division Group Planning was asked: 'How will the oil price develop in the long term, after the expiration of the Tehran Agreement (1971–1976)?' Henk Alkema, who had just been transferred from Research to Group Planning, was charged with formulating an answer. As a newcomer in Group Planning he was not hindered by reigning preconceptions. This enabled Alkema and Newland to develop a set of scenarios which were outside Shell's usual field of vision: three controversial scenarios in which the oil price increased by up to four times. These scenarios were backed up by their analysis of possible OPEC strategies and events that could cause a sudden price explosion. The depicted images deviated radically from the prevailing image of the future. Data from the past and even a Delphi investigation among 'experts' all pointed in the direction of stable prices and increasing volumes. No wonder that in the first instance the scenarios were met with a lot of resistance from within the organization. However, it was soon evident how valuable they had been as a means to get the organization to think about these possible situations. When in 1973 the first oil crisis broke out, because a number of OPEC members proclaimed an oil embargo against countries which had supported Israel in the Yom Kippur war, and oil was in fact employed as a weapon, Shell was mentally prepared for it. This enabled the company to react smarter and faster than the competition. At Shell, the above-mentioned scenarios were the first scenario exercise. Scenarios have since become an integral part of

---

1   Kahn and Wiener 1967.
2   Wilkinson and Kupers 2013.

Shell's strategy process. When other major trend breaks occurred, such as the dissolution of the Soviet Union, a possibility presented by Group Planning to the Board of Directors as early as 1984, scenario thinking within Shell again proved its benefits.

After Shell's success in scenario thinking other organizations also started to show their interest in this method of strategy development. Dutch Rabobank, for example, has continuously been thinking about possible futures since the end of the 1990s, in a number of scenario projects. Before the introduction of the Euro in 1999 Rabobank thought through possible consequences, before 9/11 the bank had already thought about a possible situation in which stock exchange values would drop drastically, and in 2003 Rabobank reflected extensively on possible analogies for Europe with the financial crisis in Japan in the 1990s and the economic crisis of the 1930s. On several occasions this helped Rabobank to see risks faster and to safeguard against them, and to seize opportunities early. In 2008, the year of the credit crunch, Rabobank made a record high profit, contrary to other Dutch banks who could only survive thanks to state aid. As in the Shell case, it proved to be possible to reflect on alternative future scenarios in advance and consequently to make profits in times of crisis.[3]

In the past, you had to explain why you use scenarios. Now, you almost have to explain why you don't use them. Among the organizations using scenarios are the International Energy Agency, the governments of The Netherlands and Singapore, the World Economic Forum, many banks and industrial conglomerates.

THE BENEFITS OF SCENARIOS

The credit crunch fits in the list which also features the first oil crisis of 1973, as well as the burst of the dotcom bubble in 2001 and the recession after 9/11: they were all events which came as a surprise to a number of key players, but which in other organizations had already been considered as a possible future and was taken into account in the strategy. One of the purposes of scenarios is self-protection, by anticipating and understanding risks. Bad scenarios do not exist, only bad preparation. Even scenarios which look bad at first sight can offer opportunities. Besides, the benefit of scenarios lies in the fact that they increase insight in the possible future context for an organization, by making explicit current assumptions. This helps to prepare for important eventualities. By reflecting on possible future situations we become more sensitive to signals from outside, we notice changes quicker and we are able to anticipate to those changes earlier.

By examining uncertainties thoroughly we gather a better understanding of their interaction. Thinking about scenarios helps to deepen our insight into the relations between developments. Compared to the predictions on which planning at Shell was based before the 1970s, scenarios focused less on predicting outcomes and more on understanding the driving forces which in the end would lead to a certain outcome; they focused less on figures and more on insight.[4] Therefore, one of the requisites for a scenario analysis is understanding the driving forces behind your business, instead of

---

3   De Ruijter 2007 and Idenburg et al 2005.
4   Wack 1985a: 76, 84.

understanding predictions or alternatives.[5] This helps to reflect on uncertainties in a structured way, without holding on to false certainties.[6]

There is discussion about the question of whether or not scenario thinking has the potential to increase our certainties. Some thinkers believe it does: by making uncertainties explicit and examining them, and by acquiring more insight into the system, one obtains more insight into what are called *predetermined elements*. Others do not believe that scenarios can help to increase one's certainties. They think that the world is inherently uncertain, and that it is only a choice to *presume* certain elements to be certain. Without taking a stand in this discussion it is important to always be critical and to realize that in the majority of cases, certainties are nothing but assumptions.

There is yet another reason to use scenarios, one which has more to do with entrepreneurship: scenarios can help to discover strategic options that one did not think of before – but this is a topic in itself which we will explore in Chapter 4.[7]

TYPES OF SCENARIOS

Since the success story of Shell in the 1970s, scenarios now can be found in all shapes and sizes. The simplest scenarios just describe single possible events, for example, what if the housing market collapses, or what if a dike breaches. Often these simple single event scenarios are used in risk management. Long lists of events are brainstormed and evaluated on their impact and probability. But mostly these scenarios are only about things that could go wrong. You'll seldom find a scenario such as what if there were no more hunger in the world. More sophisticated scenarios describe a complete situation in a specific date in the future: we call these end-state scenarios. Often these scenarios have the format of 'a day in the life of...' which allows us a sneak preview of how people will live in the future. End-state scenarios are very helpful for R&D, product development and marketing purposes. The most elaborate scenarios describe the full story from the past and present towards the future. They describe more than just events and the end state, they tell the story of how an internally consistent chain of events leads to the end state. This helps us to understand why things could happen and thus strengthen plausibility: it also helps us to see the early warning signals later on. For strategy purposes this type of scenario is recommended. Single event and end-state scenarios for risk management or R&D purposes can easily be derived from the elaborate scenarios, event and end-state scenarios can be a good starting point when developing a set of elaborate scenarios.

TWO SCHOOLS

In the last 40 years two schools of thought have developed in the scenario literature and practice: one focuses mainly on the content, whereas the other primarily focuses on the process.[8] The content-oriented school emphasizes the correctness of the content of the scenarios, a thorough foundation and internal consistency. The emphasis in this content-oriented school is on the existence of multiple, equally plausible futures packaged in

---

5   Wack 1985b: 140.

6   Alkema 2006.

7   Wack 1985b: 1.

8   Janssen et al. 2007.

scenarios which help the organization to avoid surprises in the future. The content-oriented school is the area of experts, of mathematical models, scientific support and of organizations like the International Energy Agency, who publish extensive scenarios for widespread use. It is the right approach to take if plausibility is important for you.

However, if engaging stakeholders in a dialogue to open them up for new ideas and to extend the boundaries of their thinking is important to you, the process-oriented school will be more useful. The *process* of scenario making can enrich the quality of the plans. In this process-oriented school scenarios are only an instrument, a communication technique which offers an alternative to problem-solving thinking.

A good example of the use of scenarios as a process instrument are the South African 'Mont Fleur' scenarios,[9] developed in 1992. To put this in its historical context: the exercise took place between February 1990, when Nelson Mandela was released from prison and anti-apartheid movements such as the African National Council (ANC), the Pan African Congress (PAC) and the South African Communist Party (SACP) were legalized, and April 1994, when the first democratic and multi-racial parliamentary elections were organized. The participants of the scenario project were 22 prominent South Africans: from politicians from different sides to economists, activists and academics. The goal of the project was not so much reaching a negotiated solution as stimulating the debate about the future of South Africa: what could South Africa look like in 2002? In this case the process was more important than the actual content of the scenarios.

The content-oriented and the process-oriented schools do not have to be contrary. It is possible to distinguish process and content, but it is not necessary to separate them: they complement each other. However, during the course of a scenario project it is wise to ask yourself which of the two is focused on more and whether or not the other area should also be given some attention.

According to Arie de Geus, former coordinator of Group Planning at Shell, the importance of scenario planning lies mostly in the creation of a common language and a common understanding of the developments in the environment which, rather than help the organization to better predict the future, enable the organization to react to new developments and opportunities in the market faster than the competition.[10] By taking a stroll in the future, one creates words for what does not exist yet. And if a future occurs which looks like the future you visited with the help of the scenarios, you are in a position to discuss it quickly and easily.

SCENARIO HORIZON

Scenarios have a certain horizon: in space, in time and in the issues covered. Which space they cover and how they are filled in depends on the organization which makes the scenarios, on those for whom the scenarios are made, and on the environment in which the organization operates. For example, there are global, national and business-specific scenarios. Multinational corporations and intergovernmental organizations play a role on the world stage and will be inclined to opt for global scenario projects, which cover geopolitical developments and serve as a framework for the organization's strategic planning. Because of their global and wide-ranging character making such

---

9   Kahane and le Roux 1992.

10   De Geus 1988.

scenarios is a large-scale undertaking that takes up a lot of time. For example, the Dutch Ministry of Defence's project *Future Policy Survey. A new foundation for the Netherlands' Armed Forces* did not only look at The Netherlands, but also – and especially – at the world: after all, the main task of the armed forces is 'contributing to peace, security and stability worldwide'.

National scenarios are used more and more as an instrument for conflict prevention. The future is then used as 'neutral ground' which all participants have an interest in. In such situations, the dialogue opened up by the scenarios is often more important than the scenarios themselves. The Mont Fleur scenarios discussed earlier illustrate this.

Other organizations benefit more from company- or sector-specific scenarios, which come in many different shapes and sizes: ranging from one-day projects, primarily focused on their own strategy, to comprehensive projects of a few months, which serve as the foundation for future plans. In short: scenarios focus on the relevant environment of the organization itself – and of course it is important that the organization is aware of its mission and formula for success.

The time which scenarios cover is an important choice. The rule of thumb is that the time should cover the period in which actions of policy can prove their value in society, including the time needed for decision-making, preparation and implementation. In the public sector this could range from 4 years when thinking about a new law enforcement policy up to 100 years when thinking about planning and building new dikes to protect a country from flooding. In the private sector the scenarios can be linked to the business case, and should cover a period long enough to include at least the payback period plus the time to really start making a return. For example, when you develop scenarios for a new oil field or refinery, it should at least cover 30 years. But the business case for a new mobile phone, for example, would look at five years at most: a new phone takes only a few years to design and produce, and it will be out of date in two years. Bear in mind that the shorter the time, the smaller the chance for real uncertainty, stimulus and surprise. And with a longer time horizon it is easier to pull people out of their regular thinking. When the time horizon is too long, the scenarios lack relevance and can be too noncommittal. Spending some time to consider which time horizon you want to use is important.

The design, construction and structure of scenarios are of critical importance for their usefulness in decision-making![11] All employees of an organization have a certain image of reality in their minds, a mental model of the organization in which the organization operates, a conceptual framework. The organization as a whole also disposes of such a model: the *scenario space*,[12] the paradigm or conceptual framework of the organization. When the images of the future presented in the scenarios do not fit into the existing conceptual framework of the employees and the organization, they will have little influence on the thinking and actions of the employees and the organization. Unless the conceptual framework of the organization changes, the behaviour of managers and employees will not change and scenarios will have no influence at all. The conceptual framework of the organization needs to be stretched. Therefore, it is essential to design the scenario process in such a way that employees and organizations will test their own images of reality and, if necessary, adapt them.

---

11   Wack 1985a: 76.

12   Alkema 2008.

It is not possible to reconstruct someone's mental model for them. What you can do, however, is link other, refreshing world views to the world view which prevails within the organization. Good scenarios provide this 'bridge' and they comprise the worries of managers as well as the outside world.[13] Scenarios have to come alive and they have to be able to root in the microcosm of the managers, where evaluations and decisions are made. Scenarios do not only have to deal with the facts, but also with the perception of decision-makers.[14] By presenting alternative ways of looking at the world, scenarios offer the chance to escape from a single point of view and to look at reality through a different pair of glasses.[15]

It is important that scenarios really stretch our field of vision. It is your task to prevent the mental world in which the scenarios take place from being too small; this is the case when the scenarios are very much alike and in fact variations on the same theme. It is important to think more broadly: another paradigm might also be possible! Therefore, we have to try to think in another dimension: in a new *scenario space*.[16]

3.2   Selecting Key Uncertainties and Creating a Scenario Framework

Actually, scenarios are nothing more and nothing less than dreams and nightmares put into words. They are a conversation about the unknowable future, stories of what events and developments in the outside world we might be confronted with. Those images are always (latently) present. When the organization has an idea of trends and developments, these have to be structured in a certain way: trends can underpin existing images and they can help to make the scenarios plausible. Moreover, the structure reveals the relations between the different trends and uncertainties.

DETERMINING THE KEY UNCERTAINTIES

In fact, there are an infinite number of possible future scenarios, but 'infinite' is not a workable quantity. Therefore we need a framework which helps us to encompass the bandwidth of possibilities and at the same time preserve as much complexity as possible. One of the ways to develop images of the future which mutually differ sufficiently and which reflect the bandwidth of possibilities is by designing a framework of two axes with mutually independent 'key uncertainties'.

Key uncertainties are the trend or influence clusters which will have the biggest influence on future developments and events if they occur, but at the same time are the most uncertain. It is important to realize at this stage that it is not about finding the truth. The point of this exercise is not to find the 'right' key uncertainties, but to determine which uncertainties are highly relevant for the organization. Although you try to indicate the key uncertainties in an objective manner, it still remains a matter of judgement. Eventually, it is about understanding which variables drive other variables,

---

13   Wack 1985a: 87.

14   Wack 1985b: 140.

15   Wack 1985b: 150.

16   De Ruijter et al 2009: 1–2.

and in which way. As we will see later, key uncertainties can be a convenient point of departure for the scenarios. Therefore it is important to involve both the initiator of a strategy project and those who will use the strategy when selecting the key uncertainties.

Determining the key uncertainties is always a difficult moment in the process. After all, at this point, we have passed the stage of thinking freely: now choices have to be made. How to take a decision about the key uncertainties? First and foremost it is important that the participants let go of (false) certainties and that they define which certainties are important *for the organization*. Consequently, participants have to distinguish between 'the' (objective) uncertainty and 'our' uncertainty: the key uncertainties are 'our' uncertainty, those which the organization believes to be important and relevant.

Furthermore, you should be aware of the fact that the way in which a decision is taken is culture-bound. Different processes can be used to reach an outcome. The 'French way' of taking a decision tends to be based on power: the leader decides and the final decision taken is 'his decision'. The 'German way' tends to be as objective, as analytical and as methodologically correct as possible: the 'correct' answer is calculated in the best possible way ('scoring'). The 'American way' of taking a decision often involves voting. Nobody expresses their opinion until the moment of the ballot, and as soon as the votes are counted everybody accepts the outcome. Finally, the 'Dutch way' is the 'polder model' of consensus decision-making. Although it may take a long time, eventually consensus is always reached and it will be seen as 'our decision'. The manner in which the group makes a decision on the key uncertainties is an important decision!

Key uncertainties can be determined in different ways. The easiest way to select the key uncertainties is to map all trends clusters on two axes: one represents the degree of uncertainty of the clusters and the other the importance of the clusters. The clusters which end up in the upper right corner are the key uncertainties (Figure 3.1).

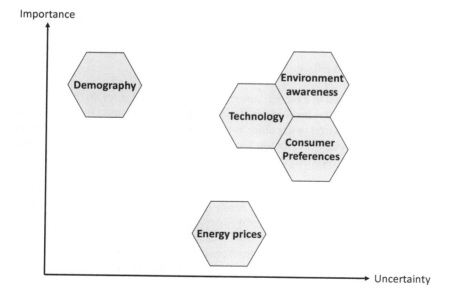

Figure 3.1   Importance–uncertainty matrix

You can also choose to decide yourself which uncertainties will be the most important for the organization and at the same the most uncertain. But when you want to create support for and commitment to the project, it is wise to select the key uncertainties in a group. This can be done by (individual or plenary) 'scoring' the various clusters for their importance and uncertainties, by voting or by discussing until consensus is reached. When the relations between the trend clusters have been mapped, this overview can be a useful tool when determining the key uncertainties. When certain clusters demonstrate several relations with many other clusters, and therefore could be a driving force of many other variables, these might just be the key uncertainties.

THE GREAT EXODUS[17]

Labour market and public task

The significant flow of talent away from the public sector – seven out of ten employees between 2010 and 2020 in the worst case – requires a common vision from the parties involved. That is why the Ministry of the Interior and Kingdom Relations carried out the project 'Labour Market and Public Tasks' together with representative associations of civil service employees and employers. On 14 April 2010 the final report was published.

The project started with a trend workshop, in which participants explored relevant trends for the next ten years. They looked at the nature of the developments, the degree of uncertainty involved and the effect on the labour market and public tasks. Then the trends which were found were gathered in different clusters with the following names:

- Demography (population ageing, declining fertility and ethnicity)
- Tight public finances (cyclical and structural)
- Changing demands of the working individual (combining work and private life)
- Labour market (flexibility, security and shortage)
- Changing forms of organization (leadership, management, productivity)
- The (dis)satisfied citizen.

The trends were elaborated in a report, supported by facts and figures. In the next workshop, the participants split into four small groups to model the trend clusters. The relations between the trend clusters differed from each other in the different models which were developed and in some models more influencing factors were added (such as ideology, politics, and media); nevertheless some issues returned in each model.

This future exploration made very clear that a great exodus of employees awaits the public sector. It is certain that until 2020, as a result of population ageing, around three out of ten employees will retire. More uncertainty remains over the number of people who will quit their jobs in the public sector for other reasons, for example budgetary concerns or because of competition for the public sector from other sectors. The size of this leaving group, for example, also depends on economic developments. The *consequences* of the exodus of

---

17   Verbond Sector Werkgevers Overheid et al. 2010: 18, 55–59, 92.

personnel from the public sector will also heavily depend on the economic situation.

In the wide range of relevant developments two uncertainties are decisive for the labour market and public tasks. One is, as mentioned above, the economic development of The Netherlands: cyclical/conjunctural developments versus more structural economic growth. The extremes of this uncertainty are stagnation (slow recovery from the economic recession combined with low growth trends) and growth (a combination of quick recovery from the recession and high structural growth).

The second uncertainty which will be crucial for the public sector is the vision of citizens, business, politics and opinion leaders on the organization of society and the role of the government. One extreme of this uncertainty is 'together', a situation in which societal problems are addressed mainly collectively and through the government: solidarity is important and people are prepared to pay for it. The other extreme is 'self', a society in which solutions must come primarily from citizens and business themselves, in a free play of market forces.

A SCENARIO FRAMEWORK: TWO, THREE, FOUR OR MORE SCENARIOS?

Before elaborating the scenarios it is important to look closely at the composition of the team which takes on this task. The scenarios should have an interdisciplinary character, and therefore it is useful to have an interdisciplinary team. The more diversity among the participants, the greater the possibility that they have a broader view on the world: from political to technological and social developments, from left or right political convictions.

The next step in the strategic thinking process is to develop a number of different future scenarios. This can be done by relating various key uncertainties which make up the framework of the scenarios. At this point we move away from data and create fictitious worlds. In this process we use the imagination of both employees and other stakeholders, for example customers and suppliers. We no longer use data, which formed the foundation of the exploration of the environment, instead we employ fantasy and creativity and we think out possible future situations logically.

The key uncertainties which we identified can be split up in their extremes and thus be used as the coathanger for our scenarios. First, for each key uncertainty we identify the bandwidth and with that the extremes. One of the criteria for good scenarios is that the scenarios have to be possible. When determining the extremes of the bandwidth of a key uncertainty it is important to take this criterion into account. The selected dimensions (key uncertainties) can be presented on two axes. For this it is essential that the dimensions of the key uncertainty are mutually independent. When (the extremes of) the key uncertainties are related, they are not independent, so some combinations will not be possible.

For example, when 'geopolitical situation' is one of the key uncertainties, you could choose to take 'more wars and terrorism' versus 'world peace' as extremes, but 'world peace' is not very plausible. In that case, it is better to go for the extremes 'more wars and terrorism' and 'manageable conflicts with limited impact'. At the same time, extremes should differ substantially from each other. Therefore, you should look for the largest bandwidth possible.

As noted before, it is not obligatory to select two key uncertainties and subsequently create four scenarios. One can also decide to create more scenarios or to confine oneself to two or three scenarios. You, with or without a team, are free to decide how many scenarios you will elaborate, as long as they are all plausible, relevant and surprising and as long as at least two scenarios are elaborated: this is the minimum number to reflect uncertainty. Because we cannot predict the future, in theory an indefinite number of future scenarios is possible. Therefore, it is important to develop enough scenarios, in order to map the bandwidth of possibilities as well as possible without reducing it too much, but at the same time not so many scenarios that the number becomes unworkable. Besides, with the help of special software the possible combinations of a large number of uncertainties can be simulated.

When you decide to create two scenarios, you can do this by describing a nightmare world and a dream world: a *worst-case* scenario and a *most desirable* scenario. However, thinking in terms of 'good' and 'bad' scenarios is risky and it is only acceptable when opportunities in the nightmare and downsides of the dream are also considered. You are not supposed to only take into account a scenario which is considered convenient for the organization. 'Every disadvantage has an advantage': for an organization it makes sense to think about the upsides of supposedly 'negative' scenarios and the downsides of 'positive' scenarios. This can lead to new, valuable insights.

When three instead of two key uncertainties are selected, a framework of eight scenarios (2 × 2 × 2) is created. However, when only scenarios which seem relevant and plausible are created, the final number can be, for example, three scenarios, as shown in the framework of the Shell Global Scenarios to 2025.[18] In this 'Trilemma triangle'

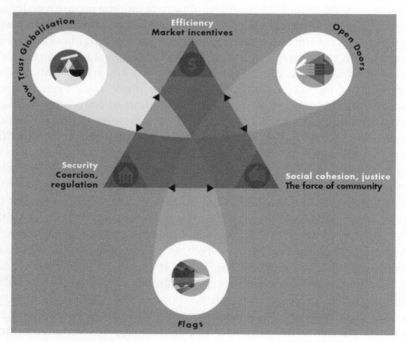

Figure 3.2   Trilemma triangle: the Shell Global Scenarios to 2025

Source: Shell Global Scenarios to 2025 (2005). © Shell International Limited

---

18   Shell 2005: 8–10.

we see the most important goals every society pursues in bold: efficiency and growth, social cohesion and justice, and security. Below these goals, we see which instruments society has to realize these goals. In each of the three scenarios which Shell made for the period to 2025 two of the goals mentioned predominate, partially at the expense of the third goal. For example, in the scenario Flags the pursuit of efficiency is cast aside under pressure of the importance given to security and social cohesion. In the scenario Low Trust Globalization security and efficiency are important, whereas social cohesion is considered less important.

It is important to realize that the method of two key uncertainties and a framework of two axes described above is nothing but a tool: it is up to you to use these tools as you think best in your conversation about future scenarios.

UNCERTAINTY SECURED

Dutch Association of Insurers[19]

The insurance industry is pre-eminently an industry which tries to prepare for the future; after the attacks on 9/11 the Dutch Association of Insurers became interested in scenario thinking and in 2005 it started an extensive future exploration. The Association wanted to get away from everyday concerns and look at the future. The purpose: making their employees better discussion partners for the members of the Association. The result was the report *Uncertainty secured*, which provided an overview of the certainties and uncertainties of insuring in/for the next ten years.

In the report two future scenarios were described: a positive scenario, 'Trust secured', in which all opportunities had been seized, and a negative scenario 'Mistrust secured', in which all threats had become reality. In an exaggerated way, these two scenarios made clear what had been discussed and thought about during the course of the project. Some developments, like population ageing and technological progress, appeared in both scenarios because the association took these as certain, although it remained unclear in what way these developments would appear. For the Association, the uncertainties resulted mainly from four external categories: economy, government, risks, and the perception of the customer.

The value of this project was that it helped the Dutch Association of Insurers to mentally prepare for the future. This became very clear with the trust crisis in 2008 and 2009. The scenario 'Mistrust secured' closely approached the situation that unfolded in reality. Because the Association had already imagined this possibility in an earlier stage, before anything was happening, it was prepared to face this trust crisis.

---

19   For a more extensive description of this scenario project, see also De Ruijter and Lassche 2006.

A decision tree can also serve as a framework for the scenarios. A decision tree contains the most important questions which an organization has with regard to the future. When for example three questions are included in the decision tree and all three can be answered with an affirmative or negative, a framework of four possible future scenarios is created. One can decide to use a decision tree instead of two axes as a framework for the scenarios when certain extremes of the dimensions selected are not worth thinking about. For the Mont Fleur scenarios, which will be discussed in more detail later, this approach was taken.

When it becomes clear that as you created the scenarios the key uncertainties were not identified correctly, or that the decision tree does not work, the key uncertainties can of course be adapted. Thus the process of selecting key uncertainties or key questions and creating scenarios is an iterative process.

FUTURE POLICY SURVEY. A NEW FOUNDATION FOR THE NETHERLANDS' ARMED FORCES: FOUR SCENARIOS[20]

Ministry of Defence, Ministry of the Interior and Kingdom Relations, Ministry of Foreign Affairs, Ministry of Finance, Ministry of Justice and Ministry of Development Cooperation

We have already mentioned the interdepartmental scenario analysis which the Ministries of Defence, of Interior and Kingdom Relations, of Foreign Affairs, of Finance, of Justice and of Development Cooperation carried out starting from 2008 to explore the future of the armed forces in 2020: the *Future Policy Survey*.[21] The result of this analysis consisted of, among other things, fours scenarios.

Two key uncertainties were selected over the course of the project, and together they formed the framework of the scenarios. The first was the geopolitical playing field, in other words the world system, with non-cooperation and fragmentation versus cooperation and integration as extremes. The second key uncertainty was the position of independent states, with high influence of states versus high influence of other actors, such as non-governmental organizations (NGOs) and multinationals, as extremes. By drawing up a framework of two axes representing these key uncertainties the basis for four scenarios was created (Figure 3.3).

The scenario Multipolar is characterized by strong states which cooperate very little and which confront each other. Here we find superpowers and power blocs; this is a world in which, at best, there is a balance of power between three or more strong states or their power blocs. These superpowers clash in many areas. There is a lot of economic and political rivalry and the degree of protectionism is high.

The scenario Multilateral sees ongoing globalization. States are strong, and at the same time there is a high level of integration and multilateral cooperation within the world system. In this scenario intensively cooperating states dominate the security agenda: global governance is reformed. Disturbances of the harmony between states are not tolerated. The west has a strong position, alongside the emergence of the BRICs (Brazil, Russia, India and China).

---

20   Ministerie van Defensie 2010.

21   See also section 2.3, where this case was used to give more insight in the advantage of interviewing in a trend study.

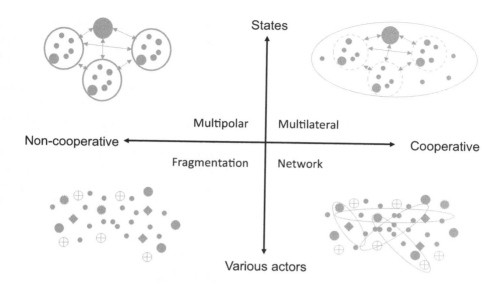

Figure 3.3   **The scenarios of *Future Policy Survey* (after Botterhuis et al. 2009)**

In the Fragmentation scenario states play a marginal role: other players such as NGOs, multinationals and other groups become more important. The world system is noncooperative and fragmented in large measure. Conflicts prevail in this world – but they are not conflicts between states. Instead, the conflicts take place between large numbers of extremely varied and varying groups or (temporary) clusters of groups. Globalization stagnates and social insecurity increases. Protection of one's own identity comes to the fore.

The scenario Network portrays a future in which states play a small role; instead, other players are integrated and cooperate on a global level. Here we see an increasing interwovenness and global cooperation in the political, social and economic areas. Non-state actors, like multinational companies and NGOs play an important role. There is a non-polar global order. We see a global market economy and a strong civil society.

Like in every scenario project, in the Future Policy Survey it soon became clear that many participants preferred one scenario, putting other scenarios aside as considerably less attractive. In this case, most participants considered the Multilateral scenario as the 'sunny scenario', whereas for many of them Fragmentation represented a nightmare scenario. Nonetheless, the participants realized that it is very useful to 'consider the unthinkable conceivable' and to think through the consequences of every scenario thoroughly, even and exactly when these scenarios are not regarded as attractive ones. For example, the Ministry of Defence would have a very important role to play in a Fragmentation scenario, while in a Multilateral scenario the power of the West would decline. As football player Johan Cruijf used to say: 'every disadvantage has an advantage' – and the other way around.

When creating scenarios it is easiest to take a few key uncertainties or fundamental questions as a starting point. From there, one can easily compile four scenarios. Creating scenarios based on key uncertainties or key questions is a deductive way of working: first you create a structure and subsequently you fill in the scenarios which follow from that structure. You work from the generic to the specific. The fundamentals of every scenario are clear from the start: they are the extremes of the two key uncertainties in a certain combination or the answers to the most important questions an organization has with regard to the future.

Nevertheless, it is also possible to create scenarios in an inductive way and to work the other way around, from the specific to the generic. The structure of the scenarios then *emerges* from the gathered data; no framework is imposed, but the storylines emerge by combining the different data in a logical way. Next, a schematic structure is derived from the stories that emerged.

MONT FLEUR SCENARIOS

Adam Kahane, the facilitator of the South African Mont Fleur scenarios (Figure 3.4), worked in an inductive way. Because of the diverse backgrounds of the participants and the sensitivity of the theme of the scenarios, in this scenario project it was very hard to reach a decision about the key uncertainties. Kahane told the participants to start by coming up with storylines, then all these different bits of stories which were made up by different people were clustered into four scenarios. Only then was a schematic structure created, which had the format of a decision tree representing different key questions.[22]

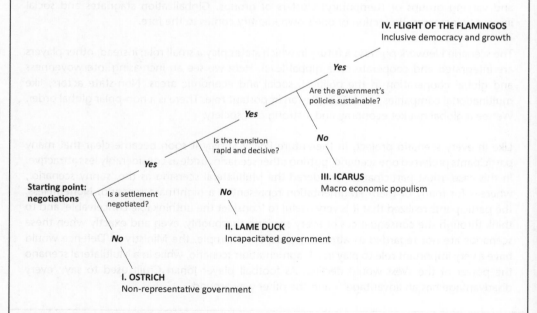

Figure 3.4   The Mont Fleur scenarios (after Kahane and le Roux 1992)

22   Kahane and le Roux 1992.

During the course of the project, which encompassed three workshops of three days each, the participants developed mutual understanding and a common language in informal, open conversations. The emphasis was not on the differences between the participants, but on what they shared: the future of South Africa. This special process resulted in four scenarios: Ostrich, Lame Duck, Icarus and Flight of the Flamingos. The scenarios, in turn, led to new, interesting insights in the possible futures of South Africa, to the creation of new, informal networks and partnerships between the participants, and to a subtle change in the language and thinking of the participants and of those with whom they spoke about the scenario project. I have visited South Africa regularly since 1992 and I am glad to see that in reality the situation looks most like the last scenario: Flight of the Flamingos. Nonetheless, the fear of the Icarus scenario still exists.

In practice, creating scenarios and the underlying structure is often an iterative process, in which the deductive and inductive ways of working alternate. It is, for example, possible to start with different storylines which are then clustered into a few scenarios. Slowly the underlying structures are revealed (induction). The structures which are thus discovered can then be used to strengthen the scenarios (deduction).

3.3   Elaborating Scenarios

The quadrants formed by two axes or the answers in a decision tree in fact provide the scenarios – but they are still very superficial. To strengthen and improve the scenarios the framework which has been created needs to be filled in further. Starting from the present, what happened to reach the end state of the scenario? How did the different events and trends relate to each other? When doing this exercise it is important that the scenarios comply with three criteria: they have to be plausible and relevant and they have to lead us to new insights (Figure 3.5).

The criterion of plausibility concerns the credibility of the scenarios. Is the emergence of a world as described in the end state of the scenario imaginable, and is the path to this

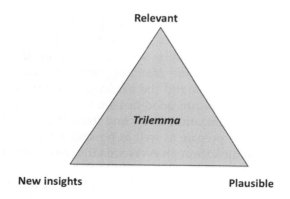

Figure 3.5   Three criteria for good scenarios

end state conceivable and internally consistent? The question is not whether the scenario is considered *probable*, but whether it is *possible*. Therefore, it is important to make the scenarios as plausible as possible.

The relevance of the scenarios is important because scenarios are not a goal in themselves: they have to be of use for the project and for the organization. Do they link to the organization concerned and do they offer starting points for further use? When this is not the case, you should try to make the scenarios more relevant.

The third criterion concerns the question of whether scenarios really lead to new insights. Good scenarios trigger people and encourage them to let go of (false) certainties, for example by touching upon taboos or by surprising, provoking emotions or inciting to act. The last is especially important: scenarios have to invite action. Scenarios should be surprising, should sharply outline possible future challenges and should widen the field of vision of the organization.

Good scenarios link separate elements to each other in coherent images or stories which mutually differ sufficiently. In addition, these images or stories should be plausible and relevant and lead to new insights. Furthermore, their internal logical consistency is important. This means that the structure and storyline of each scenario should be logical; there should be a good 'theory' to underpin the scenario. The better and more thorough the images of the future are composed, the more functional they are: people who did not participate in the process can virtually walk into these futures and imagine what that world would look like. This enables them to 'suspend their disbelief', virtually visit a possible future and benefit from it. They can catch up with the story and even add their own input. This will make the scenario more complex, rich, credible and useful.

People will be put off if scenarios are not well composed or if they are very superficial, for example because they only describe the two dimensions selected as key uncertainties and other ideas generated in the exploring phase of the project are used insufficiently, which results in a poor image. Then the scenario does not provide enough guidance to imagine it happening in reality.

At the same time, when enriching a scenario with details, you should take care: although details make a story easier to imagine, if you overdo it they can undermine the credibility of the story. To find the right balance between plausibility and credibility it is important to take into account the type of public you are dealing with. Some users prefer analytical scenarios with a clear logic, whereas other users are more susceptible to scenarios written in a creative way.

It is also essential to elaborate less attractive images of the future, as was stated before with regard to the scenarios composed for the Dutch armed forces (see the *Future Policy Survey* case earlier in this chapter). Of course some images of the future are more attractive than others; nonetheless, every future offers opportunities and threats for different actors. It is good to remind yourself and the participants every now and then that the future scenarios in themselves are not good or bad: they are only models of a possible environment in which the organization could find itself. The models serve as a tool for the organization to be able to prepare as well as possible for all those future situations. Therefore it is important to think through every scenario, especially those that you would rather not think about.

Bear in mind: no options to act or no solutions for the organization are incorporated in the scenarios. Scenarios only give us an idea of the external factors an organization might have to deal with in the future but which it cannot choose. Scenarios describe issues which the organization should take into account, because they could have a big impact.

ELABORATING THE SCENARIO LOGIC

Having created the scenario framework, one can start to further elaborate the scenarios. When elaborating the scenarios, it is useful and important not only to describe the key uncertainties or fundamental questions, but also determine how the trends, developments and events found earlier in the strategic process would work out in each of the scenarios. This will make the scenarios easier to imagine. When a number of basic plots have been set out, the challenge is to return to the long list of trends and uncertainties to make them part of the scenarios in which they are relevant. When modelling has been part of the strategic process, the relations revealed can be used in the scenarios. Of all the trends and developments which you found earlier, those with a high degree of certainty will appear in all scenarios. Ageing for example is a given fact in almost all scenarios describing The Netherlands in the next ten years that I have been involved in; for instance in the project Labour Market and Public Tasks mentioned earlier. At the same time, every scenario displays its own specific trends and developments.

Sometimes a single question, like 'What if house prices decrease?', suffices as a scenario, especially in a management team which understands the implications, which believes in the possibility of such an event and which is trained in this way of thinking. But when millions of Euros are involved or political interests are at stake, it sometimes is desirable to further elaborate and underpin the scenarios: this can increase the relevance and the plausibility of the scenarios and their ability to surprise. And with this, the chance rises that the scenarios will lead to new insights and that they will actually be used for better decision-making.

When elaborating the scenarios, for each one the most important developments and events leading to the end state will need to be determined. By shaping these into a logical plot, a story is created which explains, in a plausible way, how the end state of the scenario could arise. By writing down every scenario as a story with a beginning, a middle and an ending, the scenario becomes more than a description of one single moment: it outlines the path of the present to the end state.

This increases the imaginability of the scenarios. It also helps not to use wording like 'It could be that...', but rather expressions such as 'When in November 2017 the energy war between China and Saudi Arabia broke out...'.

When elaborating the scenarios it is important that the timeline is likely. Some transitions take time, for instance for technical or political reasons. In the year 2013, a scenario for 2020 in which the complete Dutch vehicle fleet exists of nothing but hydrogen cars lacks plausibility for the mere fact that the mass production and marketing of such cars takes time and because a method still has to be found to produce hydrogen at low cost and at large scales. And even if those things could be arranged within a couple of years, it would still be highly improbable that the hydrogen car would have ousted all other types of cars by 2020. First of all petrol cars which have already been developed still have to be sold before the supply of new cars will consist only of hydrogen cars. In addition, we have to take into account the replacement rate of cars: every year only a percentage of the Dutch population replaces their car with a new one. So even if in 2020 all new cars use hydrogen as a fuel, a large part of the vehicle fleet will still be made up of older cars that use petrol as a fuel.

If it proves that after elaborating the scenarios each of them is still relevant and plausible and leads to new insights, it is time to further enrich them. This enrichment consists of creating an integral and detailed story, which starts in the present and ends with the end state of the scenario. As mentioned before, the scenarios are now filled in with the developments, trends and uncertainties found earlier.

At this point, the storyline is consistent and logical to make sure that users can identify with the scenarios. To increase the imaginability of the scenarios, personal or micro stories work well. They touch emotions and they ensure users get a strong impression of the issues in a scenario. This increases the chance that the scenarios will evoke a sense of urgency or action. A housing crisis, for instance, is an abstract fact. We could make up a story of a couple which, just married, signed the contract for their dream home deliriously happy five years ago, and who now stand at the counter of their local bank, desperate because of the huge debt which has developed since. Bewildered, the woman calls out to her husband: 'It was you who wanted to buy that house!' By making the story about the housing crisis as concrete as possible, it will be easier for the bank employee to imagine the scenario. The consequences of a housing crisis now will become visible in their full magnitude.

When the goal of the scenarios is first and foremost to put certain issues on top of the agenda, the imaginability is less important and the broad outlines of the story may be enough (possibly in snapshots of the beginning, the middle and the ending of the scenario time frame), possibly even in key words. The degree up to which the scenarios are elaborated depends on the group and the goal they are made for.

Elaborating the broad outlines of a scenario is something which is preferably done in a workshop setting, or for which an initial impetus is provided in a workshop setting, in which participants work on a scenario in small groups. It is surprising how easily a group of people can do this. Give a group of people a flip chart with the instruction to make a plausible and relevant story that leads to new insights, that begins in 2010 and ends in 2030, about a world in which housing prices rise and a similar story about a world in which housing prices decrease – and two hours later one will have a first, rough version of the scenarios. Elaborating them in detail usually involves more research and certain writing skills. Of course you can take on this task yourself, but you can also leave it to a professional. Like writing a good news article or a scientific paper, writing good scenarios also requires certain skills which not everyone possesses automatically. If you need well imagined scenarios for a large target audience, it is advisable to deploy an experienced scenario maker. Experience shows that this is not an unnecessary luxury.

When elaborating the scenarios a catchy title which covers the content, the essence and the atmosphere of the scenario is very important; after all, the title strikes one immediately and can evoke a lot of reactions. A part of the added value of scenarios compared to single lists of events, trends and ideas is that a good story, including a catchy title, is able to communicate large amounts of complex information.

Ideally, the title of a scenario consists of one single word or a short slogan. Further, it helps when the titles of different scenarios together form a logical set. In 2008, when the credit crunch broke out worldwide, the Paying and Saving unit of Rabobank created four scenarios about the world *after* the credit crunch, with the titles Blues, Classical,

Techno and Rock. One of the advantages of these titles was that presentations of the scenarios could be adorned with music. Often, metaphors or symbols will do fine as a title – although it is important that the used metaphors or symbols have more or less the same associations for everyone. Therefore, clichés are not spared in scenarios. Everything which adds to the atmosphere and the image which one tries to outline in the scenario is justified.

QUANTIFYING

Sometimes it is essential to quantify the scenarios. Imagine that the value of an oil field is estimated based on a crude oil price of $50 per barrel. For the company which considers exploiting this field it matters a lot whether the future price of crude oil of will be $20 per barrel or $200 per barrel. Therefore, the relevance of the scenarios increases when they have been quantified: then they can be used for the evaluation of an investment proposal. In addition, quantifying the scenarios also adds up to the degree to which they are surprising, because it can evoke reactions such as 'Is it *that* much?' or 'Is it *that* expensive?'. Finally, the imaginability of scenarios also increases when they are

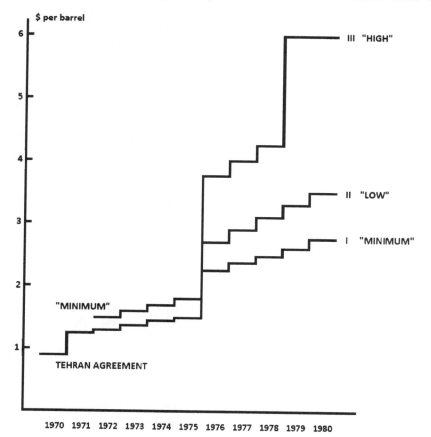

Figure 3.6   Quantified price scenarios (graph adapted from personal notes of Henk Alkema)

quantified. Take for example the future interest rate: although in reality a margin of '4–8 per cent' or 'a high interest rate' is more plausible, '7.8 per cent' *sounds* much better. A percentage of 7.8 is more suited to get across the message of the scenario than '4–8 per cent' or 'a high interest rate'. The message has to be: 'We made a calculation and this could happen'. After all, the other scenarios contain other figures, and together the set of scenarios reflects the margin.

Quantified scenarios are useful, for instance, when decisions have to be made about budget cuts. When making an important decision like that, there is no sense in basing it on one single scenario; it is better to be prepared for multiple scenarios. The bandwidth of a budgetary deficit is the consequence of both political and economic uncertainty. Quantifying this uncertainty is important to get an idea of the consequences of the uncertainties.

The first oil price scenarios created at Shell mid-1971 (see p. 57) consisted of three scenarios. The scenarios were based on macro developments, such as the development of the economy and the costs of alternatives for oil and gas, like coal and nuclear energy, but more importantly Shell's transactional environment was also taken into account. Henk Alkema studied how much the governments of the countries in the Organization of Petroleum Exporting Countries (OPEC) needed for their oil and how much they could ask. By quantifying this information, the graph in Figure 3.6 was created. Figure 3.6 visualizes what would happen to the amount which producing countries charged, the so called 'government take', for every barrel of oil produced in each of the scenarios. It was this quantification which shocked the board, and made them think.

As part of the project *Viewing Futures*, in 2003 Rabobank developed three quantified scenarios, namely for the interest rate. Those interest scenarios contained analyses of a number of factors, such as inflation, economic growth, consumer confidence, and monetary and budgetary policies. With the help of models Rabobank mapped which behaviour several actors, such as central banks and consumers, could exhibit and which consequences this behaviour could have for the price of money (the yield curve). This gave Rabobank an idea of the discontinuities which might happen in the future. The next step, representing the scenarios in graphs (Figure 3.7) increased their imaginability. A profound quantification made a scenario of low interest rates, in which we would end up in 2009, imaginable and plausible. Moreover, the usefulness of the scenarios for

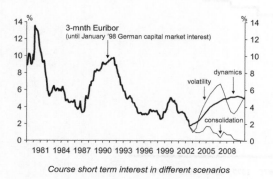

Course short term interest in different scenarios

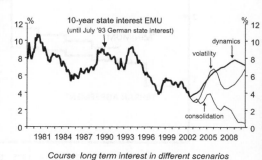

Course long term interest in different scenarios

Figure 3.7   Interest rate scenarios of Rabobank (after Rabobank 2003)

Source: Rabobank 2003

investment decisions increased. When scenarios are quantified, it is possible to calculate investment proposals for different possible scenarios, to assess risks. We will come back to this in Chapter 4.

In 2008, two key uncertainties emerged in the project Labour Market and Public Tasks: on one hand the economic development, with growth and stagnation as its extremes, and on the other hand our vision of society and the role of the government, with the extremes 'together' (better supervision and regulation and a government which intervenes smarter and quicker) and 'self' (the willingness to show solidarity with others via collective arrangements is under pressure). The extremes of those key uncertainties were combined and four scenarios were created: Bingo, Volleyball, Fishing and Climbing.

Each of these four qualitative combinations was quantified in an indicative way, to get an idea of what this scenario could mean in quantitative terms (Figure 3.8). The economic growth could vary from 0.75 per cent (stagnation) to 2.5 per cent (growth) and the collective burden could increase from 38 per cent (in 2008) to 42 per cent (in the scenario Bingo, together and stagnation) or decrease to 36 per cent (in the scenario Fishing, self and stagnation). In 2020, collective financial resources could have increased by €66 billion (in the scenario Volleyball, together and growth), or they could have decreased by €11 billion (in the scenario Fishing) compared to 2010. Indicatively quantifying the scenarios made it easier to get the message across. Whereas in 2010 the Dutch press

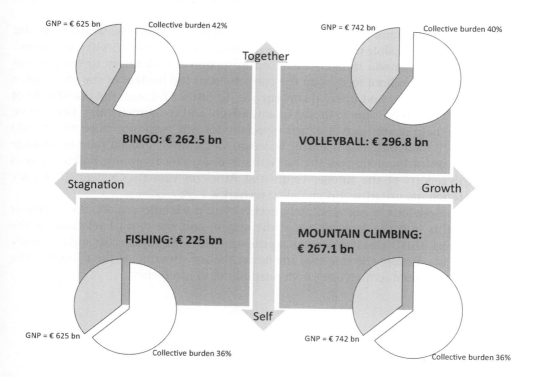

Figure 3.8   Quantification of the collective financial resources in the Labour market and public tasks scenarios (after Verbond Sectorwerkgevers Overheid 2010)

predominantly spoke about the necessary budgetary cuts worth €18 billion, the scenarios showed that the degree of uncertainty was a multiple of the €18 billion, both up and down.

MODELLING

When elaborating the scenarios you can also try to model the trends and developments which are part of the scenarios.[23] This means that you try to represent the relations and coherence between the trends and developments. A model can show the structure of the field of influence in which the organization operates, how the different elements influence each other and how the system acts as a whole. Modelling is done by considering the relations between the developments, the character and the direction of these relations, the dependencies of the relations and the possible existence of remarkable subsystems. What is found can be represented in a scheme accompanied by a clarifying text. An example of a model representation of reality is found in Rabobank's project *Viewing Futures* (Figure 3.9). This model represents how, in years of economic growth, self-reinforcing loops of positive feedback can emerge.[24] It is important to realize that a plus symbol indicates an equal relation: this can be a reinforcement, but also an abatement. The model only applies to the scenarios Survival and Growth, where the focus is on individual welfare. When, as in the scenarios Meaning and Support, social welfare is found to be important, there will be interventions in the model, leading to changes in the relations.

Modelling can be done as a group, to get an idea of the coherence between actors and factors, but it is also possible to opt for a more scientific method which fits in the content-oriented school of scenario thinkers described in section 3.1. Contrary to the process-oriented school, this school focuses on the correctness of the content of the scenarios, a thorough underpinning and internal consistence. To further increase the plausibility of the scenarios it is also possible to model quantitatively and econometrically. This can be done with the help of software designed especially for this purpose. Those who would like to approach modelling in a scientific way can, for example, deepen their knowledge of system dynamics. Predictions of the Netherlands Bureau for Economic Policy Analysis (CPB) or the reports of the Intergovernmental Panel on Climate Change (IPCC) are examples of such quantitative and modelled scenarios.

Although modelling is not absolutely necessary in a scenario project, it can deliver valuable insights into the functioning of the system and the mutual relations of the different clusters. This makes it easier to make the scenarios logical, plausible and internally consistent. It is generally the case that the better the construction of the scenarios, the better they can be used to map one's own possibilities to intervene.

---

23   Janssen et al. 2007.
24   Idenburg et al. 2005: 81.

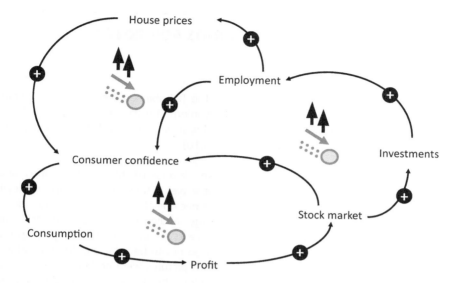

Figure 3.9   Causal model used in Rabobank's project, *Viewing Futures*

3.4   Visualizing Scenarios

Both the quality of the content of the scenario and the quality of their graphic design is important. The scenarios must have a certain 'presentation power'. For example, this can be the result of their illustration with figures, charts, graphs, pictures or drawings. The scenarios can be presented as a story, but also as a newspaper, a poster, a news bulletin or a movie. A striking representation can increase the effect of the scenarios. Sound (music, recordings...) can also strengthen the scenarios.

Al Gore's documentary *An Inconvenient Truth*, which outlines a doom scenario of a world which is ruined as a result of climate changes caused by human activity, gains in power of persuasion from the 'evidence' in the form of statistics and experts which Gore cites and from the frightening images he deploys, of melting icebergs and dying animals. Martin Luther King, who tried to transmit a dream scenario of a world without racial discrimination in his world famous speech *I have a dream*, strengthened his story by making it personal and involving himself, by drawing a visual image – we will come back to this comprehensively in Chapter 5.

When choosing the way in which the scenarios are presented, it is of course important to take into account the target audience (is it focused on figures or keen on emotions?) and the intended effect of the scenarios.

CONSUMER SCENARIOS FOR 2012[25]

Rabobank

As part of the project *Viewing Futures*, in 2003 the Rabobank developed four consumer scenarios called Survival, Support, Growth and Meaning. The scenarios described what the world could look like in 2012 and what needs and wishes with regards to financial services the consumer would have in these worlds (Figure 3.10).

Initially, Survival, Support, Growth and Meaning were somewhat superficial scenarios. Above all, they described the factors in the system. The initial axes of these scenarios were somewhat abstract: economization and socialization. When it became clear that the scenarios did not work well and that they did not appeal to the target audience, it was decided to rename the axes into 'alone/together' and 'fat years/lean years' – concepts that conjure up more of a particular image. However, this alteration proved not to be sufficient: the scenarios still did not come alive to the target audience. Relevant pictures were added to the scenarios, but although they were strengthened by this addition, the stories were still abstract. Then Rabobank decided to ask a number of actors to interpret the consumers in the different worlds of the scenarios. This step to micro stories made it much easier for the target audience to imagine themselves in the scenarios.

Because demand for a presentation of the scenario was high, movies were made: an appealing and simple way of presenting the scenarios. Although the movies were simple and short – 10 minutes per scenario – they turned out to be very effective. Each movie contained one storyline, a voiceover and matching images and music. The movies indicated a common

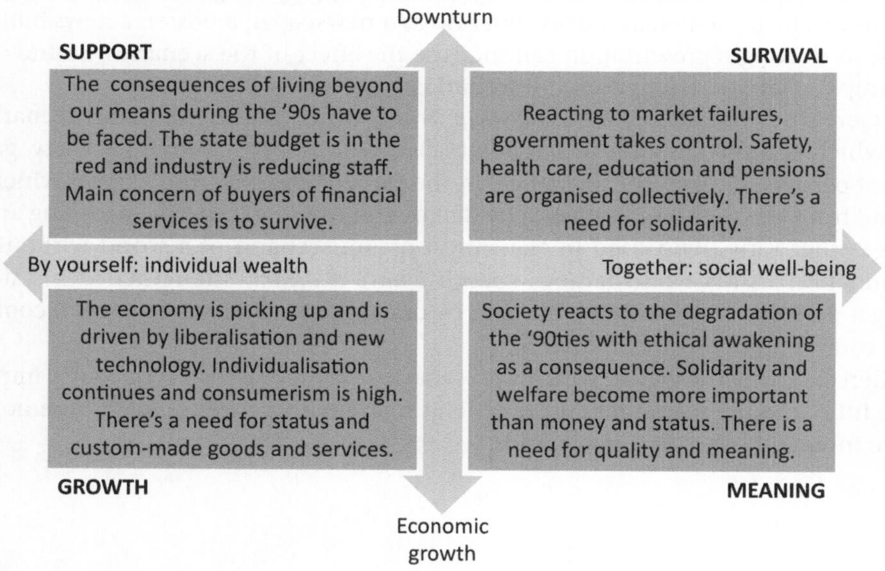

Downturn

SUPPORT

The consequences of living beyond our means during the '90s have to be faced. The state budget is in the red and industry is reducing staff. Main concern of buyers of financial services is to survive.

SURVIVAL

Reacting to market failures, government takes control. Safety, health care, education and pensions are organised collectively. There's a need for solidarity.

By yourself: individual wealth   Together: social well-being

The economy is picking up and is driven by liberalisation and new technology. Individualisation continues and consumerism is high. There's a need for status and custom-made goods and services.

Society reacts to the degradation of the '90ties with ethical awakening as a consequence. Solidarity and welfare become more important than money and status. There is a need for quality and meaning.

GROWTH   **MEANING**

Economic
growth

Figure 3.10 The framework of the Rabobank consumer scenarios

25   For an extensive description of Rabobank's project Viewing Futures, see also De Ruijter 2007 and Idenburg et al. 2005.

playing field and served as a starting point for further debate about the future. Moreover, they helped to reach a large audience, for example because with the help of the scenarios, local banks could independently go ahead and work with the scenarios. Then the scenarios were used as input for, among other things, planning, product development, and vision on sponsorship which will be discussed in Chapter 5. As the interest in the scenarios from outside the Rabobank increased, eventually a book was written about the project: *Viewing Futures*.

The example of the consumer scenarios proves once again that developing scenarios is an iterative process: a continuous feedback loop makes the scenarios ever-richer and more usable.

Sometimes articulating the scenarios directly leads to action, but more often it is desirable to enrich and adapt the scenarios as Rabobank did. This is not a goal in itself, but often it is necessary to increase the imagineability, to make sure the organization can eventually use the set of scenarios and translate them into a long-term strategy or concrete plans. A scenario is a sequence of possible future developments which together lead to a certain end state. The future will never unfold exactly in line with one of the scenarios, but thinking through the different scenarios introduces a new way of thinking: the scenarios help us to get insight into certain mechanisms, risks and opportunities. Most of the time, the process of scenario thinking is more important than the scenarios themselves. Subsequently, the scenarios can be of help when creating options and taking well considered decisions. In the next chapters, we will come back to the use of scenarios.

CONCLUSIONS: SCENARIOS

1. Determine the most important uncertainties for the future and put them in a framework. This can be two axes representing two key uncertainties, but also a decision tree containing the most important questions for the future.
2. Elaborate the scenarios: fill them in with the developments, trends, uncertainties and possible actions of actors from the transactional environment, until each scenario forms a plausible and relevant whole leading to new insights.
3. Re-present the scenarios to make them appealing stories about possible future situations and the path leading there.

4 Options:
Is our current course future-proof and, if not, what can we do to make it so?

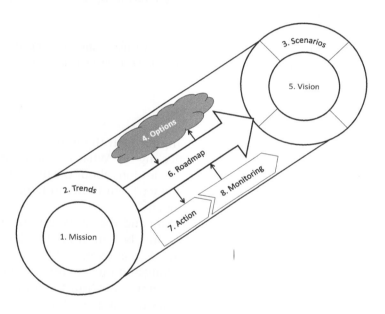

The steersman keeps the ship on course, but it is the captain who reflects on any course of action. Should they add another sail or, alternatively, put a reef in the sail? Which harbours are close by, in case the ship needs to anchor? In short: what options does the captain have, given the destination and the circumstances? This is a good analogy for your next step once you have generated the scenarios: you need to determine how the organization could act, given the possible future circumstances.

Mapping options provides more freedom to act, and vice versa. This was the case in 2000 at the UMTS-frequency auction for the telephone industry. According to the official view on the future, UMTS (also known as 3G) would be the next 'must-have' technology. Thus telephone companies thought they had no other option than to buy a frequency at any cost. The CEO of a Dutch company described the UMTS auction as an auction of parachutes in a burning aircraft: all of the players needed a parachute (i.e. a UMTS frequency) as it was their only option for the future. However, this option was based on a false certainty, dictated by the organization's direct environment. At the time there were also signs of a situation in which UMTS would *not* be an instant success, but these were disregarded. And in retrospect, the UMTS network did not become successful until 2008, when the iPhone and other smartphones entered the market. The world cannot be considered to be fundamentally deterministic. And because it is not predetermined what will happen and how things will develop, you always have options, fortunately.

As we said earlier, scenario planning did not become popular as a way of predicting the future more precisely. On the contrary, the scenario methodology proved that the future *cannot* be predicted. However, it is possible to react quickly to changing circumstances. According to Van der Heijden the time that passes between a change in circumstances and the moment of taking action can often be expressed in years rather than months.[1] This is why the added value of scenarios for generating options has been underlined repeatedly. Arie de Geus expresses it as follows:

> *Nobody can predict, therefore we should not try. The only relevant discussions about the future are those where we succeed in shifting from the question whether something will happen to the question: what will we do if it happens.*

Arie de Geus[2]

De Geus emphasizes the importance of thinking through the implications of scenarios for planning: the value of scenarios lies in reflecting on 'What if's', in creating options and in increasing the speed of changing course. Questions about the future should not be put in terms of 'What will happen exactly and when?' but rather in terms of 'What will we do if this happens, regardless of when it happens?'

It is important to use the images of the future and the conversations on scenarios, mission and vision effectively; to work with and benefit from the knowledge and opinions which arise from these conversations. Scenarios offer the means to replace reactive problem-solving with anticipative thinking and proactivity in terms of creating options. There is a tension here, however: we do not know how the future will develop whereas and yet, in the end, we can only pursue a single strategy. But it can be a dynamic strategy; a strategy with *planned flexibility*, ensuring enough space to change direction if the circumstances change. We can use options to bridge the gap between the scenarios and our plans. It is up to you to help the organization to take the step from those (theoretically possible) future conditions to actions and to the development of a strategy for the present.

Keeping Plans Alive

Every organization makes plans. It is important to review these plans on a regular basis. Are the goals still realistic? What are the limits of existing plans? Is the road to our goals still feasible? What should we take into consideration if we want to adjust the plan?

---

1   Van der Heijden 1996: 4.
2   De Geus in Schütte 2008: 3.

Verifying plans against the scenarios is a way to keep an organization's plans alive. Considering current developments, is the selected course still suitable and can we stick to it? It is often essential to avoid drifting about; the organization should stick to the existing plan and not let itself be distracted from its course by cross winds. However, in some cases it *is* essential to change direction or even adjust the entire plan. In that case, previously developed options can be used to rebuild the plan

---

THE FUTURE OF LEBANON

Interministerial workshop

In 2002 I moderated an interministerial workshop in Lebanon. Beirut felt just as it had always been: the Paris of the Middle-East, a hospitable and beautiful city, even though the scars of the Lebanese civil war were still visible here and there.

The interministerial workshop offered the first opportunity at which various ministries reflected on strategy and policy in their entirety. The ministries all had their own plans and ambitions. The ministry responsible for water supply had a long-term plan to provide sufficient water for every Lebanese citizen. The ministry for tourism, in turn, wanted to promote Lebanon as a holiday destination.

There was no formal connection between the plans of the separate ministries. The interministerial workshop, however, generated awareness that the plans were indeed going to affect each other, both positively and negatively. Tourism, for example, could provide the financial means to realize, among other things, the plans for water supply. At the same time, tourism would significantly increase the demand for water. This raised the question whether the water supply plans would be sufficient in a scenario of increasing tourism.

At first, each ministry's plans belonged to the contextual environment of the other ministries. The interministerial workshop enabled the plans to move from the contextual to the transactional environment. It turned out to be possible to work together on the separate plans in a coordinated manner. Moreover, the ministries found a common topic which was important and threatening to everyone and which needed to be thought through to create options. Apart from the many potential threats (and opportunities) which the plans of the each ministry could represent to each other ministry, a nightmare scenario was threatening them all: another war. A new war would frustrate all their plans. Yet, in 2002 no options were at hand for such a scenario, even though it was far from implausible.

Sadly enough, the scenario became reality in the summer of 2006, when the Israel–Lebanon crisis took the lives of about 1,200 Lebanese.

The example of Lebanon illustrates how large organizations often work with concurrent plans, many of which are interrelated in a complex way. One person's dream plan could represent someone else's nightmare scenario. Therefore it is important to review the various plans coherently and highlight both the interdependencies and the *common* contextual factors. Of course, every organization dreams of having a resilient or future-proof plan: a course which can brave adverse wind and a few freak waves; an organization which is able to go with the flow, for example by putting a reef in the sail or adding another sail.

4.1   Determining Future Challenges

The most important difference between an organization which first and foremost deals with problem-solving and an organization which acts strategically is that the latter deals not only with yesterday's *problems*, but also with tomorrow's *challenges*. This organization does not have to improvise because it just hit an iceberg, it sees the iceberg on its course while it is still 10 kilometres ahead and the organization has enough time to act. It is up to you together with the rest of the organization to think about future challenges beforehand, to make sure that the organization can turn these challenges into opportunities and to prevent the organization from lingering until it is actually too late.

To get more insight into future challenges, both opportunities and threats, scenarios can be directly applied in investment proposals – something which requires self-reflection and clarity about the direction of the organization. Which opportunities and risks do the different scenarios carry? What are the implications of the scenarios? These may be opportunities as well as threats: the rise of a million independent contractors, the emergence of an iceberg or a serious drop in the consumer's purchasing power. Whether these are opportunities or risks depends largely on how well-prepared you are. You need to invite the organization to think about the implications of the scenarios for the organization itself and for its area of work. A sharp decline in purchasing power in the future, for example, could mean that the turnover of a specialist shop drops by a third, while on the other hand the turnover for market vendors and discount stores increases.

Implications of the scenarios can be derived using a checklist to represent the different perspectives of the various functional parts of the organization which appear in the plans: IT, production, human resources, marketing etcetera. When doing this, you may find the following questions helpful: what implications has each scenario for (this part of) the organization, what risks and which opportunities do the circumstances outlined in the scenario offer for (this part of) the organization? You can run through these steps yourself. However, it is better to discuss them within the organization, for example in a workshop. If possible, make sure participants are already familiar with the plans of the organization. In a brainstorming session, you may decide to discuss the implications of the scenarios in plenary, or alternatively split the participants up in different groups each focusing on one scenario, for which they then present the implications to the rest of the group. As when exploring trends, for which a multiple perspective is also used, the process of mapping the implications will benefit from the involvement of people with alternative perspectives. They may see other challenges and opportunities than the participants from within the organization itself.

The value of scenarios is in their use. Scenarios can be a window to new options, new opportunities and new risks.[3] In 1992, Shell developed a set of scenarios which

---

3   Alkema 2008 contains a list of technologies that became relevant as a result of a scenario with a higher oil price. This made options visible and possible for Shell.

involved more than 30 man-years of work, the Global scenarios 1992–2020. The next step was to introduce the scenarios to the entire organization and to invite everyone to think about the implications of the scenarios for the business division for which they served. In the subsequent six months Group Planning presented the scenarios in 67 workshops involving the different functional divisions (HR policy, marketing, IT, Research & Development, and so on), the different geographical regions and countries, and the different business lines (gas, oil, non-traditional business, and so on). Group Planning also entered into discussions with governments about possible future policies. The Rabobank is another example of a company which used a road show to talk about their consumer scenarios as soon as they had been completed in 2003: in this way, 1,600 employees – from local banks to the supervisory board and from the financial division to the sponsorship division – were directly introduced to the four scenarios.[4]

Sometimes, the process of thinking through the implications of the scenarios makes it clear that there is a need for more specific scenarios; for example because the scenarios raise new, specific uncertainties for certain divisions of the organization. In the case of Rabobank, discussion of the consumer scenarios eventually led to the development of interest rate scenarios and ICT scenarios.

It is important to make the implications of scenarios as explicit as possible, if you want to ensure everyone keeps them in mind. Making the implications explicit can raise a sense of urgency in the organization and encourage people to act. The clearer the challenges are formulated, juxtaposing dry analyses with issues to address emotions, the greater the chance they are followed by action. The mere fact that instructions on how the organization should deal with these challenges are not included gives space for creativity in the organization; the self-organizing competences of teams are engaged. That is one of the reasons why it is best to determine the implications of the scenarios in a workshop setting, and not by yourself: it helps if people formulate challenges themselves, because seeing is believing. Evoking creativity and a sense of urgency is useful when the stage of generating options is reached and action is needed.

4.2   Generating Options and Wind Tunnelling

When you have mapped out the implications of the scenarios, two follow-up steps are possible. You may 'wind tunnel' existing plans against the scenarios and/or generate new options. These two activities do not necessarily take place in this order. It is possible to test existing plans (wind tunnelling) and subsequently, using the gaps and shortages found in the plans as a starting point, to generate new options. However, it is also possible to look at the implications and to explore in which ways the organization could anticipate future challenges without taking into account existing plans. In this last case, generating options is the starting point, and only once you have generated options do you consider the implications of the scenarios for existing plans.

---

4   De Ruijter 2007 and Idenburg et al. 2005.

WIND TUNNELLING

Every organization has strategic plans in which activities, goals and budgets are listed, see for example Figure 4.1.

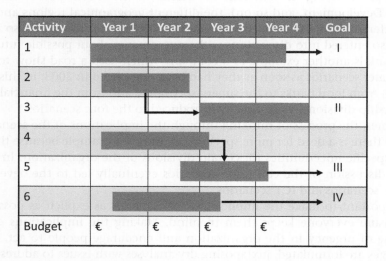

Activity	Year 1	Year 2	Year 3	Year 4	Goal
1					I
2					
3					II
4					
5					III
6					IV
Budget	€	€	€	€	

Figure 4.1   Strategic plans: activities, goals and budgets

When defining the challenges, as described in the preceding paragraph, the organization is confronted by the scenarios. We can also use scenarios to confront concrete plans which are already underway in the organization or which are planned (Figure 4.2). By confronting planned activities, budgets and goals with the scenarios, you can check these activities, budgets and goals for their relevance and success in the future. We call this process 'wind tunnelling' because the scenarios offer the turbulence which may sink future plans. During wind tunnelling you start from the inside, the 'self': those who own the plans and have to execute them. At this point it is important to know who the 'self' is: is it, for example, Rabobank Netherlands, Rabobank Amsterdam, or the HR division of Rabobank Amsterdam?

In practice, you can do this by taking existing plans as a starting point and then checking for each scenario whether or not (1) goals are feasible, (2) budgets are either too high or too low, and (3) activities should be brought forward, postponed, started or stopped given the specific conditions of the scenarios. In their capacity of test condition, the scenarios highlight the strengths and weaknesses of the current plan under extreme circumstances. Is what the organization plans to do realistic, sensible and feasible in different scenarios? This is also referred to as a 'stress test', and since the start of the credit crisis, central banks have used stress tests to supervise financial markets. One condition, however, is that scenarios should have been developed with the very purpose of testing limits, not as a tool to create confidence.

Wind tunnelling is used to work towards a strategic plan which is flexible: a plan which will work perfectly under all circumstances, because it already includes alternative routes which can be taken should certain circumstances occur. To realize this level of

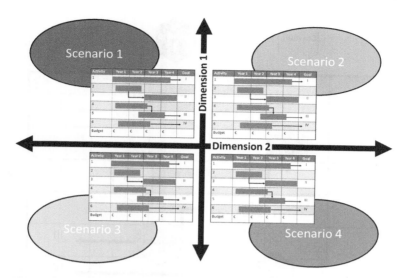

Figure 4.2   Wind tunnelling: confronting the plans with the scenarios

resilience, the current plan may need some adjustments: some activities are not quite right, should be accelerated or delayed. If this is not sufficient, new options will also have to be deployed.

GENERATING OPTIONS

Generating options can take place as a follow-up after wind tunnelling, during which an analysis has been made of the additions the existing plan needs. You can also start from scratch, without worrying about existing plans, as soon as the implications of the scenarios have been mapped out, and comparing the new options with the existing plan at a later stage. The advantage of thinking about new options regardless of the existing plan is that it is easier to come up with creative thoughts and innovative ideas.

Options represent the opportunity – *not the obligation!* – to take a decision in the future; to do something or to not do something. By imagining ourselves in the different scenarios and thinking through their implications, we can imagine options for actions we may adopt in those particular situations which will allow us to seize opportunities and to avoid or manage risks. We generate options to create the range of alternative actions which would be at our disposal and which would be effective under different possible circumstances, and with the help of which we can anticipate these circumstances. This creates freedom – see Figure 4.3.

In the 1970s, Real Option Theory was developed to allow financiers to include uncertainty when valuing investments. Shell had already used real option valuation in the 1980s when the company needed to take decisions about the exploration and the operation of oil and gas fields. The investments needed for operating an oil or gas field are huge and they are surrounded by considerable uncertainty. In this kind of situation, various alternatives for action, which can be deployed depending on the circumstances, are very welcome. In the case of Shell, investing in the North Sea only became attractive

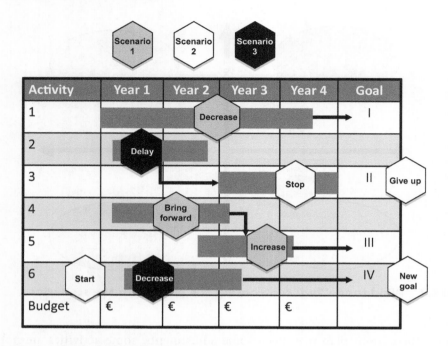

Figure 4.3   A strategic and flexible plan

when the oil price rose above a certain level – a possibility which Shell had already thought through with the help of quantified scenarios.

In the business context the concept of scenarios is sometimes also used to indicate different options or possible strategies (for example, various restart scenarios were mentioned in the newspapers after Fokker Aircrafts went bankrupt). However, in this book the word 'scenario' is used to describe the possible external environment of the future which the organization cannot directly influence, but which influences the organization. Scenarios concern the world of events which are happening to you and which you cannot choose. We use 'options' to refer to the possible courses of action which the organization has and between which it *can* choose. Scenarios serve as a tool to generate and to check options and to determine which options are future-proof or robust, and which ones depend on specific circumstances. Consequently, the options are about the inside world, the organization itself, and they explicitly take into account the uncertainties of the future and important developments in the outside world. Once again it is important to have a clear picture of the 'self-definition', 'transactional environment' and 'contextual environment'. To the HR division of Rabobank Amsterdam, Rabobank Netherlands is probably part of its contextual environment, which it cannot influence, rather than of the transactional environment. Therefore, the options of the HR division of Rabobank Amsterdam are different from the options of Rabobank Netherlands, even within the same scenario.

Of course, generating options can be done in a small group, perhaps in cooperation with a few others. However, given that more people with different perspectives are likely to think of more insights and more novel insights, this underlines the value of an inclusive approach to option generation. Involving people gives them a grasp of the bigger picture: the organization in its future contexts. When you start a brainstorm on possible options, it is important that the challenges are clear – something for which wind tunnelling can be of great help. At this stage, the scenarios are not only applied to divisions of the organization, but also to budgets, activities and goals per business activity, region and function line. The purpose is, of course, to come to new options, but it also allows you to share with everyone the challenges for the organization as a whole. At first sight, it might seem inefficient to involve large groups of people in completing the old plan and thinking of options for a new plan. But in reality, the fact is: the more options you map out, the more freedom and flexibility you will have to react to changing circumstances. The top team cannot do this on their own and besides: the more people in the organization are aware of options and plans, the faster they can act.

In workshops it is crucial to immerse the participants fully in the scenario for which they are brainstorming: this is important in order to make sure that the options will fit into the possible future circumstances, it can also encourage inspiration and new perspectives. Scenarios work well as a brainstorming technique which enables you to remove the taboos which surround some received ideas and to replace the reasoning 'We don't do that kind of thing' with 'We would not do that kind of thing at the moment, but if this scenario becomes reality, we should!' Of course it helps when the scenarios are presented in an attractive and appealing way. It is also wise to discuss the options per scenario, and avoid dumping all the scenarios on the table at once. After every scenario presentation, the group should think about possible options for future plans (in plenary or subgroups). If you have already determined the implications of the different scenarios beforehand, these can help to determine where opportunities or threats lie. All of which helps, in turn, to generate options in a focused way. Once you have completed the brainstorm, you can collect the ideas, summarize them clearly (for example by clustering them) and document them.

4.3   Evaluating Options: Robust Options, Call Options and Put Options

The options which have been created can be used as potential ideas for future plans. However, you may choose to go one step further and to evaluate to what extent the options are future-proof in all scenarios; what is their effectiveness and their feasibility. What effect do they have on the long term and under changing circumstances? The results of this analysis offer interesting insights for the development of dynamic and future-proof plans and strategies. The scenarios then serve as a context for evaluation, just as wind tunnelling does.

To keep track of the big picture, it helps to make a table of options, as shown in Figure 4.4. For all options, plusses (++ or +) and minuses (— or –) or a zero (0; neutral) represent to which extent they are successful, appropriate, relevant and feasible in the different scenarios. It is important that every option is mapped against all scenarios, and not just against the specific scenario in which a particular option was originally generated. Remember that at the moment of the evaluation it is not yet clear how the future will actually unfold, and therefore all scenarios have to be taken into account. Please note that at this stage we only evaluate the options against the future context. Other criteria which can be used to test the options are financial criteria, congruence with the mission, the availability of people or technical feasibility.

SCORING POLICY OPTIONS FOR SUCCESS;[5] ARTICLE 20 OF THE DUTCH ALCOHOL LICENSING ACT

Netherlands Food and Consumer Product Safety Authority and the Ministry of Justice

In 2001 and 2002, the Netherlands Food and Consumer Product Safety Authority and the Ministry of Justice executed a scenario project to gain insight into the enforceability of Article 20 of the new Dutch Alcohol Licensing Act: 'It is illegal for business purposes or otherwise than for free/gratis, to provide an alcoholic drink to a person of whom it has not been ascertained that he or she has reached the age of 16 years.' Article 20 obliges companies which sell alcohol to verify whether those who want to buy alcohol from them comply with the minimum age requirement.

After an exploration of the environment, scenarios were developed. The scenarios were used to check the proposed enforcement regime and the new alcohol legislation and to determine which implications each scenario had for the Netherlands Food and Consumer Product Safety Authority. Then, new ideas for enforcement of and compliance with Article 20 were generated in a workshop. Based on a discussion between the participants, the policy options were scored for their degree of effectiveness in the different scenarios. Figure 4.4 gives an idea of the policy options generated and their effectiveness per scenario.

Finally, based on the robustness of the different policy options, a coherent policy of robust and specific policy options has been formulated which makes it possible, under different scenarios, to respond dynamically to changing circumstances.

Policy option	Scenario			
	I	II	III	IV
Selective action	+	++	++	++
Shaming	+	++	0	0
Back-tracing	0	++	−	++
Introducing certification	+	++	−	++
Implementing quality systems	+	++	+	++
Stimulate licensees to know their customers	0	++	+	++
Educate licensees	−	++	−	++
Stimulate alternatives for alcohol	−	−−	+	++

Figure 4.4   Classification of policy options for enforcement of the Alcohol Licensing Act (after Janssen et al. 2007)

5   Janssen et al. 2007: 101–10; Noordik and Blijsie 2008: 209.

When an option is appropriate and feasible in every scenario, and thus scores plusses for every scenario, it is a future-proof option. An option which fits in all scenarios and always produces something positive is called a robust option. In other words: no matter how the environment will develop in the future, this option is always a good idea.

There are also situation-dependent options: those which do not produce something positive in every scenario. In some specific situations you might want to be able to start a new activity. This type of option is referred to as *call option*. In other cases you might want to be able to stop an activity. This is referred to as *put option*, see Figure 4.5.

Please bear in mind: in this context, we use the concepts of call options and put options as real options. Their names are derived from the call and put options in the financial world, which are traded at the stock markets. These financial options, for which a premium is paid, represent the right – not the obligation! – either to buy or sell a stock at a fixed strike price or exercise price before a certain expiration date. A call option represents the right to buy a stock. A buyer will only exercise an option if and when the real value of the stock is higher than the exercise price of the option plus the premium. A put option is the right to sell a stock: this option is only profitable if and when the real price of the stock is lower than the exercise price of the option minus the premium. Financial call and put options can be used to insure oneself against price rises and price falls. This creates the possibility of profiting from price fluctuations, both rises and falls. Real call and put options are the equivalent of financial call and put options, and they apply to real activities; they are the alternatives for action which an organization may pursue to realize future plans under different circumstances.

Some activities score well in most scenarios, but less well in others. Such activities can be combined with a put option: in other words, they are introduced as a part of the plan, but a 'stop' is put in place to make sure the organization can pull the handbrake in case certain circumstances occur which make the action irrelevant. Having a put option means an action can be withdrawn in a particular situation. Put options apply to those actions which are appropriate, relevant and feasible in current circumstances, but which have to be stopped when certain specific developments occur. There are alternatives to a dead stop; you may choose to postpone, decrease, or sell. Examples of put options are the cancellation clause in a hotel reservation, the interim evaluation of a project to review

		Scenario A	Scenario B	Scenario C
Option 1	Robust	+	+	+
Option 2	Call	-	-	+
Option 3	Put	+	+	-

Call: Start, speed up, bring forward, scale up
Put: Stop, slow down, postpone, scale down

Figure 4.5   Robust, call and put options

whether or not it will be continued, or the temporary employment contract often offered to new employees.

When you realize that you have put options, it is of the utmost importance to make sure that the activities concerned can genuinely be stopped if need be. Therefore, the organization should focus both on the things it has to do, but also on the things which, in certain cases, it must stop doing. You need to ensure that the stop mechanism is clear and you may need to work out an exit strategy.

SHELL'S PUT OPTION (1970S)[6]

In Chapter 3 we mentioned the first scenarios developed by Shell in 1971 before the first oil crisis. As soon as it became clear that circumstances could arise which would cause oil prices to increase substantially, Shell's management decided that it was necessary to prepare for this. After all, a slow reaction to a change in the environment would be expensive.

In fact, the management of Shell seized the scenarios as an opportunity for a fire drill: what do we do in case the oil price doubles – or worse still? In such a 'what if' situation, the natural reaction of a multinational like Shell might be to centralize. On reflection, however, this turned out to be a less than clever move in an oil crisis. In the 1970s, before the era of the Internet and email, managing a multinational company of Shell's size in a centralized manner would be a recipe for trouble; not least because, if oil is expensive, room for local policies is needed. In France, this might mean increased nuclear activities, in Germany a focus on coal and in the Netherlands a transition to gas.

A second important effect of this 'fire drill' was the fact that Shell was able to interpret information from the environment in a different way to its competitors, because different possible future scenarios had been given thought within the organization. At a very early stage, Shell employees recognized certain developments in the Middle East as indicators of an energy crisis such as the one which had been discussed in one of the scenarios. Because they saw the crisis coming so early, they were able to take a number of crucial strategic decisions, the most important of which was a rebalancing of investments in refining capacity, which allowed Shell to shift investments quickly. In the autumn of 1973, the focus was moved from the expansion of primary capacity to the increase and improvement of the output of refineries. This enabled Shell to gain a considerable advantage over its competitors.

Statistics tell us that from the start point of 1973 it took the oil industry as a whole two years to realize that the market had fundamentally changed. During those two years the competitors to Shell kept developing extra refining capacity, to be able to keep up with the 6 per cent yearly increase in the demand of oil which the world had seen before 1973. It subsequently took five to six years before the competition tailored its refining capacity to the real demand for oil. The number of orders for the construction of new refineries did not decrease until 1977, four years after the start of the oil crisis. Needless to say the excess capacity which was maintained all those years cost a lot of money – money which Shell had saved by adjusting its strategy to the changing circumstances in time. Shell was ready for change!

---

6   Van der Heijden 1996.

Alongside robust and put options, there are also options which only score well in one or two scenarios. These options do not have to be deleted immediately. Instead, you can increase the sophistication of your plan by enabling the option to be taken up in the specific case that the circumstance occurs in which such an option is relevant, appropriate and feasible. This is a call option and you prepare these to allow for cases in which the outside world unfolds in a certain way. As with stopping, starting can be done in various ways: investigating, pre-investing, building up, expanding, increasing, intensifying …

In 2003 I was involved in an integral housing study of the District Court of Zutphen. During the project, it turned out that one of the available call options would be a very good idea: to take an option on the site of the vocational training centre neighbouring the court. Because the site was not available at that time, the court took the strategic decision to settle temporarily elsewhere in town: it rented a part of a former tax collector's office. At the same time, the court contacted the municipality, the vocational training centre, the Council for the Judiciary, the Government Buildings Agency and the Public Prosecution Service in order to be able to acquire the site of the vocational training centre. The court created a real call option, which eventually would be executed.

In 1992, Shell Group Planning applied the Global Scenarios 1992–2020 internally to evaluate Shell's strategies. The most important question in those scenarios was whether the economy and politics would face liberalization and internationalization (New Frontiers) or not (Barricades). Before the workshop, the Middle East region of Shell (which included India, although at the time it did not have any activities there) did not consider investing in India. However, under the New Frontiers scenario, the world would be open and an investment in India would be a good idea. In the Barricades scenario, on the other hand, the world would be engaged in identity politics and an investment in India would probably not produce the outcome wished for. Because of this uncertainty, Shell decided to create a call option. They decided to start selling lubricants in India. In this way, the company gathered insight in the market and built up relationships, while limiting its investment. When, at the end of the 1990s, the Indian economy started liberalizing, Shell was able to capitalize this call option and it used its presence in India to expand its investments quickly. In 2010, having investments worth almost a billion dollars, divided among different activities, Shell was the biggest and most diversified international investor in the Indian energy sector – something which had been unthinkable before the scenario workshops in 1992.

Another example of a call option is a pilot, which keeps open the possibility of expanding the project if successful. Most R&D activities in the pharmaceutical industry are actually call options: they create the possibility – but not the obligation! – to continue the search for a certain drug if the early stages are successful. R&D is a very appropriate place for strategic thinking, because this division deals, by definition, with the long term.

CALL OPTION AT MSD[7]

In the pharmaceutical industry, investments often entail risk: they involve research projects over many years, the results of which, at the time of the initial investment, are surrounded by a lot of uncertainty. At the outset, it is hard to assess the strategic value of such projects. This sector often struggles with traditional techniques of evaluating investment proposals because of the long lead times and the associated risks.

The financial division of pharmaceutical company Merck Sharp & Dohme (MSD) uses the real option theory to decide on investment proposals. According to CFO Judy Lewent, option analysis provides a more flexible approach to value research investments because the real option theory allows the company to evaluate those investments at successive stages of a project. Options can help to examine the uncertainty surrounding of investments and to value it. The two crucial factors determining a project's option value are the length of time the project may be deferred and the project volatility.

When an initial investment in a research project is made, the possibility – not the obligation – is created to continue that research at a later stage and to expand it. The first up-front payment can be followed by a series of so-called *progress payments*: payments made as progress is made in the research. Each of these payments gives MSD the right – but not the obligation – to make further investments later. On the contrary, MSD can also decide to withdraw, and in that case the contract can be terminated without further investment having to be made.

_____

7   This case has been taken from an interview with Judy Lewent, who was CFO at MSD between 1990 and 2007. It was published in Nichols 1994.

Together with the relevant people inside your organization, you can determine the criteria which will be used for the selection of options. Of course, relevance and feasibility in the scenarios are important. But perhaps the organization or the management thinks that the options should comply with more criteria, such as costs, support from particular target groups, ethics, or compliance with competences which already exist at the time. These criteria can also serve as test conditions for the options, and for this purpose a matrix (see Figure 4.4) can be a useful tool.

Making the selection criteria transparent and the used scoring matrixes can help to explain how the classification and selection of certain options was established, and thus contribute to the legitimacy of the plan. In addition, scoring matrixes can come in handy at a later date, when new circumstances occur and options have to be reconsidered. By reviewing the scoring matrixes made earlier, it will be easier to recall why it was decided at the time (not) to go with certain options. It also preserves the learning process of the people in the organization; they don't have to reinvent the wheel each time and they can learn from the past.

Robust, put and call options can be combined to form a coherent, future-proof and dynamic strategic plan: we will come back to this in Chapter 6. In this plan, options are sorted in the right order, because a logical sequence of options is important. Such a strategic plan is special because on one hand it is sufficiently flexible to move along with developments in the contextual environment of the organization, on the other hand it is sufficiently robust to withstand a number of external developments. The plan has not been set in stone beforehand, with just one vision of the future in mind and without the possibility of changing along the way. On the contrary: throughout the execution of the plan the organization has alternatives for actions at their disposal, depending on the circumstances. Planned flexibility, both upside and downside, has been built in. This extends the lifespan of the plan.

4.4   Investment Proposals

To support investment proposals, many organizations use traditional business cases, in which they weigh future costs and benefits of certain decisions to decide whether the investment is worth the money. The problem posed by this method is that the calculation includes a lot of external components, for which forecasts and assumptions are used. Once one of the external components turns out to be different in reality, the entire calculation becomes useless.

Imagine that airline carrier KLM wishes to expand its fleet or replace aircrafts. Which type of aircraft would be best for the airline to opt for? A variety of contextual factors are relevant for both costs and benefits of the business case. Cost-influencing factors include the interest rate, the price of kerosene and the wages governed by collective agreements. Factors influencing the benefits of the business case include the consumers' spending power, the demand for beach holidays, the popularity of videoconferences as an alternative to physical meetings, and the macroeconomic circumstances. These are all factors which partly determine the number of (business) trips made and whether business people fly business class or economy class. And then there is also the possibility that an ash plume (or other short-term event) makes flying impossible for KLM for a period of time. Hence, when choosing between a business aircraft for short distances or a super economic economy class aircraft for long distances a variety of contextual factors are at work which KLM cannot directly influence, but which are definitely important for the calculation of the case. Generally, in business cases, assumptions are used for all these contextual factors. But if one of those assumptions is wrong, this has an immediate influence on KLM's plans: if the Netherlands enjoys a beautiful summer, fewer flights will be booked than suggested in a business case which assumed an 'average summer' in their calculation.

In a traditional business case such as KLM's, investments are seen as 'now-or- never' activities, which are irreversible, not divisible and confined. This makes it hard to decide about an investment, because uncertainty surrounds the result of the investment. Fixed assumptions have to be made for all variables, whereas in reality they are very uncertain. As a result, the outcome of the calculation is in fact an accumulation of uncertainties! Organizations tend to ignore uncertainties which surround a project and instead look for assumptions about future cash flows that favour the investment.[8] It is, however, very important that those who take strategic decisions explicitly take into account uncertainties and change, stick to an integral approach (thus, not thinking project by project) and hold on to clear criteria for decision-making.

---

8   Leemhuis 1985: 33.

Different options encompass different costs and benefits, as stated before. It is possible to design business cases in which the value of certain options is calculated, in order to be able to take a better-informed decision on investments. The real option theory is a better method of valuing investments than the traditional method. When it turns out that, based on different 'forecasts' (the scenarios), options are not robust, call and put options are needed to guarantee the flexibility of the plans and to manage risks. Here the most important question for the organization is how much is it willing to pay for this flexibility. The call and put options can then be valued for their costs and benefits.

Ultimately, every option is an investment proposal. In terms of investments, a call options means that the investment required for the activity is divided into different parts. This approach enables you to make as small an investment as possible initially, without precluding the subsequent possibility of making the entire investment. In the case of a put option, the organization considers the potential of making the investment, while at the same time creating the opportunity to pull back from the investment when certain circumstances occur. For both call and put options it is important to be able to identify the requisite warning signals: we will come back this in the last chapter.

As soon as you understand the value different options have, it will be easier to evaluate investments and reach a decision. To that end, the different options which an organization has will have to be calculated, in order to create a structured method of evaluating costs and benefits. This facilitates decision-making, regardless of the background of uncertainty. It leads to better decision-making, which takes into account uncertainties in an explicit and structured way.

CALCULATION EXAMPLE

I often use the simplified calculation below in workshops to illustrate the value of real options for strategic decisions on investments. Here are the data you have on a fictional investment in a new technique:

- **Pilot** (development and test phase of the technique) costs €5 million; the success rate is 50 per cent
- **Roll-out** costs €45 million; the success rate is 80 per cent
- **Potential revenue** €100 million
- Based on these data, would you invest or not? The classical method of calculating is as follows:
- **Calculation 1** The total success rate is 50% × 80% = 40%. The expected value of the investment is (40% × 100) – 45 – 5 = – €10 million. Conclusion: do not invest.

If you take into account the possibility of stopping after the pilot, however, the calculation is different (see Figure 4.6):

- **Calculation 2** The expected value of the investment is (50% × –5) + ([50% × 20%] × –50) + ([50% × 80%] × 50) = + €12.5 million. Conclusion: do invest.

The difference between the two calculations lies in the put option to stop investing further if the pilot fails. To be exact, the value of this put option is €12.5 million + (−€10 million) = €22.5 million; the put option raises the expected value of the project from loss-making to profitable. And of course, this requires that the investment for the actual roll-out is not made until the pilot has been completed successfully. Too often, organizations have already decided to start the roll-out and undertake the biggest investment before the pilot has been completed and evaluated properly. This makes calculation 1 the de facto solution and the put option does not have any value (Figure 4.6).

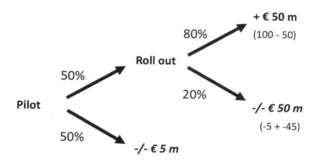

Figure 4.6   Calculation using a put option

The calculation also shows that it is wise always to run several pilots simultaneously, to make sure the organization has several irons in the fire in case a pilot fails. A portfolio of options decreases the risk that you end up with nothing, since you have multiple alternatives if some pilots fail. When you execute a test phase for several activities, you can decide subsequently which activities are to be continued and which activities are to be stopped, because they ran less well, without the need to invest a considerable amount of money. There is also a second way of looking at this calculation. The pilot project can also be seen as call option which, if the evaluation is successful, offers the possibility of expanding the project ('Provided that the pilot project succeeds, I will invest further in the project').

When a business case is not approached in the traditional way, but several real options are taken into account, you get a better idea of the various uncertainties which surround a project and of the way these uncertainties can be dealt with. For example, it is often possible to delay, adjust or split up projects which ask for investments into different strategic components, and consequently, to reduce the risk. Most of the time, the least expensive option is to invest first in the activity which eliminates the biggest part of the risk at the lowest costs.

Imagine an investment which consists of the technical development of a new product and its marketing. In a situation where the technical development is very uncertain and therefore risky, whereas on the other hand the chance of success of marketing, although costly, is quite certain, you will start by investing in the technical development. The calculation example explains that it is unwise to start investing in expensive marketing if the investment in the technical development might be unsuccessful. On the other hand when the success rate of a very expensive technical development is quite certain, whereas the interest of the market is uncertain, you would ideally start by marketing (a prototype of) the new product. Only when it turns out that the market is interested should you move on to the big investment in the technical development. Thus, the timing and sequence of investments are of vital importance.

The difficulty of business cases with real options lies in obtaining the percentages and key figures. To that end, you will need to attach probabilities to the scenarios: quantitative assessments of the likelihood of the scenarios. This can be done by using statistics which provide information on the success rate of the marketing of a certain new product or of its technical development. Measuring risk requires three things: the law of large numbers (there have to be many examples from the past), mutually independent events (these examples cannot be correlated) and identical circumstances ('*ceteris paribus*': the circumstances in which the events took place should be comparable). On this basis, you may try to quantify the (value of the) options. This is possible for common, simple issues. Statistical data exist on common uncertainties, for example related to market introductions and technical successes.

It may also be possible that exact figures are not available, or that the figures do not meet the criteria mentioned above: the figures are from a one time only event, the events are correlated, or they occur in a very different context ('*ceteris non paribus*'). In that case, you can try to estimate the relative probabilities and to divide the investment conceptually into several uncertainties, such as 'technical development' and 'marketing'. Please note that percentages are not new certainties. On the contrary: percentages indicate that the whole is *not* certain. In the end, the purpose is not to make one single static plan for the investment, but to build in put and call options, to be better able to manage uncertainties. Indeed, you will also find that the estimates of the probabilities will change over time. The options can then be recalculated.

The options which you found do not have to be implemented all at once and with great fanfare; it is not necessary to turn the wheel brutally on your ship. It is also possible to steer in a very subtle way by having several call and put options open at the same time. For example, take the question of whether a bank wants to focus on savings or on investing: the ratio between the popularity of the two differs according to the state of the economy. When a bank offers both savings and investing possibilities, it covers a large part of the market. With the economy flourishing, the main focus of the customer will automatically shift from saving to investing, whereas in lean years the opposite happens. The direction or management does not have to push for this: the circumstances inevitably ensure that the focus is on one option, while the focus on the other option is partly (perhaps temporarily) abandoned.

I experienced this myself, when I worked for the Royal Netherlands Academy of Arts and Sciences in the mid 1990s. An exploration on the future of chemistry highlighted the opportunity to focus more on nanotechnology. It was highlighted as a trend and a scenario was described in which nanotechnology played an important role. Since a large group of Dutch scientists, both in the public and private sector, were involved in the process, there was no need to decree later that less time and money should be spent on biology, physics or chemistry, since this development occurred automatically when the opportunity materialized. The scientists involved simply deserted other subjects when they jointly gave more attention to nanotechnology. Here, the self-organizing competences of the network of faculties and universities came in handy. When you take the time to explore the challenges and generate options for action in a way that involves the organization (or a network of organizations), you do not have to impose a course of action. Often, the organization automatically starts to move as soon as threats or opportunities start to appear.

Formulating opportunities and risks in different scenarios and generating options sometimes automatically leads to action, but this is not a given. In both cases it is important to keep in mind the vision of the organization. What does it want to achieve in the future, using the generated options? In the next chapter importance of a vision and the ways in which you can work with a vision will be discuss.

CONCLUSIONS: OPTIONS

1. Discuss the implications of the scenarios: which opportunities and challenges will they pose to the organization?
2. Do make use of 'wind tunnelling': confront the existing plans with the appropriate scenarios. Discuss which parts are robust and which parts are not.
3. Generate new options, using the scenarios. Which activities should we be able to stop or start?
4. Assess investments in the light of the scenarios and discuss them in terms of real options.

CHAPTER

5 *Vision:*

Where do we want to go, who do we want to be?

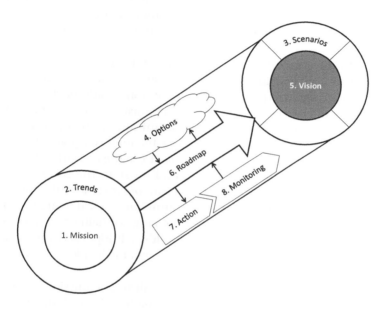

When you board a sailing boat, it is most unlikely you plan to sail the seas without any destination in mind. You want to go somewhere! And you want to go there for a reason: to win a regatta, to trade or to visit other lands. You have a particular harbour in mind at which you want to arrive. It is important that before boarding all the passengers have the same destination in mind so that this does not need to be discussed while travelling.

What is a Vision?

Just as in the sailing example, thinking about strategy is pointless unless the desired goal of the organization is clearly stated. It is essential that you make sure there is a mental image of a realistic, plausible and desirable future for the organization and that you understand the role of the organization in this future: a vision.[1] Therefore the conversation about vision (derived from the Latin *videre* which means 'to see') is an important activity.

---

1   Bennis and Namus 1985: 89.

The future is not a fact and does not look the same to everyone. We can't predict the future, nor can we choose the circumstances. However, taking the scenarios into account, we can sketch an ideal image to ourselves of where we want to be in the future. By thinking as one about what you want, whether you are a company, a city, a community or an association, a common vision emerges. It is important for organizations to seek a mutual agreement on this desired future and of the steps which need to be taken to reach that future. At the same time it is important that there remains some room for alternative views, space for experimentation and for checking the vision from time to time. Broad ownership of the vision is important, and the responsibility for development and implementation lies at the top of the organization. But everybody with a long-term interest in the organization can be involved or even initiate the conversation about the vision.

There is a strong connection between the strategic conversation about vision and other strategic conversations. The trends and scenarios show possible future circumstances for the organization in which the vision should be achieved – despite or because of those circumstances. These external circumstances can be taken into account in the conversations about the vision for the organization. The options will be used to realize the vision, but the vision also determines which options you will use. A roadmap, which we will discuss in Chapter 6, shows the road from the present to the desired future. There is a strong connection between vision and mission: the mission formulates the field of activity and the reason for existence of the organization, the vision formulates what the organization wants to achieve in the future. In an ideal world the vision follows the mission. However, the vision can include a change of field of activity, which would transform the mission. In short: the vision builds a bridge between what is outside your zone of influence (trends and scenarios) and what is inside your zone of influence (mission and options).

Some find it hard to distinguish mission and vision. The mission formulates who or what you are and for what reason(s) you exist, while the vision desribes what you want to be, starting from your mission – or: what do you want to achieve. For example, the mission of a government is to serve its country, while its vision could be 'working together, living together'. With 'mission' we describe the fundamental reason for the organization's existence, the philosophy which underpins all activities and decisions. 'Vision' on the other hand refers to an image of what the organization wants to achieve in the future. The mission describes the starting point, while the vision describes the imagined, ideal future.[2] The mission expresses why the organization exists in the first place, for example 'to deliver sustainable energy'. The vision expresses what the organization wants to achieve, e.g. '100 per cent sustainable energy in the Netherlands by 2030'.

5.1   The Usefulness of a Vision

THE VISION AS A GUIDE, AS GLUE AND AS A SOURCE OF INSPIRATION

The future vision serves as an end point when making plans and designing a strategy: it gives direction to the goals of the organization and helps to show how to get there. These

---

2   De Wit and Meyer 1998: 813.

steps will later be detailed through options and roadmaps. The vision can also serve as a reference point to explain future strategic choices. A vision is not a straitjacket, but a guiding point on the horizon from which you may consciously and deliberately deviate. It is a reference point in the future, which indicates a desired destination.

SPONSOR VISION OF RABOBANK

In Chapter 3 we explored Rabobank's consumer scenarios for 2012: Survival, Support, Growth and Meaning. In November 2003 Rabobank's sponsorship division decided to develop a vision on the sponsorship policy for the future with the help of several scenarios. We described a deductive way of working in which the overall vision and scenarios were used as a basis to generate (robust) options for a divisional vision.

Sponsorship policy is one of Rabobank's most important communication tools. One of the reasons for developing this vision was the fact that Rabobank had to make important choices for its sponsorship contracts in 2005. Old contracts were due to expire and had to be terminated or renewed. New contracts were in many cases likely to last a number of years and should therefore be entered into deliberately.

In the period 2001–2005, as in the preceding four-year period, cycling had been the most important element of Rabobank's sponsorship policy, followed by hockey, the Museum Card Foundation, equestrian sport and others. Research had shown that Rabobank had a unique position as a cycling sponsor compared to their sponsorship of hockey and equestrian sport. However, on the basis of the consumer scenarios, should they continue to sponsor cycling?

Rabobank wanted to distinguish itself by being 'involved with and close to' the customer. Sponsorship activities should also fit with that vision. When cycling sponsorship was added in to the scenarios, it turned out to be a robust choice, with differences scenarios providing alternative emphasis on its value.

In a Growth scenario (fat years and individualism) 'winning' would appeal to the customer, entirely in tune with cycling sponsorship. In a Support scenario (lean years and community spirit) the emphasis would be on recreational cycling rather than competition. In this scenario cycling offered the positive image of a sport which you can enjoy together and in your own neighbourhood. In a Meaning scenario (fat years and community spirit) cycling would be popular just as in the Support scenario, because of its association with health, fitness and the environment. In a Survival scenario (lean years and individualism) over-generous sponsorship would be considered extravagant, and this needed to be taken into account. The bank would also need to stay close to the customer and to emphasize the individual and open character of cycling.

Sponsoring cycling turned out to be a robust option; one that supported the values 'involved' and 'close' with greater or lesser emphasis on the recreational or competitive side depending on the scenario. Bearing in mind the long-term nature of sponsorship it is important that it fits into the the long-term strategy of the bank and meets the future needs and expectations of the customer. In addition, a sponsorhsip policy that seems future-proof helps the bank to demonstrate that long-term relationships are what matters to them. The bank was anxious that they might look like an organization which opportunistically changed its sponsorship goals every couple of years. The robustness of cycling as a sponsorship target in the scenarios helped to make it the basis of the vision for the sponsorship division.

The Rabo Cycling plan, which was set up in 1996, still exists today and includes sponsorship of the Royal Dutch Cycling Society (KNWU), several cycling clubs and local cycling events and races, in cooperation with the Dutch Recreational Cycling Society (NTFU) and encouragement of recreational cycling. However, by the end of 2012, in response to the doping scandals in the sport, Rabobank stopped sponsoring the professional men's team, after 17 years of support. The decision was made with great regret, but that element no longer seemed a good fit with the core values of the bank. And no, the doping scandal was not foreseen as a scenario, but it could have and (in hindsight) should have been.

(The development of) a vision is a useful tool to align everyone in the organization. The vision is a direction-indicating tool for decision-making, but it also can be used to communicate with stakeholders: staff, customers, suppliers, partners and other parties. And when everyone is engaged, it helps the organization to start moving and to sustain that movement, as illustrated in Figure 5.1. In short, when all energy is aligned in the same direction, more forward power is available than when the energy is scattered.

In workshops I sometimes illustrate this with the story of the three masons. The only reason the first mason works is because he needs to the €10 per hour he can earn. The second mason works harder than the first, because he is motivated not simply by the money but because he also knows that his fellow masons and other workers count on him. The third mason works the hardest of the three, because he hopes that by working together in this way, someday in the future the cathedral, on which he is working today, will rise for his children and for all citizens of the city. We use a vision like this to give everyone the missionary zeal of the third mason. We build on something big for the future, something long term, and something that is here to stay. The vision functions as a source of inspiration. When you try to win the hearts of people with your vision, you will engage their support behind the goal of the organization as a whole. When everyone in the organization knows the vision, each of their modest actions collectively generates great things!

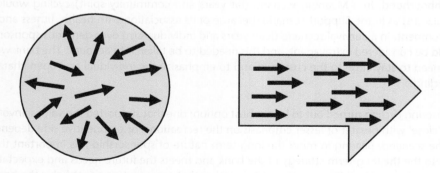

Figure 5.1   Aligning the organization

The vision not only enables the organization to start moving, it can also be useful in other ways, for example, as a tool to check whether the organization is still on track and to distinguish between important and less important issues. There is a paradoxical feature of a vision: the further you look ahead, the better you can navigate. Anyone who has ever sailed knows that it is easier to navigate on a distant point on the horizon rather than on the compass right in front of you. The further you look ahead, the quicker you can sense any slight deviation – and therefore the more accurately you can navigate.

SELF-FULFILLING AND SELF-DENYING FUTURES

In Chapter 3 on scenarios we described the development of the first scenarios at Shell in 1971, before the first oil crisis. Three scenarios were used to portray a world with higher oil prices. In these scenarios possible OPEC strategies were considered. After the event some people believed that the Shell scenarios may even have inspired several OPEC countries to engineer an artificial lack of oil in 1973. Perhaps one of the Shell scenarios was a vision for the members of OPEC. If this was genuinely the case, it means that the Shell scenarios actually contributed to their own fulfilment. Ultimately it was the Yom Kippur War which was the immediate cause of the first oil crisis rather than the expiry of the Tehran Agreement in 1975, as had been assumed in Shell's oil price scenarios, but the message was clear. When images of the future describe a complete picture and they are grander than the organization which creates them, a self-denying or self-refuting or a self-fulfilling effect can arise. Sometimes images of the future are used like this deliberately, and sometimes for exactly this reason some images of the future are *never* made public.

A self-denying vision works like this: imagine a vision or an image of the future, a nightmare rather than a dream, that is so repellent that people clamour to prevent it from ever happening. This visceral response spawns an alternative future. Something along these lines actually happened in the case of the Millenium bug. The fear of worldwide computer meltdown and the related technical problems in the transition from the year 1999 to the year 2000 was so huge, that organizations took extraordinary precautions to prevent it from happening and the Millenium bug had little impact. In a similar way, a self-denying effect occurs when the authorities deliberately warn of another Black Saturday (the first Saturday of the holiday season in Europe, when roads get blocked with traffic jams) is coming. They hope that this image will keep people from traveling to their holiday destination that day and that therefore problems on Black Saturday will be limited.

In 1972 the Club of Rome sounded the alarm bell with the report *The Limits to Growth*: the Club presented a model which showed that our resource supplies would be so low within a few decennia that industrial growth would slow disastrously. Today, it looks as if this prediction was incorrect: we still have enough resources to make industrial growth possible. But it is also possible that the scenario described by the Club of Rome did not come true, simply because the idea caused such a great stir that precautions were taken to prevent it from happening. This form of feedback in the system – a feedback loop in which scarcity and the resulting higher prices of resources spawns innovation – had no place in the model which the Club of Rome presented. The model simply showed what would happen if we would did nothing to prevent the prophecy from happening. In reality a single scenario is effectively a prophecy, often motivated by political expediency and designed to influence us to transform it into a self-denying of self-fulfilling prophecy!

Al Gore also aspired to this self-denying effect when presenting *An Inconvenient Truth*. He painted a nightmare-like vision of the future in which he showed what could happen should global warning continue, hoping that people, mobilized by this future vision, would take action to prevent further climate change.

A self-fulfilling vision is the exact opposite of a self-denying vision. It creates an image so attractive and so empathetic that it encourages actions to make it reality. The vision effectively fulfils itself. Sociologist Robert Merton described the self-fulfilling prophecy: 'The self-fulfilling prophecy is, in the beginning, a false definition of the situation evoking a new behavior which makes the original false conception come "true"'.[3]

A good example of a self-fulfilling statement was that of Pieter Lakeman on the television programme *Goodmorning Netherlands* on 1 October 2009. Lakeman advised savers of the DSB Bank to collect their savings as soon as possible, to create a run on the bank to force the bank into bankruptcy, which would be in the interests of the disadvantaged parties (including those in the Foundation Mortgage Burden of which Lakeman was chairman). His call had swift effect: within a week more than €600 million of savings were collected. On 19 October 2009 the bank was declared bankrupt. Without his call there may never have been a bankruptcy or it would at very least been delayed.

It is difficult to prove whether a vision was self-fulfilling or self-denying. You only ever know the reality as it really happened, you can never prove why other possibilities were not realized. Take the Millenium Bug, which eventually caused far fewer problems than expected. Was this simply because the impact was much smaller than assumed, or was it because precautions were taken? We will never know.

And when it comes to things which did happen, it is hard to distinguish between those which happened spontaneously and those which were suggested by someone's vision of the future. Take the example of the accommodation strategy of the District Court of Zutphen, which we mentioned in section 4.3. The accommodation strategy was assessed by the Council for the Judiciary and drew on the scenarios of the number of cases which the District Court would deal with in the upcoming years. It is very possible that the Council, when reading the scenarios which accompanied the request for more space for the District Court of Zutphen, thought: 'What a good idea. We can transfer cases from the busy District Courts in the western part of the Netherlands to the District Court of Zutphen.' Something which had been written into one of three scenarios for the District Court turned out to be an option to the Council. Thus the scenarios which the District Court of Zutphen had drawn up may actually have created a self-fulfilling effect, since the increase in workload subsequently happened. Scenarios that are designed for one party can turn out to be a vision for others on a different level. Both are stories about the future and will give people new ideas.

VISION AND CONTEXT

The fact that it is not clear to what extent the actual situation has been inspired by the vision illustrates how the line between what is inside of our control and what is outside is rarely fixed. We see 'reflexivity', mutual dependence between thinking/vision and reality. The founding father of the principle of reflexivity was sociologist William Thomas. The Thomas theorem states that 'If men define situations as real, they are real in their

---

3   Merton 1968: 477.

consequences'.[4] A good example of this theorem is the panic which broke out on the Dam Square in Amsterdam on 4 May 2010 (Commemoration Day) when a man suddenly screamed during the two-minute silence. The situation was entirely benign, but because people in the public audience thought there was some danger, they behaved accordingly; and the result was mass panic, with 60 people injured. The fear of danger created danger.

George Soros, billionaire, famous for his speculation against the British pound in 1992, is a well-known believer in the reflexivity theory. He describes reflexivity as a two-way street between our thinking and the course of events. Reflexivity does not apply to physical sciences. Thus, when you study gravity, gravity itself will not change. Economics is a social science and Soros asserts that in economics there is reflexivity, since our thoughts about the economy do, in turn, influence it.[5] And he proved this; by speculating on a falling British pound, he helped the pound to actually fall. Reflexive statements have a certain effect on reality. This effect is exaggerated in financial markets when compared to the real economy: when we make negative statements about the value of (the shares of) a company, this can immediately have negative impact on the its share values.

A vision is a an aspirational image of the future which you try to realize, but it could just as well be a frightening one which you try to avoid. This is a reflexive expression, because an interaction between the vision and reality exists. Someone who creates a vision is not simply an observer of reality but a participant who affects reality with his or her statement.

With a particularly powerful vision you can often affect many more people and events than you first anticipated to be in your transactional environment. Sometimes the opposite is true: when you overestimate your level of influence, your vision may simply be a sign of narcissism or megalomania. You often read vision statements along the lines of 'We want to become the number One', yet clearly we can't *all* be number one. There is a thin line between overestimating and underestimating what you and your vision can accomplish.

Imagine a local Rabobank with only local clients. One of the clients, a flower bulb grower, extends its field of activity to Kenya and the bank decides to support him. The Kenyan flower industry, which earlier belonged in the contextual environment of the bank, is now within the transactional environment. The local bank has contributed to the trend of 'globalization' and affects an industry which the bank originally saw merely as context. The implications of this mean that when you change your 'self' – for example, in reaction to the trend of 'globalization' which you have observed – you reinforce the trend. Which means that the trend is not within your contextual environment, but in your transactional environment.

Once a strategy project is completed it can become apparent that the contextual environment was much more open to influence than first expected. We have already noted how the line between the 'self', the transactional environment and the contextual environment is rarely as clear as first assumed. Think of the dreams of Martin Luther King and Nelson Mandela and the nightmares of Al Gore, or even the destructive vision of Joseph Stalin and Adolf Hitler.

---

4   Merton 1995.

5   Soros 2008.

THE LIMITATIONS OF THE VISION

Be careful, however, because a vision can be as disempowering as it can be empowering. This is exactly what happened to Henk Alkema when, as head of the strategy division of Shell Chemicals, he developed the 'Select & Focus' strategy for the reorganization of the highly fragmented chemical branch of the enterprise. The chemical activities of Shell had been focused on petrochemicals from the outset: processing oil fractions into chemical products. In the 1970s the company developed a vision in which Shell would be a strong organization with greater resilience through offering a wide range of products, and the strategy of diversification was introduced. This led – amongst other things – to the expansion of new company divisions, including the chemical division. When it became apparent that many chemical activities were anything but profitable, the 'Select & Focus' strategy was developed. As a parent Shell lacked the appropriate competences to be of added value to its offspring, particularly those that had little in common with the petrochemical industry and with technology. During the 'Select & Focus' strategy these activities were closed down. This unbundling was also suggested by the academic insights of Goold and Campbell, who argued that a mismatch between parent and subsidiaries can sometimes be at the heart of poor subsequent performance. When the parent company cannot be an effective parent to its offspring (the parenting advantage), or when parent and subsidiary do not fit together well enough, then it is wise for the offspring to become independent or find another parent.[6] This was exactly the case for the new chemical activities in Shell: the connection between oil and gas, in which Shell excelled, had been lost through the new vision.

A vision is nothing more than a tool to formulate and achieve a goal collectively. It involves setting a course which should not be followed unquestioningly; with the passage of time you need to revisit and retest your vision against the background of the prevailing circumstances and the internal skills of the organization.

5.2   Developing a Vision

When you are aware of the circumstances in which your organization could end up and and you are clear on the reason your organization exists, you can create an image of how, ideally, it would look like what you *want* to achieve. This desired image is a long-term aspiration and is called a 'vision'. By undertaking this exercise together, as an organization, a community or an association, a *common* image starts to emerge. The vision is what the organization wants to build, for example the design of the cathedral which we mentioned previously. Designing the vision is less work than for example developing the scenarios. Although it is useful in the vision to take into account the opportunities and the threats in the environment, you don't need to explore the (future) environment of the organization. The important question here is to find the deeper motives of the organization: what does it want?

In most organizations a vision does exist, implicitly or on paper, but they are rarely in the hearts and minds of the people involved. In such cases it is useful to start a conversation about the vision. The vision can be narrowly formulated to relate to the

---

6   Goold and Campbell 1991.

organization itself (for example, to achieve a certain market share), but it can also be larger than the organization (for example, 'to eliminate poverty in the Netherlands'). The same applies to the time horizon: the vision can be for 2020, but equally for 2030 or 2050. You can make a vision relate to a single division, a company, a group of companies or even a country.

A vision can be created in several ways. You can build a vision around the opportunities and threats which the scenarios offer, but you can also review the current activities of the company and then aggregate the desired outcomes of those activities into a single picture. Whatever method you choose, you always need to make a choice about the level on which the vision is created: the strategic conversation about the vision can take place *top-down* and *bottom-up*. A top-down conversation means that the vision is created on the highest level of the organization and then imposed on the lower levels. A bottom-up approach of visioning implies that you search for existing desires and visions mainly with the operational levels of the organization, consolidate these into one big vision and present that to the top management.

In both approaches it is useful to convene a session in which you have the participants think about the time horizon of the vision. Is the vision for 2020, 2030 or 2050? You can then ask the participants to imagine where the organization will be by the chosen year, what it will have accomplished and what would the world look like ideally. A good, common vision is ideally not an answer to the question 'What do we want to avoid?', but an answer to the question: 'What do we want to create?' For me a vision should not driven by fear, but rather by ambition: a vision reflects what the organization wants to accomplish with the mission.

It is an art to describe a vision as visually and attractively as possible. The more visual and attractive the vision, the easier it is to share and translate into concrete targets and actions, both within and outside the organization. This requires focus on what is really important: you need to be able to tell the difference between major and minor issues and to formulate clearly. Do you want zero net energy consumption or zero net carbon dioxide emissions? Do you want to have at least 200 employees in 2020, or is it important that the organization is known as a good and appreciated employer, regardless of the number of employees? A vision describes how the ideal image looks and is therefore more elaborate than a simple short headline. A vision becomes more powerful when it is more detailed and highly visual.

A good vision meets a number of substantive criteria (in the subsequent paragraph we will discuss the criteria for an effective presentation). A vision is an *inclusive* story. This means: it is important that the vision is of interest to all involved; not simply to employees of the organization, but also to customers, shareholders and other stakeholders, all of whom should also be able to relate to it and join in. The *internal consistency* of the vision is also important: the vision needs to be logical with a coherent storyline to be believable. The vision should be *attractive* and engaging. The next criterion is the *level of stretch*: a good vision challenges employees and other stakeholders to make an effort. This demands a delicate balance: if a vision is easy to realize, it does not challenge. On the other hand: if a vision is unrealistic, it paralyzes. Peter Senge introduced the concept of 'creative tension', which refers to the tension between a vision and the reality. The gap between vision and reality is like a rubber band: when vision and reality are to close to one another, there is no tension and the rubber band is slack. When a vision and reality are too far apart, the tension is too high and the rubber band breaks. It is an art to find the right balance between vision and reality.[7]

The ultimate criterion for a vision is as follows: a vision should be meaningful to the organization. Therefore it is important to use value-driven words in the vision. And a vision should also address the emotions of the target group if it is to *inspire*. The idea is that people in the organization, on hearing the vision, want to get up and go to work. The final prerequisite is authenticity: the genuineness of the message can make or break a vision.

Put another way: the true, the good and the beautiful are the triangle which make up the vision. People want to create something they perceive as true (credible and coherent), beautiful (aesthetic and attractive) and good (ethical, inclusive and meaningful). The overlap between the vision and the mission is substantial. In fact mission and vision need to be aligned because they both touch the core values of the organization.

When developing the vision, conversations about trends and scenarios are a good starting point. Addressing these elements enables you to design the components of your vision. Scenarios are a tool which you can use when you want to evaluate how realistic your vision is. You'll find that simply by talking about scenarios and trends, normative statements about the desired future often emerge by themselves. If you gather these statements together and visualize them, a more complete image can be generated.

Once a set of scenarios has been developed, you can make a strategic choice to present a particular scenario to achieve a specific effect. You can present your dream scenario as a vision or a nightmare scenario as a spectre. In either case you are playing with perceptions in a bid to change the contextual environment.

My own experience is that formulating the vision is easier when it is preceded by strategic conversations about trends and scenarios. Thinking about trends and scenarios makes it easier to develop a common vision, because you have already become acquainted with things which are inevitable in the future. Consequently a *sense of urgency* arises around the need for change along with an awareness that *business as usual* is no longer sustainable. And when you hold your trend and scenario interviews and workshops, you will most likely come across elements which involve the future of the organization itself. On that occasion you will have set them aside because you are focused on the outside world, but in the subsequent strategic conversation about the vision you can revisit them, and they may well be a source of inspiration.

This vision can be divided into provisional milestones which are mini-visions in their own right. Then you can use the (conversation about) options to design a roadmap, which indicates in detail and step by step what the organization should do to achieve the vision. For example, Eneco has set itself the target to produce only sustainable energy in 2030, with a milestone in 2012 of 30 per cent and another in 2020 of 70 per cent. In Chapter 6 we will discuss roadmaps in more detail.

---

7   Senge 1992.

DUTCH LEADERSHIP 2015 (1)

Netherlands' Shipbuilding Industry Association

In 2005 my team was asked to help develop a vision for the Dutch Shipbuilding industry for the Netherlands' Shipbuilding Industry Association (VNSI). This vision project was inspired by the report *Leadership 2015, Defining the Future of the European Shipbuilding and Ship Repair Industry* by the European Commission, which sketched the future of the European shipbuilding industry. VNSI wanted to connect to this report and to elaborate it into an ideal image, one which focused on the Netherlands and translated the ideas into an action plan; something which reflected the aspiration of the Dutch shipbuilding industry to become leaders in Europe.

In a short scenario exercise we mapped external developments by interviewing shipbuilders amongst others. A threat scenario soon became apparent; one in which no one invested in shipbuilding, the government refused to support the industry and consequently there was no future for the Dutch shipbuilding industry. Slowly it dawned on the VNSI that this threat scenario could become a self-fulfilling prophecy. If many people began to think that shipbuilding had no future, investments would decrease as a direct consequence of this perception and the industry could indeed get caught in a downward spiral.

It was up to the VNSI to prevent this from happening, to ensure that investors, employees, the government and other actors had faith in the shipbuilding industry again. Starting from the trends and scenarios we looked for opportunities in the shipbuilding industry. We tried to connect the rich history of the Netherlands in shipbuilding with trends such as globalization and sustainability. We were careful to involve both the older generation of shipbuilders, who mainly represented the past, but especially the new generation. We asked young people why they had chosen a shipbuilding trade and what future did they see for this industry.

During the process VNSI slowly regained faith in a positive future for the industry. The outlines of a great opportunity for the Dutch shipbuilding industry appeared before them, they were able to capitalize on these by focusing on topics like entrepreneurship and technological knowledge. This all was accumulated in the vision *Dutch LeaderSHIP 2015*, which stated that in 2015 the Dutch shipbuilding industry would be leaders in innovation and sustainability. Five success factors were expressed in this vision:

- highly satisfied customers and new markets
- supply chain reinforcement
- entrepreneurship and professional management
- knowledge and innovation
- integrated and innovative government policy.

Promoting synergy in the supply chain and investing in the knowledge of (future) staff became priority number 1 for the first two years. Concrete actions were linked to the success factors to realize the vision.

This optimistic vision attracted the attention of investors. Potential employees saw the shipbuilding industry as a promising industry and the political attention for the industry increased. In 2005 Rabobank (sponsor of this visioning project) took a stake in the second largest shipbuilder, IHC Merwede. The tone of press reporting on shipbuilding improved following publication of the vision and government support for the industry grew after the final symposium in which some Members of Parliament were asked to comment on the vision. Perhaps all of this was mere coincidence, but the upward spiral had started.

DEDUCTION AND INDUCTION

In Chapter 3 on scenarios I mentioned the difference between deductive (from general to more specific) and inductive (from specific to more common) processes. The same two perspectives apply to a vision.

Let me explain the difference between them with an example. Remember, you can make a vision for an individual organization or a collective of organizations, but you can also do so for a single department or a specific branch. When you are working on a vision for a department, there are two methods you can use. You can, where available, make the vision of the whole organization your starting point and then make the relevant parts specific for your department. In other words, you are deriving the vision of the department from the vision of the whole organization and one story is translated into several stories for several departments. This is a deductive way of working and it is how, for example, IHC Dredgers derived its vision from the vision of the mother company IHC Merwede.

Another deductive way of developing a vision is by elaborating and visualizing the vision of your managing director or founder of the organization. Your job is 'to find the sweet spot for the soapbox'; to make sure that managers spreads the vision through presentations and meetings. Your role, in this case, is to bring the vision to the surface and to spread it as widely as possible. When the vision is developed in a deductive way, you are often working *top-down*. The dream of one or a few people is transferred to many others. When these others can connect to the (imposed) dream and find that (at least a part of) their own vision fits within this bigger picture, a deductive process can work very well. On the other hand, if people do not succeed in making the vision their own, it will never have the desired result.

However, you can also work inductively and derive one big vision by combining elements of many smaller visions. When you work in an inductive way, it implies that some visions already exist, perhaps within the minds of people in the organization or in organizational documents. If you can unite the visions of employees, customers, suppliers and other stakeholders, you will arrive at a shared vision. The material you have collected in interviews and workshops needs to be integrated into the larger organization-wide vision. Effectively, you create a new vision by putting the pieces together, rather like a jigsaw puzzle – although in this case, the process is one of dialogue with the relevant decision-makers and stakeholders.

An inductive way of working often goes with a *bottom-up* approach. You listen to and involve as many people as you can. The final vision is later shared widely. In the process you might find that there are some opposing and incompatible interests and wishes within the group. Sometimes during such a process you even stumble over strongly conflicting visions, e.g. between the management, the employees and the shareholders and even within these groups. In such cases a shared vision does not exist, a priori. In order to set course, people will have to reconcile, or even battle, the different visions to reach a compromise. Alternatively, you may decide to go in one direction and accept that not everyone naturally wants to follow. In such cases, you have the difficult task of searching for something everyone wants: a shared aspiration, or make something so attractive that it might become that. When real negotiations about the vision are needed, there will always be winners and loosers. This makes the challenge to have the whole organization promote this vision (see also pp. 118–119) even more difficult.

5.3   Formulating and Visualizing a Vision

To realize the vision it is important to formulate and visualize it. Inherently, you will be designing what doesn't yet exist. You are, with the help of the organization, creating something new. But the vision can only materialize if enough people truly believe in it. This last point is essential in realizing the vision: developing, visualizing and sharing the vision is something which is ideally done together. The more people believe in the vision, the greater the chance that it will actually come true.

This is why the aesthetic side of the vision deserves attention. In the introduction to the chapter I explained how a vision requires imagination. Thus it is important to make the vision attractive. It should draw an image that is as clear and strong as possible. This image should appeal to people at both a rational and emotional level. If you succeed in that you will find it easier for people to incorporate the vision into their view of the world and to start moving towards it. Authenticity is crucial, otherwise the audience will not be touched and addressed by the ideas.

Ideally the top of the organization can inspire the rest of the organization and wider stakeholders by walking around inside and outside the organization to spread the word. Formulating and visualizing includes the need to develop a good story; one that is real and sincere. To make the story more appealing, try and be as clear and specific as possible. Aristotle said 'the soul never thinks without an image'; it is also true that concrete images can strengthen a vision. It is also important to realize that the arguments used as evidence to support the vision should appeal to the motivation and emotions of people.

Imagine an organization operating predominantly in one single country which has a vision to become multinational. You can help people in the organization to feel the 'internationalization', by giving reasons for it: 'we need to follow our customers who are going international' or 'wouldn't it be great to be able to travel more?'. The particular arguments you choose depend on what appeals most to your target group, which makes it wise to understand fundamentally what makes your vision attractive for them. And that, in turn, needs to be done as a conversation, a two-way process of presenting and listening.

'I HAVE A DREAM'

Visualizing doesn't need to be taken literally; a figurative vision can also have strong visual qualities. I like to use Martin Luther King's speech 'I have a dream' to enable participants in a workshop to experience what a good and appealing vision feels like:

I say to you today, my friends, so even though we face the difficulties of today and tomorrow, I still have a dream. It is a dream deeply rooted in the American dream. I have a dream that one day this nation will rise up and live out the true meaning of its creed: 'We hold these truths to be self-evident: that all men are created equal.' I have a dream that one day on the red hills of Georgia the sons of former slaves and the sons of former slave owners will be able to sit down together at a table of brotherhood. I have a dream that one day even the state of Mississippi, a desert state, sweltering with the heat of injustice and oppression, will be transformed into an oasis of freedom and justice. I have a dream that my four children will one day live in a nation where they will not be judged by the color of their skin but by the content of their character. I have a dream today.[8]

Apart from the fact that the black American reverend appealed to the public through his qualities as a public speaker, the images which he evoked underpinned the power of his story. Martin Luther King used several rhetorical techniques to communicate his powerful message. For example, he created visual *images* in the minds of his audience: of the red hills of Georgia and the desert of Mississippi – whereby he also, by referencing two different States in this fragment and a futher ten in the rest of his speech, clearly shows that his message applies to all of the US. Moreover King makes sure he addresses his audience *directly*: it is about the sons of former slaves, but also about the sons of former slave owners. In this way he is careful to include all listeners in his vision, no matter what their social background. King connects his dream vision to older, deeper underlying stories of the American past evoking an 'American dream'. The story is *authentic* and has an *emotional* appeal, e.g. because he makes it personal by referring to his own children. And as far as rhetoric is concerned, the repetitions – for example, of the phrase 'I have a dream' – strengthen the power of his speech.

---

8   King 1963

When formulating a vision it is important to choose a language and words which appeal to the target groups. Ask yourself: 'Who do I need to tell, what and how should I tell them this to achieve what I want?' The choice of words is important and ideally concentrates on the target group: customers, shareholders, employees, government. When you approach these groups in their own language, the power of the vision will increase.

So a vision can be expressed in a story. Alternatively, you can literally use physical visualizations, for example, by making a scale model or a drawing. A vision becomes stronger when the design is consistent with the message, with what or who the organization wants to be. And then you also have the choice between the language of numbers or the language of words. This will be different in every organization. In an engineering firm or a financial company the vision will most likely contain more numbers, while the vision of a municipality will focus more on people, with words and images.

THE SECRET OF IJMOND

Municipality of Heemskerk

In 2008 and 2009 the municipality of Heemskerk explored the future of the municipality up to the year 2040, in order to formulate a long-term strategy. The project started with trend-watching. All of the trends which were important to Heemskerk were researched and published in a first report called 'Municipality of Heemskerk 2040: Trends and developments in and around Heemskerk'. They then developed three scenarios: Silver, Sub-hub and Beach. Each scenario showed opportunities and threats for the municipality and were visualized by a graphic artist in three large posters.

A workshop with members of the Council and municipal executive board members was organized, at which they discussed how the municipality could react to the opportunities and threats as made visual in the three scenario posters. They also described what Heemskerk would ideally look like in 2040 if all opportunities from the scenarios could be grasped and all the threats could be controlled. This enabled the muniplaity to design a new vision: 'Heemskerk, the secret of IJmond', a story written out in a second report. Elements of the vision included a population of 40,000, strong social cohesion, increased tourism, improved access and a higher level of sustainability.

The final report also included an artist's impression of Heemskerk in 2040. They felt that a simple two-dimensional map would not be inspiring enough and would look too much like a zoning plan, whereas the vision was about the future of community and not simply about the physical design of the area. Which is why Heemskerk chose a graphic representation 'at eye level' instead of just a map. A professional artist helped to realize a drawing which showed a map incorporating snapshots at eye level. Each of the snapshots showed an important aspect of the vision: how the citizens of Heemskerk would live and work in 2040 (see Figure 5.2).

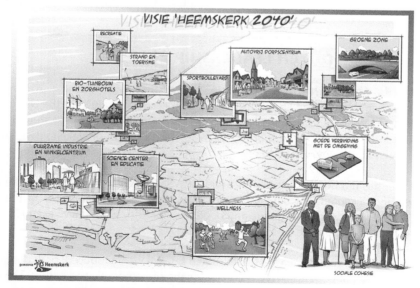

Figure 5.2   Vision 'Heemskerk 2040'
Credit: JAM Visual Thinking

They added an explanatory text which was extensively edited to make the vision feel good, concrete, local and most of all 'their own'. The choice of words played an important role. The members of the Council and the municipal executive board members of Heemskerk preferred words such as 'wellness' which they associated with 'fitness' and 'energy' over words such as 'health', which they associated too closely with 'cure', 'healthcare' and 'illness'. The exact formulation of the vision is an art and a collective process in itself.

5.4 Sharing a Vision

The strategic conversation about the vision is not an easy one to have because the desired future which the vision describes requires imagination. The conversation about the vision is also difficult because there will be conflicting interests and desires. Once the vision is developed and visualized, the next step is sharing it, and since both the context and the people inside the organization change all the time, visioning is almost a continuous process. You constantly need to remind (new) employees and stakeholders of the vision of the organization.

It is essential that everyone in the organization, but also the external stakeholders, become acquainted with the vision. After all, if the vision is kept a secret, it will be impossible to realize it. You also want people to see the meaning of their work, feel connected to each other and the organization and see themselves having a place in the vision. All this helps people to be focused, feel inspired and to make the vision come true. There are many ways to share the vision, from billboards in a factory to credit-card size cards to carry with you. Most importantly, whenever you walk around in the organization you need to question whether everyone is familiar with the vision: do people know where we are going? And if not, what is the best way to talk with them about the vision?

DUTCH LEADERSHIP 2015 (2)

Netherlands' Shipbuilding Industry Association

Earlier in the chapter we talked about the vision Dutch LeaderSHIP 2015 of the Netherlands' Shipbuilding Industry Association (VSNI), in which a promising future was shown for the shipbuilding industry. This vision aroused interest from all sorts of stakeholders, such as investors, potential employees and the government.

But of course, this did not just happen by accident. VSNI did all it could to make the vision well-known and accepted. For different target groups different presentations of the vision were put together, varying in language and design so that they would have as much appeal to the target group as possible (see Figure 5.3).

A small film about the vision and a heavily illustrated booklet were produced; both designed to attract the attention of potential investors, trade unions and other relevant parties. The report included *tags* in the margin and bullet lists so it would appeal to entrepreneurs who were mainly interested in the outline of the story. For the report politicians were interviewed to learn about their vision on shipbuilding and to ensure that they became part of the vision too.

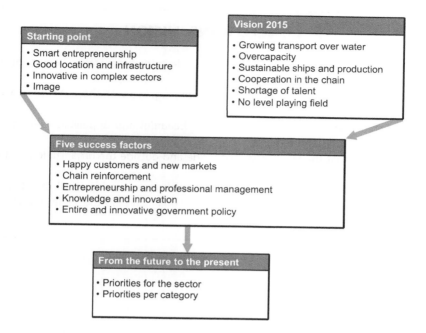

Figure 5.3   Dutch LeaderSHIP 2015: five success factors (after VNSI 2005)

In the various representations of the vision (film, report, presentation) rather than describing all scenarios we very deliberately chose to focus just on those which represented opportunities which might contribute to a prosperous future for the Dutch shipbuilding industry. We avoided conscious references to possible negative trends and scenarios and limited the discussion. The focus was on the dream, not the nightmare. There was already plenty of negative thinking within the shipbuilding industry; a vision of hope was what was most urgently needed!

When you hold a strategic conversation about: who or what the organization is (mission); what it wants to achieve (vision); what happens around the organization (trends); in which situations it might end up (scenarios); and which possibilities it has for action (options) one subject is missing: how will the organization put the acquired knowledge into practice and get from A to B? For this you need a roadmap, which shows in detail the route between the present and the desired future. This roadmap is the subject of the next chapter.

CONCLUSIONS: VISION

1. Discuss, *top-down* or *bottom-up*, what people in the organization want to achieve in the future: what are their visions?
2. Combine the visions to one collective vision, e.g. in a workshop. Where do we want to go together?
3. Elaborate the vision into a convincing, beautiful and appealing message, using words, numbers and pictures.
4. Make sure that the vision is shared inside and outside the organization and repeat the story.
5. The leadership of the organization should show leadership in all the steps above and step on the soapbox. And every individual can help the leadership to actually take this role.

CHAPTER 6

Roadmap:
How do we get there?

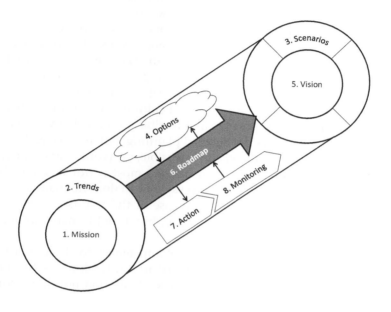

Before you leave port, you set your course. But you also check if the cargo is all loaded, whether you have enough fuel and decide which sails you will hoist. Once you are at sea, it is not enough to know in which direction you want to head. You need maps on which you can draw your waypoints and see how you get from where you are to your final destination. You also need to know who is running the engine room, who is steering and who is keeping watch. When establishing a course you need to take into account the manoeuvrability of your ship and anticipate any circumstances you might encounter along the way. And finally you need to know the latitude and longitude of your destination. Do you want to set sail for New York or for Dover? Are you planning to unload, take on more cargo, or make it your base for further trade? And what are your stopovers on the way?

The strategic conversation about the roadmap is a conversation about 'strategy' or 'strategic planning': the steps between the present and the desired future. In many organizations the word strategy is used in a more limited sense; the strategic plan of the organization for how to achieve their vision. We call this plan the 'roadmap', to avoid confusion between this and strategy in its broader sense. The roadmap bridges the gap between the present – the mission – and the desired future – the vision – of the organization. Your task therefore is not only to help to define this future, but also to make sure that it is clear how this can be achieved through provision of a rough strategic plan: our roadmap.

Strategy is often seen as 'the plan for the longest-term and on the highest level'. This strategy or, as I call it, roadmap will need to be translated into concrete business plans, policies, department plans, medium-term plans and long-term plans. These plans are part of the way in which you will *execute* the corporate strategy, and they will be discussed in the next chapter. But when you spell out the strategy for a smaller part of the organization, these plans can each in turn be examples of roadmaps: descriptions of the road to be travelled from A to B within a certain amount of time.

Roadmapping is not something you undertake in isolation. It involves interaction with the other strategic conversations. In collaboration with the organization you can test the success formula, the mission and the vision against the scenarios, and look at the options to reach a concrete plan: the roadmap. There is a direct link between the vision and the roadmap. In this case, we are dealing with an iterative process: you will know whether the vision you have formulated is realistic once you have decided how you will try to realize the vision. In some (corporate) cultures a vision can only be embraced once it is clear that this vision is possible and feasible, and for that you need a finalized roadmap. Nothing is done during the detailed planning, but as soon as the roadmap has been finalized and it is clear that the vision is feasible, everyone starts acting.

It is important to recognize that what matters most is not whether the roadmap has been drawn well, but that everyone knows what to do. The roadmap is an 'object' to hold on to during the ride. Just as in the case of the results of the other strategic conversations, the roadmap is not a destination, but a tool to make strategic thinking and acting possible.

During roadmapping you will need other competences to those you have already used. You need to be able to organize your work and to work to a schedule. It is your responsibility to check and double-check with everybody that nothing is forgotten and that everyone knows what to do.

6.1   What is a Roadmap?

The roadmap links the mission to the vision. The mission describes where the organization came from, the vision shows where it wants to go in the future and the roadmap describes which steps we need to take to get there. The roadmap sketches the route between the target (point B) and the present (point A). It is a complete series of internally consistent and coherent steps which an organization needs to take.

When you design a roadmap, it is important to ask yourself what is the sphere of influence of your organization? If you include activities in the roadmap for actors over whom you have little influence, the map will be less realistic. A good plan is a realistic plan. Every step must be feasible and executable.

What distinguishes a roadmap from a classic, one-dimensional strategy is the fact that a roadmap contains alternative routes. These can be taken when particular circumstances arise or when the original route doesn't work out as intended. This is dynamic planning. We use a roadmap as a hard plan, which we can model and for which we can calculate the effects: the diversity and the uncertainty which were still present while exploring the scenarios and options are now past. At the same time we take into account possible changes in circumstances and we make sure we have alternative options ready.

A roadmap consists of three W's: Who does What, When? The 'Who' in the roadmap depends on who or what is included in the 'self' (see Figure 2.1). Often this will be the organization itself, or people or departments within it (production, finance, human resources). But it is also possible for the organization to take the line of a 'greater Self'; in other words a network which extends beyond the original parties. If this is the case, you will count target groups outside the organization (politicians, subcontractors, investors) as part of your list of actors and include them in the roadmap. Sometimes you will intentionally do so. You'll need to be confident of your influence over actors from outside your own organization or your sphere of influence, before you include them. The 'What' in the roadmap describes which actions need to be carried out to realize the final goals. The 'What' and the 'When' are connected. The 'When' describes when or in what time the actions need to be carried out.

When we formulated the vision for the Netherlands' Shipbuilding Industry Association (VNSI), Dutch LeaderSHIP 2015 (see Chapter 5), we include a list of 18 actions. These actions were mapped against several success factors, with discrete schedules and amongst the target groups within the association (sea-shipbuilding and mega-yachts, ship repair, minor shipbuilding and associated members). The roadmap became an integral part of the vision document. Allthough the scale of roadmaps can vary a great deal, the principles on which they are created remain the same: the roadmap is a logical set of steps which show who does what and when, and against which activities and sometimes also budgets and targets are formulated (see Figure 4.1).

6.2   Designing a Roadmap

How do you design a roadmap? The first step is to look backwards from the desired future – the vision – to agree which steps should be taken between the present and the future to achieve your ideal picture. You use these steps to trace out a course of action which can lead you from the present to the future, thus shaping the dynamic strategy into a concrete form. Finally, you should assign the roles to the actors and decide on the allocation of tasks.

As you start to design a roadmap, you need to ask yourself three questions which serve as a guideline for the whole process:

1.   For whom (which parts of the organization) are you making the roadmap?
2.   What are the goals and milestones?
3.   Which actions need to be taken and what is the connection between these actions?

A ROADMAP FOR ENERGY-EFFICIENT BUILDINGS[1]

World Business Council for Sustainable Development

In the developed world, buildings are responsible for 40 per cent of all energy consumption. Energy use could be reduced substantially by designing, building, using and finally demolishing buildings in a more sustainable way. The World Business Council for Sustainable Development (WBCSD), an association of multinationals working together to foster sustainable development, has explored if and how we can achieve zero net energy buildings in 2050. We facilitated a number of workshops to translate their vision into roadmaps.

During this process the WBCSD formulated the following vision: 'By 2050 new buildings will consume zero net energy from external power supplies and produce zero net carbon dioxide emissions while being economically viable to construct and operate.'

To fulfil this ambition, seven different groups need to take action:

1. government authorities
2. developers
3. investors
4. utilities
5. suppliers and manufacturers
6. architects, engineering, contractors and craftsmen
7. occupiers of the buildings.

To derive the roadmap from the vision we adopted the method of backcasting from the ideal picture and quantified the resulting actions: a deductive way of working. The roadmap was divided into actions/milestones on the basis of the short and medium term with final goals in 2050.

Workshops with representatives of the seven target groups were held, followed by one integral workshop. We used an inductive approach: gathering and combining the ideas of the several target groups. The results of the backcasting and the quantifications were connected to the output from the workshops and from that a roadmap emerged. You can see the result in Figure 6.1.

By developing the roadmap together with the target groups in workshops and by publishing and communicating the roadmap the members hope that the plans it contains will indeed be realized.

---

1   World Business Council for Sustainable Development 2009.

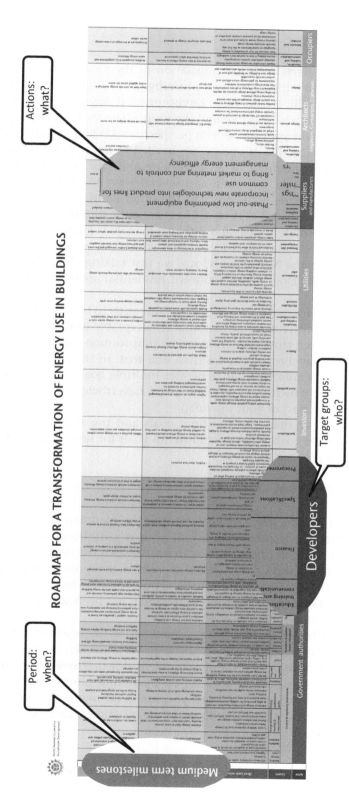

Figure 6.1 Details from the roadmap of the WBCSD for energy efficiency in buildings

FROM VISION TO GOALS

The design of a roadmap starts with the translation of the vision into strategic goals. This is an important step in which a focused phrasing of the final goal and the interim goals is important. At the PBL Netherlands Environmental Assessment Agency (PBL) I conducted a strategy project which elaborated the vision 'The Sustainable City in 2040', for which we generated roadmaps from several perspectives.[2] When we started designing the roadmap from the perspective of energy, we needed to figure out whether the PBL wanted to achieve a climate-neutral or an energy-neutral city. A climate-neutral city doesn't produce carbon dioxide, but there are several ways to achieve this goal, e.g. by offsetting the carbon dioxide emissions. On the other hand, an energy-neutral city produces as much energy (or more) as it uses. These are quite different concepts.

You also need to be absolutely clear about the scale of your goals. Imagine your goal is a sustainable city by 2040. You need to indicate which city you are describing: just Amsterdam or all cities in the Netherlands? Are we just talking about the city centres or also about the outskirts? Does it only concern residential areas, or commercial and harbour areas as well?

For the purpose of the roadmap the abstract vision needs to be translated in strategic goals. A goal is a simple SMART (Specific Measurable Acceptable Realistic Timely) version of the vision. The vision is a story that needs to be transformed into measurable items. Often a vision can be unravelled into more than one goal. In the public sector, visions are usually broader, which automatically generates multiple goals. In the private sector a vision is often narrower which leads to fewer goals; nevertheless it is possible to state more than one goal at the start of your roadmap.

You need to state more than just the final goals and the scale. A well-structured roadmap will split the final goals into several interim goals for specific parts. These form the waypoints which mark your journey.

MANOEUVRABILITY AND BACKCASTING

An important element to remember while designing the roadmap are your *lead times*. The lead time describes the manoeuvrability of your organization. It is very easy to underestimate just how slow an organization can be. Between the order and the delivery of goods or services you'll always have some delay: the delivery time. In the same way, you need to calculate the delivery times for the actions in your roadmap. You need to plan ahead and make sure each element in the roadmap has been scheduled far enough in advance to deliver on time.

During the Internet boom in 2000 I was a member of the board of a fast growing IT-company which wanted to develop new software very quickly. So they hired more staff. Unfortunately this only slowed the development down. There was a simple error in reasoning: some processes can't be speeded up by adding more people. Sometimes, the lead time is fixed and you cannot increase your room for manoeuvre. Make sure you understand exactly what you are: a speedboat or an oil tanker, and reckon with your response time, accordingly.

---

2   For a more extensive description of the PBL project 'The Sustainable City in 2040', see the case study later in this chapter.

For a company such as Nokia it takes about a year to develop a new type of mobile phone and a year to recover the costs: thus looking forward for a period of two years is sufficient. But building a new facility for the production of a new phone, from the start of the design process until the actual use of the facility, takes more than a year and the pay-off time for the investment in this facility is much longer: perhaps even five years. The pay-off time of an oil or gas field can be even longer; between ten and twenty years. In that case you need to project even further forward. The manoeuvrability and the response time of organizations varies; it can vary between different departments and between different scales of activity (developing a new type of mobile phone or developing a new production facility). The hiring of people, R&D and IT investments all have their own rhythm and dynamics and you should know what they are.

And it's not only lead times you have to deal with: you also need to address windows of opportunity or momentum. Sometimes an opportunity comes along for which you only have limited time to react. The momentum is the short period of time in which you can seize the opportunity; if you don't, it's gone. Timing is of decisive importance to failure or success. The end of your lease is good example of momentum; you can choose to end it and move (a put option) or you may extend the lease. Political elections provide a momentum which politicians need to use to push themselves into the reckoning. The same is true when a good candidate company for merger presents itself, something which only happens once in a while and with a limited window of opportunity.

Because of the existence of lead times and momentum which show that time and timing are crucial to roadmaps, it is sensible to use backcasting. Backcasting is the opposite of forecasting. You look back from a future picture and determine the distance between that future and the present. Instead of thinking about the current trends in a continuous line, backcasting involves thinking of solutions to achieve the desired future, the vision. Backcasting is where developing a roadmap really starts because now several paths, from the future back to the present, begin to emerge. When you have insight into the difference between the static and the dynamic, into the preferred order of actions and into the lead times, you can complete the roadmap much more effectively and therefore enable the organization to steer itself more accurately.

SELECTING OPTIONS

Who specifically do you need to realize the goals of the organization? What do you need to do when and what do you need? The options you have charted before can be considered a reservoir of ideas and used as input when you start filling in the roadmap. It is likely that you have generated more options than you actually need to complete the roadmap, in which case you can, as suggested on p. 91, formulate extra criteria to select the options: in addition to relevance and feasibility you can calculate elements such as costs, support or connection to present competences.

The most important and robust options (see p. 93) make the kernel of the plan. They fit and are relevant and feasible no matter what the detail of the plan. The use of call and put options in the roadmap prevents the roadmap from becoming a static blueprint, it remains a dynamic and future-proof plan. They allow you to adjust the course in response to changing circumstances. Thus during execution there is space for alternatives of action. And although it sounds like a paradox, because we defined the options and their respective conditions, we have built flexibility into the plan. The scenarios can help you to describe when and under which conditions the organization should start or stop certain activities.

Call options can also be part of a roadmap. If you are using them it is important to describe the circumstances in which these actions should be taken up. Call options are often connected to milestones (interim goals): these are perfect moments to check the progress on the roadmap and to decide whether certain actions should be stopped or phased out. It is therefore important to be clear about the conditions under which a change of direction becomes necessary: all this makes it much easier at a later stage to recognize the circumstances in which you need to use your call and put options – but more about this in the final chapter. The milestones form the structure of the planning cycle: they offer opportunities to judge the roadmap and progress. You can also use these moments to evaluate the call and put options.

The options can refer to activities, budgets and goals. You can arrange them in order and on the basis of their relationship to each other. To do that you need to have an image of how the options relate to one another. When using the options which you included in your roadmap, you should not only use backcasting, but also look at the relationship between the options. Each of them may be feasible in isolation, but are they feasible when connected? In other words, can you execute the planned options several at a time or all at once? And is the whole set of actions internally consistent? For instance, you might have built in the option to go international with your organization, and you might have opened the option to enter three or four new markets. But it is unlikely that you will have the resources to do all of this at once, or that you will know in advance which markets will pick up first. The more scenarios and options you prepare, the more flexible you become. However, you don't need to make all of this explicit in the roadmap.

Most organizations find it difficult to include uncertainties and options in the roadmap. They prefer to list the risks and uncertainties in a separate document which is added to the roadmap under the name of 'Strategic Risk Management' or 'Sensitivity Analysis'. This is the traditional way of planning, in which uncertainties are not mentioned in the plan. Including different options in a roadmap can make it complex and divergent, but it is good to realize that you need to have some options, whether you include them in the roadmap or collect them in a separate document. It is necessary to realize that uncertainties simply exist and that a plan which reckons with this fact offers more security.

ALONE OR TOGETHER?

Selecting options and filling in the roadmap can be done on your own at your desk. Nevertheless it is advisable to involve the different parties concerned in the design of the roadmap. Collaboration will create support and ownership. Just as in other strategic conversations, we see that in this conversation about roadmaps it is as much about the process as it is about the content. In the case of a small project, you can organize a workshop to select the options. This can be done initially by identifying the options individually, by writing them down on Post-it notes, possibly including the name of the person or department which should execute the action, and then as a group recording these on a big timeline; moving them around while discussing the options. Each target group can use Post-its of one specific color. The Post-its can be connected by arrows to symbolize the relationships. In this way a roadmap is literally filled in iteratively. In large projects this process is essenially the same: they simply involve more people, more workshops and more analysis and writing.

THE SUSTAINABLE CITY 2040

PBL Netherlands Environmental Assessment Agency

The PBL Netherlands Environmental Assessment Agency (PBL) makes strategic policy analyses in the field of environment, nature and spatial planning. One of the PBL projects was The Sustainable City 2040; an independent scientific project which was started to support the Dutch government in designing policy contributing to a sustainable urban environment. As part of this project, PBL organized a dialogue among the concerned parties from the business community, NGOs, government authorities and research institutes. Four angles were defined: health, viability (split between growing and shrinking cities) and energy. For each of the angles PBL wanted to come to an ideal picture and then use backcasting to translate them into roadmaps: what would a sustainable city look like in 2040 in the eyes of each of the parties concerned and what needed to be done in the mean time to achieve the ideal picture? For this purpose two workshops (one about the ideal picture and one about the roadmap) were organized for each angle with a final conference which I was asked to conduct.

The first workshop of The Sustainable City 2040 project explored the context of health and was held in February 2009. 'Health' was defined in detail in the workshop. The participants then considered the demands which could be made on a healthy, sustainable city in 2040. These demands were clustered in several themes which were then elaborated. Emphasis was placed on why the theme contributes to a healthy, sustainable city. Then participants worked in small groups to develop a vision of a healthy city in 2040, based on the pre-noted demands. The ideal pictures, made during the workshop, described an urban environment which protects and encourages health and contained a lot of comparible elements.

Following the workshops the employees at PBL tried to summarize all the ideal pictures into one integrated vision which was described in a story and presented in drawings. The primary goal of the integration of the ideal pictures was to visualize the future and to make it less abstract. At the same time people were actively looking for differences which were given their place in several scenarios.

The integrated vision was used as input for the second workshop for the Health context which was held in May 2009. Participants first had the opportunity to sharpen the vision. Backcasting from the vision of the healthy, sustainable city was a fundamental element. What should be done between the present and 2040 to make our cities healthy and sustainable? The participants were asked to record the actions on Post-it notes. They then split these actions into four timelines, which represented different fields of policy-making: public space, mobility, facilities, and employment and housing. This was followed by three rounds of discussion in which the four timelines were mapped out in more detail. The first round explored 'what and when': the actions were arranged in the correct order on the timeline and where possible given a completion date. In the second round the participants considered the rules of the game and the sources which would be needed to make it a success. In the third round they considered the actors and coalitions involved.

After the workshop the results were elaborated further. All of this resulted in a roadmap of a healthy, sustainable city which was built up from smaller timelines for public space, mobility, facilities and employment and housing (Figure 6.2). Both the integrated roadmap and the smaller roadmaps consisted of the same elements: the starting position, the ideal picture and the timeline with actions, rules and sources and actors. For the other angles – viability in growing cities, viability in shrinking cities and energy – similar integrated and smaller roadmaps were developed.

Figure 6.2 Vision of a healthy city in 2040

Credit: JAM Visual Thinking

6.3 Using a Roadmap

In many organizations the ability for staff groups to self-organize is often much greater than many managers think. Self-organizing ability implies that the employees act independently, furnish solutions and make plans. Staff involved in this way is often innovative and managers find they need simply to let go and provide space. This concept is often illustrated by comparing a traffic light to a roundabout. At a traffic light, authorities take care of you and as a road-user you are subjected to 'the system', which tells you what to do. At a roundabout the authorities trust the self-organizing ability of a road-user. In an organization with a high self-organizing ability, the employees of all departments know that they are essential to the whole and they take the responsibility that comes with that. This makes it very important in such an environment that everyone knows the bigger picture and knows where they stand: what is their own role and their expected contribution to the whole? In such cases people know the potential bottlenecks and it is easier to formulate solutions to them.

A roadmap can be used to steer top-down (the roadmap as a traffic light) as well as to have people steer themselves (the roadmap as a roundabout). These are the two ways in which you can use a roadmap, to encourage an organization to start acting. The WBCSD developed roadmaps for energy efficiency in buildings. Prior to that everyone played the blame game: financiers, contractors and architects blamed each other for the lack of action in the field. The roadmaps of the WBCSD were developed to make them end the deadlock and start acting by making clear what needed to be done and by when, in order to realize the ideal picture: a world in which buildings consume zero net energy.

FROM VISION TO IMPLEMENTATION PROGRAM

Municipality of Heemskerk

In 2008 and 2009 the municipality of Heemskerk developed a vision for 2040 (Heemskerk, the secret of IJmond); this process has already been described in Chapter 5. Once they had formulated the vision, the municipality was keen to realize it. Within the municipality no one considered the vision as something that could be connected to policy. It was therefore decided to generate a roadmap; the 'implementation programme'. The goal of this implementation programme was to place the abstract future images from the vision for 2040 into the present and the near future. This enabled the municipality to connect the vision to policy and the municipal plans and the vision became an internal force amongst the municipal staff.

In the summer of 2009 our team conducted two workshops with civil servants from the Department of Policy and Strategy. Prior to this several tracks were derived from the vision. These themes formed the starting point of the workshops in which the policy-makers discussed how the vision for 2040 could be translated into specific policy plans such as for transport and environment, tourism, education and welfare. They then needed to backcast: what had to be done in Heemskerk between the present and 2040 to realize this vision? Because 2040 was a distant planning horizon for the organization, they chose to focus on the road to 2020 and on practical issues such as 'who', 'what' and 'when'. Some parts of the vision, for example to open up the beach by lightrail, turned out to be unrealistic in the short term. One of the most difficult issues during the development of the implementation programme turned out to be the fact that thinking about a vision can be done, more or less, without committing oneself; a roadmap requires you make choices and deal with practicalities.

An implementation programme was designed using the results of the workshops. For each of the tracks several categories were articulated: the desired effect of the intervention, the wishes of the public and requirements (if known) of the parties involved, the neccesary first steps, a timeline and an allocation of actions. This overview, which presents starting points for concrete policy, was presented in April 2010 to the new city council and the new municipal executive board members, so that it would be anchored to the municipal organization and the municipal policy.

When the roadmap is completed, you need to connect it to the official plans to ensure it becomes part of the planning and control cycle, as we mentioned at the end of Chapter 4. Turnover, budgets, goals and efforts need to be connected to the roadmap. They are the levers by which the organization can steer at the roadmap.

The actions described in the roadmap should also be quantified. What are the costs of a certain action and what benefit does it bring? Is the action feasible? Therefore it is important to link to the financial and HR departments. You need to work as a team with these and other departments, so that a connection starts growing between the roadmap and the financial and staffing possibilities of the organization.

A roadmap should not just be a static document. It needs to be used, updated and kept alive. Strategic thinking should be transformed into strategic acting. In the next two chapters I will explain how you can use the roadmap to keep organization moving forward and on track.

CONCLUSIONS: ROADMAP

1.   In consultation with the parties concerned, translate the vision into strategic goals and interim milestones.
2.   Backcast from the goals; define the distance between the desired future and the present and define the requisite solutions.
3.   Select the most important options to design your roadmap; describe the conditions under which they should be used or withdrawn, so that a flexible plan arises.
4.   Discuss who does what and when. Map the actions onto a timeline and allocate the roles.

7 Action: From talking to acting

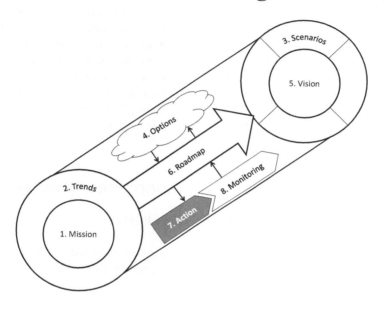

The American writer William Arthur Ward is attributed the following quotation: 'The pessimist complains about the wind; the optimist expects it to change; the realist adjusts the sails.' This defines the moment at which you change from talking to acting. On a ship it is not enough to agree about the final destination, the weather conditions and the mapped course. You also need to work to put into practice everything which has been discussed in the previous chapters. There is often surprisingly little to do on a ship, but what you have to do – hauling, getting to the wind, paying off, hoisting the sails, changing the jib – needs to be done at the right moment. And, just as importantly: you have to cooperate. Thus, when you change tack you haul close to the wind, the jib is released, everyone's heads should be down as the boom comes over, the jib is furled again and the helm goes back to position – and all this in one smooth movement. In a similar way plans in your organization need to be transformed into concrete and synchronized actions.

You have taken care to open a strategic conversation in your organization. At the right moment you introduce each subject: the mission, the environment, possible scenarios for the future, options for action, the vision or concrete plans. But there is another task too: taking care that people actually use the knowledge and insights which result from the strategic conversations. Thinking and acting should be connected to each other if the organization is to start moving. Here lies the power of having debated the mission, vision, scenarios, options and roadmap: it makes it easier for an organization to move along in its ever-changing context. Strategic thinking is transformed into strategic acting. For example, if the vision of your organization is to internationalize successfully, you start acting in sync, from division mangers opening offices abroad, to the receptionists speaking the necessary foreign languages with fluency.

All previous strategic conversations should have unleashed new energy. This energy now needs space to flow and at the same time to be canalized. The organization should start to manifest new behaviours. It is up to you to orchestrate this change. Therefore in this phase you will need to understand how the organization is structured and who is responsible for the execution of the strategy. In many organizations processes are executed on autopilot. If you want to change these processes, you will need to practise them. Most of us intuitively have a sense of the reorganization which should get an organization out of trouble. Your role, however, is not reorganizing, but preorganizing: continuously preparing the organization for challenges which are not yet in view, in order for it to be ready to go about.

7.1 Strategy Within the Organization: Preorganizing

TRANSLATING THE ROADMAP INTO ACTION PLANS

Once goals or milestones are known and the options are selected, a course plan has been formed: the roadmap. You will now elaborate the roadmap in detail into action plans, which involves a series of questions:

- Which call and put options should be used and under which conditions?
- Who will handle which action?
- In which order will the actions be executed?
- Which means are needed and who will assure them?
- Who should be notified and informed?

At this stage it is essential that the departments which are required to execute the plans consult with each other. Several parts of the organization think on different abstraction levels. Because the roadmap needs to be elaborated into concrete actions and placed in a logical sequence, diverging parts of the organization need to work together to design the action plan(s). Remember to keep one eye firmly focused on the bigger picture and the other on the essential details. This will ensure that plans emerge which are attuned to each other and which together realize the strategic roadmap. The outcome you are looking for is a set of medium-term plans, one for each department; a strategic document and/or policy plan per department. Regardless of the number of plans it is important that they are collectively consistent and congruent.

There are several points on the timeline where possible bottlenecks will arise: moments where the sequence and schedule estimation of options require the greatest care. Details often play a decisive role. An important concept here is the 'critical path'. In action plans a critical path emerges at points where actions are dependent on other actions, in other words when an action can only be started once another action has been finished. The critical path shows which activities in a plan define the course of your route. When

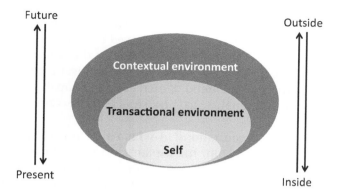

Figure 7.1   Filling in the roadmap: from future to present and from the outside to the inside

you shift activities which are on the critical path, this influences the whole route. It is these activities, those upon which other activities depend, that cause bottlenecks. Let us imagine that in one year you can set up an international sales organization which can bring in twice the demand your factory can deliver, but it takes two years to double the capacity of your factory. In this example it is the factory rather than the sales organization which is on the critical path. The factory, not the sales organization, is the potential bottleneck. While planning and defining the order of the actions to be executed you should reckon with possible bottlenecks and identify which elements are or are not on the critical path (Figure 7.1 above).

The transactional and the contextual environment both play a role during action planning. You will often need to design 'strategy for the strategy'. This can mean, for example, that you fill in the roadmap with the intention of taking the CEO from the contextual to the transactional environment. You can co-create a roadmap to enlarge your sphere of influence. This was actually what the World Business Council for Sustainable Development (WBCSD) did: in the roadmap for energy-efficient buildings they sketched an ideal picture, following which the roads to this desired future were traced out – not only with actions for the WBCSD itself, but also for other parties concerned. The WBCSD was not content to leave everything in the contextual because it wanted to change the world. By engaging in new relationships, armed with a good vision and a roadmap, its domain of influence was enlarged and it was able to set the whole playing field in motion.

When we plan we are creating two-directional focus: we do not only think from the outside in and from the future to the present, but also from the inside out and from the present to the future.

TOP-DOWN OR BOTTOM-UP?

The way an organization is organized and structured influences the way the organization is set in motion. The organization may be geographically organized, or it may also be organized on *business lines*. Prior to the 1980s, most large companies like Philips, Unilever and Shell were organized accordingly to a geographical structure: with divisions in countries and regions. From the 1980s onwards, the business lines became the dominant structure, in conjunction with some functional divisions, such as planning, research and development and IT. These divisions no longer served national or regional interests but the entire organization. In fact the structure often reflects the customers and the external reality: it was no accident that the change from geographical regions to business lines coincided with the macroeconomic trend of increasing ICT capability and globalization. It is important that you understand that the strategy is also organized differently in different organizations.

I regularly come across organizations in which it is not clear who has the final responsibility for strategy. On a ship, the captain and the helmsman are two distinct roles. In many organizations I see these roles confused: many managers act mainly as helmsman to steer the ship, therefore they have little or no time left to act as captain, to walk around and look at what is happening.

In organizations the highest levels of management can choose to shield themselves as far as possible from operational troubles, or they can go to the front line and stay in touch with the inside and the outside world. The better connected you are to both perspectives, the more likely you will see changes coming and when necessary, you can act quickly. At the beginning of the nineteenth century Carl von Clausewitz was already convinced of this:

> *Strategy must go with the Army to the field in order to arrange particulars on the spot, and to make the modifications in the general plan, which incessantly become necessary in War. Strategy can therefore never take its hand from the work for a moment.*

Carl von Clausewitz[1]

The point at which the strategic conversation is initiated in the organization, can vary considerably from one company to another. Sometimes strategy gets started by a manager or by the board, but often it is an individual department (for example HR or R&D) that puts the future on the agenda. Ideally, strategy is an inherent part of the whole organization. You need to find ways to encourage all staff to think critically and be constantly alert. Everyone should be aware of possible futures and be able to imagine themselves in those scenarios.

It makes sense to incorporate strategy in the operations of the organization and likewise to incorporate the operations in the strategic process. For me the strategic planning process is a process of co-creation involving a broad spectrum of people in the organization, through interviews, workshops, presentations and team work. This will enable you to bring operational perspectives into your strategy and also mean that you have a growing body of employees who can help internalize strategic thinking.

The strategy can be put into practice in several ways. We distinguish *bottom-up* and *top-down*.

- **Top-down**   When proposals emerge top-down, this means that the top of the organization imposes the vision and roadmap on the rest of the organization, so that they can be converted into actions by the operations.[2] In this approach the

---

1   Clausewitz (1832) 1997: 141.

2   Leemhuis 1985: 32.

roadmap can very well be used as a tool in line with the classic hierarchical *command and control* philosophy: the roadmap serves as a starting point to give instructions and then to check to see if they are followed. The top-down approach allows you to implement strategy with almost military precision.

HOECHST: *TOP-DOWN*

In 1999 I conducted a scenario process of the WBCSD which addressed the future of biotechnology, more specifically of genetically modified organisms (GMOs) in agriculture and food. At that time expectations of this technology were high. The process resulted in three scenarios. Only one of them showed a bright future for biotechnology and GMOs in the short term; in the beginning the risks would be very high. The best strategy for chemical businesses would be to completely abandon this type of activity, but that would require a lot of courage, especially since the industry had still high expectations of the technology and was underestimating the risks.

Some companies had invested a considerable amount in biotechnology and GMOs and had minimized the possibility of exit. However, this was exactly what Hoechst (nowadays subsidiary of Sanofi-Aventis) did. It was an enormous decision to exit before the rest and to make use of that momentum. Such a drastic decision can only be taken top-down, and in the end Hoechst saved itself huge losses by having the courage to adopt an exit strategy.

- **Bottom-up**   When proposals emerge bottom-up, this means that change emerges from the operational level of the organization and then moves upwards level by level to the top. Very large proposals float all the way to the top and become part of the strategy when they are approved by the board.[3] Thus the plan is written while the organization is already in motion, and forms a conformation and reinforcement of the direction the company is already taking. We noted earlier that you are jointly responsible for transforming talk into action and for connecting thinking and acting. That means it is important that you liaise with doers, with the operational level of the organization. Although we have associated the top-down approach with the military way of working, in many modern armies you will find bottom-up approaches too. Even admiral Michiel de Ruyter (1607–1676) worked with self-organizing teams and *empowerment*.

IHC DREDGERS: BOTTOM-UP

IHC Merwede, of which IHC Dredgers is a division, was originally a shipyard. Over time IHC has changed and is no longer a shipyard, IHC now *owns* shipyards. IHC Dredgers had a rosy outlook in 2008, but there was also a real risk that orders would be cancelled because of the credit crisis. Within the business environment in which both entities operated structural changes were happening. In the trend analyses, they identified both a growing overcapacity

---

3   Leemhuis 1985: 32.

in the industry, and at the same time, new markets emerging. IHC Dredgers consequently wanted to think about a Medium-Term Plan 2012.

In 2008 and 2009 I supported several strategic workshops in special locations, including a windmill called 'Look over the dike' and a fort built in the nineteenth century. In these workshops we explored the transactional environment and how this would develop in several possible scenarios. We undertook role plays in which we modelled the behaviour of the clients and the competitors. Several strategic options for IHC Dredgers were identified, such as the internationalization of production, standardization of ships, disconnection of product and product location and adjusting the organization structure.

Following a number of workshops the company wrote the Medium-Term Plan 2012. However, it is interesting to note what happened next: even before the plan was finalized and officially approved by the board, the participants of the strategy sessions had started to execute the ideas which had come up in the workshops. They themselves developed bigger strategic initiatives, on the basis of the options that surfaced during the workshops. The decentralized execution of the options in practice (bottom-up) went much faster than the official publication of the results of the workshops and the confirmation by top management (top-down).

Strategic decisions are ideally taken at the junction of top-down and bottom-up, where – if everything works – the right communication takes place very naturally: it is up to you to facilitate this interaction and to make it a smooth and effective process.[4] There are challenges working in this space, for example, language: in general top-down proposals are abstract. They describe broad outlines and are based on the official strategy. Bottom-up proposals are often described in quantitative terms: they are often more concrete and more detailed and not necessarily based on the official strategy.[5] A sensible technique for overcoming this problem involves you helping to place concrete proposals within the bigger, abstract picture. Likewise you can help to translate the broad outlines into practical proposals.

UMTS: GREAT SCENARIOS, BUT A FAILED STRATEGY PROJECT

1998 was a busy time for us. At the end of the 1990s the prevailing image of the future – or better the official future – was that UMTS- or 3G-networks were *the* future of mobile communications. All telecom operators wanted to get hold of a UMTS licence, no matter what. Within several of our clients, the lower levels in the organization had conflicting images of the future. In the mobile division of one large global telecom company we made scenarios for the future of UMTS. During the trend exploration we discovered that alternative technologies for UMTS were already available, and that content for UMTS was not available, no phones with UMTS were available and production lines were not yet ready.

Based on the trends and some modelling, we described four possible scenarios for UMTS.

---

4   Leemhuis 1985: 32.
5   Leemhuis 1985: 32.

Three out of four scenarios showed unfavourable outlooks for the period we were exploring. This spurred our client into coming up with a way to win, even in the 'bad' scenarios. The company would participate in the auction of UMTS frequencies and through their bidding inflate the price, whilst at the same time ensuring they did not win the auction. One of the foreign competitors would then build the network, following which, when UMTS devices and content were available, our player would hire network capacity from this competitor to operate as a *virtual mobile network operator*. In a successful scenario for UMTS the company would win by buying or hiring capacity and thus be a successful trader instead of owner. At the same time, in those scenarios which posited a less successful future for UMTS, the client could avoid or mitigate the main risks: they would not be spending any money on acquiring the frequency and therefore would have lower costs than their competitors. Although no unambiguous prediction could be made about the future success of UMTS, it was possible to design a robust strategy which would work positively in all scenarios.

Unfortunately, we made one big mistake. We had forgotten to include the CEO of the parent telecom company in the process. Our client was a very hierarchical organization. This made it impossible for the board of the mobile division to discuss the plan on equal terms with the CEO of the parent company: he was *blinded by foresight*, and therefore determined to buy a UMTS frequency. He had hired expensive consultants and they all predicted a great future for UMTS. He was not interested in scenarios and options, there was only one way to go; to obtain a UMTS licence at all cost. So, although the scenarios and the proposed strategy were solid, the project failed. We did not have the buy-in from the top. The mobile division was not in charge of its own future.

In 2000 the CEO went ahead, and bought his licence (using borrowed finance) at an eye-watering price. In less than a year the company was almost bankrupt: the expensive licence had proved almost fatal. The UMTS market took much longer to develop than was officially predicted by most experts. It wasn't until 2008, when the iPhone entered the market, that UMTS really took off.

This experience illustrates why thinking about strategy makes no sense if the right people are not involved. When you think about strategy at a level in the organization where decisions are not made, it is difficult to transform thinking into acting. So in every strategy project it is essential to consider who should be involved.

Even when there is agreement that the complete board should decide about the strategy, differences between organizations exist. Often the personality of the manager is the decisive factor. Is the CEO a conductor who takes a coordinating role, or a 'rockstar'? Rockstars have big egos. In the organizations they lead, there is a risk that a personality cult may arise. Successful rockstars occur less often than successful conductors. Steve Jobs from Apple was the exception to the rule, an example of a rockstar CEO who was able to secure success. Many organizations with a rockstar as CEO run the risk of following a strategy based simply on ego. Overestimating oneself is the biggest mistake you can make as a leader.[6]

---

6   De Ruijter et al (2009).

It is advisable to spend time considering how best to connect the results of the strategic conversations to the official systems within which an organization operates: the planning and control cycles. This is an essential step to make scenario thinking useful. At Shell there is a tight connection between scenarios and the planning and control cycle: every business plan and each investment over a certain amount is linked to and tested using the scenarios. At the same time some people may deliberately choose to avoid a tight connection between the options and the official decision-making process, because there is the imminent danger that options become too much of a part of internal politics. You may also wish to maintain a certain amount of freedom, and to rely on an informal route to place options into the planning and control cycle. Whether you choose to link the strategy to the existing systems of planning and control or not is a choice you will have to make based on your specific situation.

PREORGANIZING: **ORGANIZING TO MAKE IT POSSIBLE TO START MOVING**

In 1998 I helped a Danish manufacturer of test and measurement equipment for analogue televisions, to prepare for the future. This company had been sold for a tiny price to a private equity firm because the original parent company (Philips) saw no future for it in the face of the rise of digital television.

Philips did allow one of its top internal strategy consultants to help the spin-off. Although the company was no longer part of Philips, there was a certain loyalty to ensure the employees were taken well care of. Together, we foresaw many developments and opportunities in the rise of digital television: analogue television transmitters would need to be replaced with digital transmitters; the number of studios would grow because of rising demand for content. The test and measurement equipment company had just the right competences to exploit these developments, but they lacked the organizational structure to grasp the opportunities.

It seemed best for the company to split itself up into smaller units; *start-ups,* but start-ups with experience. The R&D department had already designed digital television transmitters: they had developed the technology to enable them to test digital televisions. This department could be preorganized as a start-up for a digital transmitter technology. The company had also developed competences in the field of studio equipment; another opportunity for a start-up. The production department served several business lines.

By looking at the company as a collection of several business lines it became more transparent to the employees what the company could do and was doing. The willingness to change made the company considerably more open to developments in the outside world and made them able to respond quickly to the new technologies which emerged after 1998. Whereas in the 1990s Philips saw no future for this company, in 2010 the two companies that emerged still exist, having proved their own futures.

7.2 Telling Stories to Move

The conclusion of a long-winded strategy process is often presented to the rest of the organization as gospel; from the top of the organization to the bottom. While the top of the business took months to reach its conclusions, the rest of the organization is supposed to understand 'the answer' in a 20-minute PowerPoint presentation. How you organize and communicate strategy is of major importance. Everyone in the organization should understand the trends and assumptions on which the strategy is based and the questions to which it is an answer. It helps to make the strategy work to share the underlying trends, possible scenarios encompassing hopes and fears, along with the several options which were explored. Only then will the 'presented' mission, vision and roadmap be fully understood and appreciated.

Sharing the complete content communicates the methodology at the same time. The various parts of the organization can then copy the methodology and borrow parts of the trends, scenarios and vision and translate these to their own specific mission, vision and roadmap. Each part of the organization, whether they are a functional division like human resources, marketing or production, or a business line such as private banking, insurance or regional divisions, can copy the process and reuse a large part of the content. The various parts must synchronize both methodology and content. Sharing information and broad communication will help you to create a forward-looking culture. It enables you to execute thinking at a level which allows other levels of the organization to offer feedback and criticism. Criticism is not to be shied away from. If you can handle the criticism well, you will break down resistance. And if the criticism is relevant, you learn!

In his article 'Planning as learning' Arie de Geus refers to John Holt's *How Children Learn* when he claims that teaching is one of the most inefficient ways to transfer knowledge: a maximum of 40 per cent of what is taught is picked up by the public, and the average percentage is usually around 25 per cent. Teaching is also inefficient if the teacher has no authority among his or her public.[7] As we have already underlined, you need dialogue, images, emotions and stories to involve people in possible scenarios or your vision for the future. The same is true for strategy: to secure involvement and to motivate employees to commit themselves to the strategy, a PowerPoint presentation will not suffice. Screenwriting coach Robert McKee observed that people are not motivated to act by ratio; you should use a story to address their emotions.[8] We have already covered the properties of good, appealing stories – repetition, visualization and addressing emotions – in Chapter 5, Vision.

In his *Ars Rhetorica*, which he wrote in the fourth century BC, Aristotle expresses the three elements of a convincing speech: *logos, ethos* and *pathos*. By *logos* he meant logical arguments, facts and data. *Ethos* refers to the credibility, the authority of the speaker and the norms and values to which he or she is talking. With *pathos* Aristotle refers to the emotions, the sympathy and imagination which are recalled in the listener by the story. A convincing message is a combination of logos, ethos and pathos.[9] This is well illustrated by Al Gore's *An Inconvenient Truth*. In his documentary about global warming Gore often refers to facts, using measurements which show that the carbon dioxide concentration

---

7   De Geus 1988: 4.

8   Fryer 2003: 6.

9   Van de Wetering 2009.

had risen quickly in the last decennia. The documentary places considerable emphasis on the credibility of Gore and to his authority in the field of climate change by referring to his political career, his experiences while travelling and his involvement in scientific research on climate change. Finally the film appeals the emotions of the public by showing intrusive images of the consequences of the warming of the earth, such as a map of only half of the Netherlands (a consequence of rising sea levels), and by referring to Gore's personal life. The combination of logos, pathos and ethos was used imaginatively in *An Inconvenient Truth*. The documentary had international influence and created a sense of urgency among politicians as well as among the private sector. Remember, a 'fact-based' strategy is often not enough!

The scientist Piet Vroon explained that the impulse to act is not just driven by our knowledge (our primate brain) but also by emotions and instinct (our mammalian brain). People and process function both rationally and, more often, in an intuitive and instinctive way.[10]

Behavioural patterns cannot be changed by knowledge alone. It is not enough that people in the organization have knowledge of the vision, of the trends, scenarios and options. They must *feel* these things too and need to respond to them emotionally. Only then can they adjust their behaviour. You can encourage this engagement by connecting these strategic elements to the incentive structure; the moment you give a bonus, promote someone or show any other sign of appreciation, you will alter behaviour.

THE FOSBURY FLOP

There is another complicating factor when you want your organization to start moving and changing. I like to explain this with a story about the 'Fosbury Flop'. When high jumper Dick Fosbury used this new high jump technique for the first time in the 1960s, he did not jump as high as he had been using the traditional technique. His body was trained to the old technique and not yet attuned to the new one. And everybody who has seen the technique can imagine this, because it looks counter intuitive; you run toward the bar, and then just before it you turn into a jump over it backwards. Another athlete might have stopped training in the new technique at this point. But Fosbury persisted, and once he was well trained, he was able to jump far higher with his Fosbury Flop. So much so that in 1968 he established a new Olympic record of 2.24 metres using his technique and since 1978 all top athletes now use this technique (see Figure 7.2).

Figure 7.2   The Fosbury Flop

Credit: JAM Visual Thinking

10   Hoeks 2002.

The same thing is happening within organizations. When an organization is trying out new behaviour this may be penalized at first; the new measure carries high costs or possibly a less effective way of working than the traditional methods. Employees are experienced in using the old techniques, while they need to practice the new. The result is a double S-curve (see Figure 7.3) in which the second S starts lower than the first but ends higher. The phenomenon of the double S-curve is very common. In fact, this figure describes the mismatch between feedback in the short term and feedback in the long term. Many organizations find themselves stuck doing what they always did, like Kodak producing film for analogue cameras, because that was what they were good at. Jumping to a new S-curve is always difficult and painful at first. When you start using the Fosbury Flop technique it feels uncomfortable and awkward, but it will prove better in the long term. In many strategic change projects, organizations seem to fall back at first, but in the long term well-considered and sustained reforms often lead to better results. The trick is to ignore your discomfort and your received ideas when you start something new. Trust instead to your logic which tells you that the new way will work better in the long term.

During the transition from the old to the new way of working, training and practice are crucial. Arie de Geus alluded to 'Planning as learning'.[11] De Geus characterized intuitional learning as a process in which you develop a language. When the implicit knowledge of a person in an organization becomes explicit, his or her mental model becomes a building brick to the mental model of the organization as a whole. How much and how fast this model changes depends on the culture and the structure of the organization.[12] According to De Geus the best learning processes take place in teams which accept that the whole is more than the sum of its parts.[13]

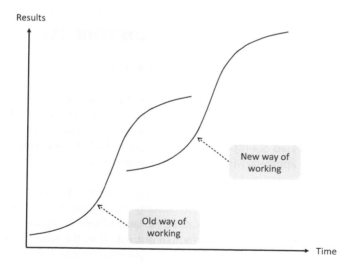

Figure 7.3 Double S-curve during the transition to a new way of working

---

11   De Geus 1988.

12   De Geus 1988: 6.

13   De Geus 1988: 6.

7.3 The Power of Example, Participation and Attention

Anyone who has ever opened a textbook will have come across the concept of 'learning by example'. There is a reason for this: children do what you *do*, not what you say. When you raise children, it is important that you give the right example, that you play with your children and you give them positive attention. Organizations are exactly the same. People in an organization copy their managers. Therefore it is important that top managers model strategic actions, that they participate in activities which they expect of the rest of the organization to undertake, and that they give positive attention to employees.

When the roles of captain and helmsman are played by two different people, the captain has the freedom to walk around on the ship, is in a position to watch how the organization handles the strategy and can listen to feedback, can give attention to employees and reward them – for their desired behaviour.

If you want an organization to digitize, you should take the lead and start communicating by email instead of handwritten notes. I have seen a German organization which established a department for 'internationalization' where only Germans worked, and a Dutch organization which in 2007 employed an IT-director who did not have a computer on his desk and who had all his emails printed by his secretary.

The new behaviour you require of the organization feels awkward to employees. In the early days this new behaviour will not be as easy for them as the old: remember the story of the Fosbury Flop. You and/or the management of the organization need to demonstrate the new behaviour.

LEADERSHIP AND LEADERSHIP (3)

Netherlands' Shipbuilding Industry Association

In Chapter 5 we talked about the Netherlands' Shipbuilding Industry Association (VNSI) which formulated the vision Dutch LeaderSHIP 2015 in 2005: one in which by 2015 the Dutch shipbuilding industry is leading in innovation and sustainability. Several success factors and actions were addressed during this strategy process. The triad of example, participation and attention was very apparent when VNSI started working with the vision and the actions.

- **Example** Greater cooperation in the supply chain was one of the spearheads of the vision. VNSI acted by example, establishing the Holland Shipbuilding Association, together with the supplier association, Holland Marine Equipment (HME), despite the existence of a fair degree of mutual distrust. Thus the board members of both associations serve as an example of the cooperation for which they aimed. They laid the basis for good relationships and cooperation, new behaviour and mutual trust.
- **Participation** Internationalization was an important issue according to the vision of VNSI. The vision formulated that the Dutch shipbuilding industry should be leading in innovation and sustainability in 2015, both within and across the Dutch borders. For this reason the VNSI organized study trips and trade missions, so that members could collectively work on their internationalization.

- **Attention**   Innovation was also high on the agenda. Initiatives in these fields were explicitly rewarded. The awards for innovation, which already existed, were scaled up and today a big annual Maritime Awards Gala is organized in cooperation with other associations in the maritime sector. *Scheepsbouw Nederland Magazine* provides column space in every edition to an element of *5x Action*, the collective vision which was developed by the new Holland Shipbuilding Association in 2008 as a translation of the visions of VNSI and HME.

Storytelling is an effective instrument for setting examples, encouraging participation and attention. It is an effective technique for involving people in organizational change programmes, so that both their brains but also their emotions are addressed.

7.4   Stopping

Thus far in this chapter we have been talking about enabling an organization to start moving. There is, however, an important issue which we should not overlook. Setting an organization in motion is not simply about starting new activities: stopping old activities is just as important. Starting often starts with stopping. Professor of Political Theory, Herman van Gunsteren, who wrote a book about stopping, noted: 'When change programs get stuck, stopping is often the hidden problem.'[14]

We see a big difference between the public and the private sector when we look at the ability for organizations to 'stop'. In the private sector many activities stop automatically: if there is no demand, production will stop. However, it remains painful saying farewell to loss-making activities or departments. Taking a loss and writing off your investment is difficult. It often involves loss of face for those in charge of the activity and can require that you literally say farewell to people with whom you have worked for years.

In the public sector the experience can be quite different. The logic to stop activities when there is no demand for them any more is often missing; the 'interest to continue' outweighs the 'interest to stop'. Agricultural subsidies are a good example. When these were introduced after World War II they were very necessary and very useful, but a few decades later these subsidies no longer fit so well. We all remember the overproduction of milk, wine and butter. Nevertheless, reforming or abolishing has been easier said than done, and the subsidies have continued for decades after the original purpose was lost.

In both public and private sector we often find cases when budgets need to be cut. Most of the time, the reflex is to cancel or postpone investments which are important for future renewal. In 2008 I was considering the best reaction to the credit crisis in collaboration with Rabobank Payments and Saving (see the case example described in Chapter 3). They identified two ways to cut budgets: cancel all planned IT investments for renewal (and by doing so cut off the future) or continue investing in a new IT system but cut budgets for keeping the old legacy IT-system alive (effectively, cutting off the past). The latter approach is very much strategic budget cutting and it is exactly what Rabobank chose. Henk Alkema was facing the same issue when reorganizing the chemical division of Shell (see Chapter

---

14   Van Gunsteren 2003: 118 and personal notes H.J. Alkema.

5). He needed to look at the complete portfolio of chemical businesses which Shell was in under the 'Select and Focus' programme: what needs to be stopped or sold to create space for the elements which are doing well and/or do fit with Shell?

You can compare these examples with the process of investing in a new car. You might try to save money by postponing the purchase of a new car. However, this could mean that you spend considerably more in the next few years on repairs on your increasingly old and unreliable car, which may also cost you more in petrol. Alternatively, you can save money by choosing to invest in a new car and getting rid of the old one; thereby avoiding maintenance costs. If you accept this analogy, you can see that in the long term continuing with something is often more expensive than stopping. It is smarter to short-cut the past rather than to constrain the future. A crisis is an ideal moment to choose the flight forward: 'Never waste a good crisis!'

MEAT, FISH OR VEGETARIAN?

Dutch Institute for Scientific Information services (NIWI)

Strategy is not only about starting activities, but also about stopping activities. In 2002 I conducted a strategic exploration with the Dutch Institute for Scientific Information services (NIWI), part of the Royal Netherlands Academy of Arts and Sciences. NIWI were responsible for the storage and accessibility of scientific research data, including document distribution (for which it was best known): the institute bought scientific magazines, copied articles and sent them on request. The most important issue for NIWI in 2002 was the ongoing digitization of the collection. What would happen to the demand for paper documents? Should NIWI continue its paper document distribution? Would there be a need for the services of NIWI in the future, or would users themselves have digital access to all the data for which they would be looking?

In the exploration project we found that there were three factors that NIWI could influence: the collection, the target group and the subsidy. Based on this we mapped five different options for NIWI:

- **Meat**   NIWI distributes to all target groups, will collect broadly and will offer their services at different prices to researchers and to others.
- **Fish**   NIW will only distribute to scientific researchers and only additional collecting will be done.
- **Vegetarian**   NIWI stops collecting, will only distribute limited materials from the old collection and then only to the academic world.
- **Vegetarian plus**   NIWI stops collecting, but will continue to distribute from the collection using price differentiation between academic researchers and others.
- **Vegan**   NIWI stops collecting and distributing all together.

The five options were elaborated with a focus on the consequences for customers and staff, and the financial consequences. It may be clear that (partly) stopping activities, whether this be collecting or distributing, was an element in all five options. The 'exit' deserves attention in every strategy process.

The problem is that stopping is often difficult. Rarely does an organization really stop old activities as soon as a new activity starts. Stopping is often seen as something negative and has the undertone that you stop because it was not going well or it was wrong. Many organizations have problems with stopping. The influence of crisis managers lies exactly in the fact that they are only temporarily part of the organization, which makes it easier for them to stop certain activities; as an outsider the crisis manager can say or see things insiders can't or will not say or see.[15] Alternatively, an outsider can stop patterns of behaviour which everyone in the organization knows should be stopped, but which nobody in the organization seems to be able to stop.[16] In many cases community relations and loyalty are important to an organization, but these things can sometimes stand in the way of necessary change.

You may prefer to take another view of stopping and see it as pruning: by removing something old, letting go or phasing out, you create space for something new. It's therefore important in an organization to avoid labelling established behaviours as 'wrong' per se, but rather to describe them as an activity which was useful in the past and which was much appreciated, but which does not fit in the *future* setting. This offers the people in your organization the opportunity to stop an activity without experiencing it as a loss of face. In such cases stopping or letting go can be both painful and a relief.[17] This is the case when the parent company and the subsidiary no longer fit well together and there is no *parenting advantage*.[18] Sometimes another parent suits an organization better than the original mother company.

There is a difference between put options, as we described before, and actually stopping something. When you announce in an organization that a certain activity will be stopped, you may immediately stir up resistance. Then you will have to face questions: 'why do we have to stop?', 'what if customers demand changes?' or 'isn't that what we were founded to do?' Stopping involves a process of saying farewell. You need to allow time for 'mourning' and to allocate the 'inheritance' of the activity which will be stopped. This means that it's best to decide early if and when you want to stop. This will give you time to think about how you phase out the activity. Do you want to sell the activity; do you want to reorganize it, or do you want to terminate it all together? When you take the time to stop, you also offer people in the organization the chance to look for something new. The preliminary process of stopping should be organized well.

Stopping well requires a process of mourning; to stop people need rituals.[19] So you may find it helps to arrange a moment for a ritual and to create space for the farewell. The Hollandse Bank-Unie (HBU) took this advice literally. In 1914 the N.V. Hollandsche Bank voor Zuid-Amerika was founded in Rotterdam. In 1933 the name changed in Hollandsche Bank-Unie and in the years after that HBU took over some local banks. In 1967 HBU was taken over by ABN and from 1991 the bank was a subsidiary of ABN Amro. In 2010 the old Rotterdam-based bank was finally sold to Deutsche Bank. This farewell was not to go unnoticed: the HBU was let go in a real 'funeral ritual'. The HBU staff offered the director Services of the Deutsche Bank the HBU flag. On the evening of the share transfer

---

15   Van Gunsteren 2003: 11.

16   Van Gunsteren 2003: 12.

17   Van Gunsteren 2003: 15.

18   Goold and Campbell: 1991.

19   Van Gunsteren 2003: 118.

people were invited to look back with pride at 95 years of HBU in a photo show. This 'celebration' of the past was really appreciated by all, and allowed mental space to look forwards to a fresh start.

Stopping creates space to start new activities and to begin a new S-curve. It requires courage to start new activities, just as it does to stop old ones. The movement may already be present in the organization. Your role then is to identify the movers and to facilitate them. In other words, it is not just a story or a vision that needs to be transformed into movement. You also need to detect existing movements in the right direction and to support them with attention, space, manpower and finances. Stopping other activities is one way to do this, since a new activity will often be financed or resourced at the expense of old activities. My experience with nanotechnology, from my time at the Royal Netherlands Academy of Arts and Sciences, is an example. It was not necessary to order the scientists to spend less time and money on biology, physics or chemistry, because their focus automatically shifted towards an exciting new technology of the future: nanotechnology.

Changing course should therefore not be quite as difficult as it seems; if the helm is on course and you adjust the sails to the wind, the ship will start moving in the right direction and you will be moving towards your goal. Good preparation will enable you to gather energy from the context and the organization will prosper. But in order to know in which direction you have to move in relation to your current condition, you would be wise to measure and monitor the state of your organization and look at developments within its environment.

CONCLUSIONS: ACTION

1. Use all the material (mission, environment exploration, scenarios, options, vision and road map) to set the organization in motion. This can be both *top-down* and *bottom-up*.
2. Tell stories to keep the organization moving; here 'examples', 'participation' and 'giving attention' are important.
3. Do not simply pay attention to starting new activities; remember to spend time stopping any old activities which are no longer relevant.
4. Exploit the energy of existing movements in the right direction.

8 Monitoring:
To stay on course

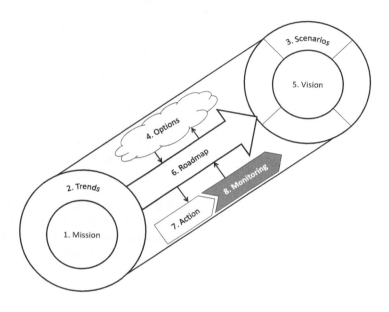

A night at sea. Nothing is more beautiful: staring at the stars in the dark; occasionally writing a note in the ship's log. We know by now that to stay on course you need to pay continual attention to what's going on around you, but also to what is happening on board the ship itself. Of course you can stick just your finger up in the air to find out roughly in which direction the wind is blowing. But it is much wiser to act in a more structured way. For example, you can keep a log and track your waypoints to monitor progress. This is important feedback, but also a starting point for new questions. And if you are in a race, you look at the ships around you. Are you making progress compared to the rest of the competitors? After all, to stand still is to regress!

Once an organization has started to move, the strategy process is by no means finished. Shaping a dynamic strategy and acting upon it is an ongoing process. Are you still on course? Is everyone still in the right place? Time continues to flow and the world outside continues to change and to develop. You should adjust the vision if necessary, start investments or exercise your options to stop them. Thanks to the various strategic conversations in the organization about the mission, the trends, possible scenarios, options, the vision and the roadmap, the awareness of the future and the environment of the organization has become more acute, which enables you to gain signals from the environment that much faster. And this is important! By comparing the direction in which you are developing to where the world is going, you can evaluate whether the route you have chosen to navigate is still appropriate. This form of monitoring can involve your own organization, your transactional environment (clients and competitors) as well as the contextual environment. Your roadmap will provide an essential anchor point, because it shows where the organization stands at any point in time and under which external circumstances certain options should be exercised or stopped.

There will be many instances when your organization is running the risk of deviating from course. When you find out you are no longer on course, it is important to ask yourself: what is the reason? Is there a discrepancy between reality and the core values stated in the mission? Are unexpected trends happening in the outside world? Is it because of a lack of action? Can we still reach the vision? Monitoring in this way will bring you back to one of the earlier chapters in this book, and is often the beginning of a strategy process.

It is therefore important to select both internal and external indicators and early warning signals which the organization should monitor. Be careful! There are many pitfalls in monitoring the world inside and outside; in Chapter 2 we already described phenomena such as selective perception, perspectivism, cognitive dissonance and group thinking.

In times of rapid change, a crisis of perception (that is, the inability to see an emerging novel reality by being locked inside obsolete assumptions) often causes strategic failure, particularly in large, well-run companies. Opportunities missed because managers did not recognize them in time are clearly more important than failures, which are visible to all.

Pierre Wack[1]

When the organization is not sufficiently open-minded to receive signals from the outside world and to interpret them, it misses valuable information and cedes new opportunities to profit to competitors.

The credit crisis shows how observations can enable different conclusions, with all the consequences which these entail. In March 2007 the Netherlands Bureau for Economic Policy Analysis (CBP) published the *Official Economic Forecast 2007* in which it predicted economic growth of 2.75 per cent for 2007 and 2008. The Dutch central bank DNB even predicted economic growth of 3 per cent for 2007 and 2.8 per cent for 2008.[2] Less than a year later, on 15 February 2008, the Minister of Finance Wouter Bos said the Netherlands should expect 'considerable economic growth' in 2008; for him, talking about an economic crisis was 'completely out of touch with reality'.[3]

But by 31 March 2007 the cover of the Dutch magazine *Elsevier* already showed a deflating balloon: the magazine published a story on a possible credit crisis.[4] And on 1 February 2008, even before the Minister's statement about the expected economic growth and before the bankruptcy of Bear Stearns, Rabobank announced precautions in case of a crisis.

---

1   Wack 1985b: 150.
2   Centraal Planbureau 2007: 78.
3   *NRC Handelsblad* 2008.
4   *Elsevier* 2007.

RABOBANK SAFEGUARDS AGAINST CRISIS[5]

Bank gets €30 billion in mortgages ready as security for ECB loans

Rabobank has taken precautionary measures to secure sufficient liquidity in times of crisis. Late last year the bank got €30 billion in residential mortgages ready as security for loans of the European Central Bank in case of emergency.

According to CFO Bert Bruggink, Rabo has not suffered from the crisis, up to now. He wants to get the bank ready for worse times in the future. 'We anticipate on a worst case scenario. I do not assume that we will need it, but at least we are ready.'

---

5   *Het Financieele Dagblad* 2008

Timing is everything: when, as Rabobank did in the example above, you anticipate earlier than your competitors the situations in which you could possibly find yourself, you can take precautions. Monitoring and interpreting signals, both from the organization and from the outside world, is of great importance to the organization that wants to be ready to tack at all times.

8.1   Monitoring the World, Inside and Outside

TRACKING PROGRESS

The crux of monitoring is finding a language in which to discuss the future and the signals relating to it. Having the kind of strategic conversations mentioned in the previous chapters will help because, by expressing collectively what could possibly be happening in the future and how the organization could respond, you will naturally start to develop a common language to talk about the future and about uncertainty. With a common language you are equipped to discuss publicly implicit assumptions about the future, therefore you can more easily separate the noise in the environment from meaningful signals. The art of monitoring is to filter noise; to receive the signals and to understand their significance.

Monitoring what happens within your organization is a way to measure progress against the roadmap. You can show the significance of registered data by interpreting it as signals. When you choose the data you want to track, it is important to consider which signals are most significant. A classic way to monitor the progress of the organization is via the annual figures: the tax authorities require the business to look back every year. Did you make any profit? How did your capital grow? Other examples of formalized opportunities to look back in organizations are personal performance review conversations and the planning and control cycle. These are all moments at which you collect internal data of the organization and its progress, from which you can read possible signals.

The Dutch government has appointed a special day to monitor its own progress. In 2000 it announced the establishment of Responsibility Day. Since then, once a year, on the third Wednesday of May, the Prime Minister and the Ministers take responsibility for their actions in executing the policy goals presented for the previous period. This is not a day where they report how much was spent, but whether the targets were met.

Monitoring your market share, stock prices, currency exchange rates and interest rates offers a starting point for monitoring progress. When an organization aims for product leadership and improved competitiveness, it will monitor the volume and the market share of its products. When an organization feels it important to increase its value to customers, it will monitor how great a share of clients' or customers' discretionary spending it is achieving, nowadays called share of wallet. Companies focused on shareholder value tend to track their share price on a daily basis, and countries often measure GDP and their currency rate to track how they are doing. For departments within a larger organization and for organizations owned by the government long lists of 'key performance indicators' will be defined and measured.

For every organization it is important to look back accurately and thoroughly and to link this process with the vision and the roadmap. You will need to design and define your key performance indicators well. They need to be within your control and have a direct link to the vision you want realize. When your progress is disappointing, you don't want people to have excuses: 'it is the oil price' or 'it is because of the recession'. On the contrary: these are external factors which you can not affect. You have to consider these factors up front and you can't use them to excuse your own delay or setback. And these external factors are very much on the agenda when monitoring the developments in the outside world. The examples of Rabobank and Shell given in the introduction show that profits can also be made in times of crisis. By anticipating external developments you can have an advantage over your competition. There are no bad scenarios, only poor preparation!

MONITORING THE WORLD OUTSIDE

When monitoring the world outside, you need to deal with two distinct parts of the environment (see Chapter 2): factors from the contextual environment (which are outside your influence, but which will influence you) and the actors of the transactional environment, those who can be influenced. Your task is to decide which factors and actors should be monitored, and then do so. Scenarios can help you to indicate which developments can be decisive for the future and therefore should be monitored. By monitoring these developments we can interpret which scenario is unfolding.

When monitoring developments in the world outside, scenarios are a helpful tool to understand where the organization is at any one moment. You can use the names of the scenarios to explain the context. For example, if you see low economic growth combined with low interest rates, you might simply call that a Japanese scenario. This shorthand is useful but there are a few things you need to keep in mind. While monitoring the environment based on a set of scenarios, you run the risk that you and the organization become too engrossed in the scenarios and that you lose track of other developments. The whole purpose of monitoring is not simply to look for those signals that fit (one of) the scenarios; exactly the opposite; signals help to determine how reality is developing, and you *then* check if there is a matching scenario. Using this priority for your activities will help you to keep an open mind for signals which may indicate patterns other than those described in your scenarios. The scenarios help to make these unexpected signals visible. It is important to also look at the signals which do *not* fit any one of the scenarios which you have described, as much as it is to look for signals which do.

Another related point of attention is the importance of regularly checking whether your scenarios are still up to date and relevant. Reality will not develop precisely in the way you have described in one of the scenarios. It is more likely that you will find elements from different scenarios occurring together, along with elements which you did not describe before. By thinking through the scenarios and monitoring them, we can recognize and explain shifts at an early stage. Naturally, we use what we discover in our environment analysis and what we have recorded in the roadmap. My experience is that you read the newspaper differently according to how you open yourself for signals which indicate how the world is developing. You shift your attention from feedback to feedforward.

When it comes to the factors there are many different signals from the world outside which you can monitor. Many of these are already monitored via regular basic surveys and research undertaken by the newspapers and trade magazines which are filled with data tracking all sorts of indicators. Make use of these surveys and choose which signals to monitor yourself, perhaps with the help of special software. What the organization finds important determines what the organization monitors.

Actors also offer interesting information about the development of the environment. How you organize the monitoring of relevant actors (customers, competitors, new entrants, politicians and government officials) – *business intelligence* – depends on your organization and on the specific actors in which you are interested. Supermarket chains, for example, use mystery shoppers because they are interested in the prices and offers of their competitors. Pharmaceutical companies work with general practitioners and ask them for information when competitors come up with a new product. And of course market research is an example of a method to monitor the behaviour of clients.

The connection with trend-watching, as described in Chapter 2, is obvious. When monitoring, the emphasis is not on sketching as wide as possible an image of the environment, but rather on measuring and collecting meaningful data. This data can then be connected to the various strategic conversations which are taking part in the organization. By keeping track of key developments regularly you can keep up with handling alternatives; which options should be started or stopped at any given moment. In this way you can meet changing circumstances proactively. When you monitor and detect signals which indicate a development in the direction of certain scenarios at an early stage, you can then exercise the right call and put options. By monitoring in which direction the future is developing, it becomes clear which options become relevant.

EARLY WARNING SYSTEM: WHY A MONITORING SYSTEM?[6]

Justice for Tomorrow (1)

In 2006 the Ministry of Justice undertook a strategic exploration of the future in a project called Justice for Tomorrow which resulted in four scenarios with two key uncertainties, 'demand for social safety' and 'internationalization'. The demand for social safety refers to the willingness of the people to sacrifice (in tax contribution, but also in civil rights) to prevent others from causing them harm or suffering. The level of internationalization refers to the extent to which the support for the European Union will increase or decrease and consequently whether regulation and legislation are predominantly organized at a national level (The Hague) or European level (Brussels).

Based on the scenarios the Ministry then formulated five strategic assignments to be prepared for the future. The way in which the ministry could or should be developing policy for these strategic assignments obviously depends on the environment. Therefore it was useful for the Ministry to be able to determine in an early stage just how the environment is developing and which scenario(s) map these developments. Consequently, they decided to develop a monitoring, or Early Warning System (EWS), to enable them to monitor the developments in the environment (see Figure 8.1).

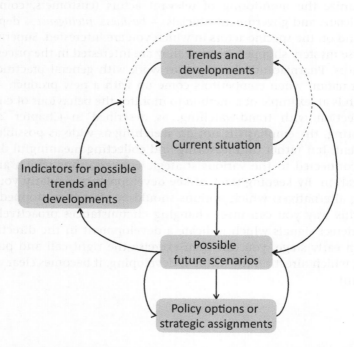

Figure 8.1   The early warning system of the Ministry of Justice (after Botterhuis et al. 2009)

---

6   Botterhuis et al. 2009.

A monitoring system can be used to track and structure signals which indicate changes in the environment. The monitoring mechanism in the project Justice for Tomorrow was aimed at identifying and explaining events connected to social, technological and economical changes, in which the four scenarios were used as a tool. By monitoring the indicators pointing in the direction of increased or decreased demand for social safety, or more or less internationalization, the Ministry of Justice could monitor how the key uncertainties developed. This knowledge enabled the policy-makers to determine proactively which strategic issues and options were to become relevant in the future.

The scenarios were thus used as lenses to filter the incoming information. By monitoring a wide range of signals you get an idea in an early stage of the direction in which the future is developing. Although a monitoring mechanism does not make it possible to predict the future, this system has the potential to connect developments and events in the short term to change in the long term. For this reason it is important that signals are not seen as independent short-term factors, but as a part of a long-term development; the exploration of the future, which was carried out previously, helps to structure and give meaning to these signals.

8.2   Connecting the Dots

Quarterly reports, risk management, benchmarking, market research, news, industry conferences ... aren't we overwhelmed with signals from both within and outside? Yes, probably, particularly when in addition to the traditional signals you may be endeavouring to follow social media like Facebook, LinkedIn and Twitter to understand what is going on. If you cannot connect the dots, you will only hear white noise. Some 'dovetailing' is required: in other words, you need to develop the capability to combine signals or compare them with what you already know if you are going to make sense of what is happening. Our use of signals involves connecting the world outside the organization in a meaningful way with the 'world' inside the organization. The trends, scenarios and roadmap in the earlier chapters form the structure, or scaffolding if you like, to connect all these dots. Every piece of relevant data is either part of a larger trend, a signal fitting in a scenario, an indication of where you are on the roadmap, or it could be a predefined trigger to exercise an option.

By correlating signals from the outside world with signals about the organization's progress, you can generate meaningful feedforward. If you want to work out which signals can be used in this way, you can use modelling (see p. 78); this allows you to understand the coherence between factors, actors and internal developments and also offers a focus to distinguish signals from noise.

USING SIGNALS AS FORESIGHT

By monitoring the developments collaboratively, you will develop a common language. Signals become not merely symptoms of the past or the present, but indicators of what could happen in the future. Once you are aware that these signs can tell you something about the future, you will automatically start looking differently at the world around you. You don't read the newspaper any more as a report of what happened yesterday, but as an announcement of what could happen tomorrow or next week. A good listener starts hearing more and more. You will start looking differently at the signals in your environment and your organization; not as a symptom of what has happened, but as a sign of things to come. Looking at the future is not simply a matter of exploring trends and developments in the environment, but also of picking up signals or events in the present which could announce a change or switch in certain trends. The data points which you gather by monitoring the world inside and outside can – when correlated with one another and with other information – be lagging indicators or leading indicators (or early warning signals): indicators which tell us something about what has happened (in the case of lagging indicators) or what will happen (in the case of leading indicators).

To illustrate the difference between leading and lagging indicators, let's look at the construction sector in the Netherlands in 2008 and 2009. The order book for many construction companies was full in 2008 and their turnover was good. But a leading indicator of an approaching crisis, for both architects and construction companies, was the way in which the capital market shut down: this meant that it would be harder for clients of the building sector to finance new building projects. In 2009 the turnover of architects fell considerably. For architectural practices this was a *lagging* indicator of the tightening capital market: a strong fall in activity levels as a result of the credit crisis. However, for construction companies this same signal was a *leading* indicator of what was to come. It often takes a year between the design of a building and the actual construction. The volume of architectural designs correlates neatly with the subsequent volume of building contracts.

Another example of a leading indicator is the structure of the interest curve. When the interest structure is normal the short-term interest rate, which is used for loans with a short duration, will be under the long-term interest rate, which is used for loans with a longer duration. Long-term loans simply bear a higher risk. We speak of in an inverse interest structure when the short-term interest rates are higher than the long-term interest rates. Banks make profit by lending money (for example in the form of 10-year fixed mortgages) which they finance by constantly borrowing for a short period (for example from consumers in their savings account, from other banks or from the central bank). Therefore an inverse interest structure is dangerous to banks: in such situations they pay more interest than they receive. This was the case in the US in 2004–2006, when the short-term interest rate at which the banks borrowed themselves went from 1 per cent to 5.25 per cent, way above the amount that banks received on their mortgage lending (sometimes as low as 4 per cent). An inverse interest structure is often a leading indicator for an economic recession: each of the six recessions in the US between 1970 and 2001 was preceded by an inverse interest structure, as a consequence of a series of raises in interest rates by the Federal Reserve and which made the short-term interest rates increase.

Predicting changes in the outside world with the help of signals is nothing new:

As any adult knows, a magician cannot produce a rabbit unless it is already in (or very near) his hat. In the same way, surprises in the business environment almost never emerge without warning.

Pierre Wack[7]

---

7   Wack 1985b: 148.

THE PIZZA INDEX

A nice example of a leading indicator is what has been called the 'pizza index'. In the 1980s and 1990s, so the story goes, the number of pizzas which were delivered to the Pentagon coincided with the course of military operations. The logic was as follows: when the American Department of Defense is preparing a military operation, officials are working overtime and because they are no longer home in time for supper, they have pizzas delivered to the office.

The weekly *Time* wrote this about it on 13 August 1990:

> *Delivery people at various Domino's pizza outlets in and around Washington claim that they have learned to anticipate big news baking at the White House or the Pentagon by the upsurge in takeout orders. Phones usually start ringing some 72 hours before an official announcement. 'We know', says one pizza runner. 'Absolutely. Pentagon orders double up the night before the Panama attack; same thing happened before the Grenada invasion.' Last Wednesday, he adds, 'we got a lot of orders, starting around midnight. We figured something was up.' This time the big news came quickly: Iraq's surprise invasion of Kuwait.*[8]

According to the *Washington Times* of 21 August 1991 the Pentagon broke a record on that day with 102 pizzas delivered; this was also the day of the abortive putsch against the Russian president Gorbachev. Incidentally, the White House ordered at least 52 pizzas on that same day.

Companies, such as oil companies and other organizations which benefit from early advance warning of pending military activities, may well like to track leading indicators of increased planning or frenetic decision-making in the corridors of power!

---

[8]   Ellis and Gray 1990.

Not all foresight is legal. Stock trading with foresight based on inside information is generally illegal. But there are other, relatively simple ways to develop foresight. Imagine you want to be able to anticipate any housing market crises. If you track data on the length of time homes are on the market prior to sale this can be a leading indicator for the development of the housing market. If you are interested in the new products by Apple, you can monitor the domain names which are registered by Apple (or simply track macrumors.com). And if you are curious about the situation at your direct competitor, you can keep track of the job vacancies they are posting. Designing these kinds of methods has a serious purpose but it involves an element of creativity, imagination and fun.

MAKING A CONNECTION BETWEEN THE 'OUTSIDE' AND THE 'INSIDE'

It is not enough simply to monitor developments and to keep track of indicators of change. The information which you gather needs to be connected to the internal progress of the organization. As soon as you have detected the warning signals for changes in the environment, you should already know how to act on that information. Does an emerging new trend influence the vision of the organization? Do you need to change the roadmap? When you see change coming early, you have time to anticipate its impact. This makes it possible to intervene with greater subtlety than those occasions when you need to react ad hoc. The detection of early indicators offers you the potential to be proactive; a process of planning rather than urgent problem-solving.

You should relate the signals to where you are and where you want to go to: the vision. Ideally your monitoring should inform you which options are 'in the money'. That is why it is good to return on a regular basis to the conversations about scenarios, trends and options, and to connect them with the information you gather from monitoring. Monitoring can help you to decide which options you will need to exercise, or might indicate that it is necessary to adjust your roadmap or even your vision.

This is also the reason why we pointed out earlier that 'It is the oil price' or 'It is the recession' are not valid excuses for disappointing progress. These are developments which you should have monitored, knowing that they could influence the progress of your organization.

8.3 Intelligence and Organizing Early Warning

To some of our clients intelligence is hugely important; not only financially, often human lives are at stake; for example when we work for the Ministry of Defence, or on issues related to water management or to national security. They have special departments tasked with measuring and monitoring. Every organization will measure its finances; commercial organizations will always measure their sales. Some will have competitive intelligence departments to monitor the movements of their competitors. All Ministries of Defence will have an intelligence organization dedicated to monitoring possible enemies. There are many ways to organize yourselves to measure progress and to monitor external developments. For tracking external developments, an internal network of intelligence gatherers is a good alternative to a dedicated department. This is the how Rabobank and construction firm BAM ensure that the organization is alert to the outside world and to the future.[9]

It is useful to have an idea of how relevant actors and factors are connected: it makes it easier to see which signals should be monitored and to which developments they are referring. Monitoring the environment and identifying signals becomes much easier when you have developed some effective scenarios in advance. A good set of scenarios also enables you to monitor the key uncertainties (see p. 62) straight away. If that is the case you need to investigate whether there are empirical sources which will provide strong evidence about the developments which have been identified as correlating to key uncertainties. You can also look at the factors which influence the key uncertainties; leading indicators which will be a useful part of the early warning system.

In a sense, scenarios themselves are already part of an early warning system; understanding which scenario is unfolding gives you a head start over your competitors, since most organizations will only react once external problems have been internalized. And it can take months or even years before a changing context actually shows up in your annual figures. Work on classifying whether the indicators you are tracking are

---

9   De Ruijter 2007 and Idenburg et al. 2005.

leading or lagging indicators. Do they give clues about trends which are about to develop in the (near) future, or do they give clues about trends or events which have happened? The best future oriented early warning systems will track leading indicators.

EARLY WARNING SYSTEM: THE APPLICATION OF A MONITORING MECHANISM[10]

Justice for Tomorrow (2)

In an earlier section we described why the Ministry of Justice wanted to develop a monitoring mechanism as part of the project Justice for Tomorrow. Let's look at how the Ministry realized this intention. How did they link the qualitative scenarios and the development of policy? The first question they asked themselves was: which empirical sources already exist and which, collectively or separately, give clues to the developments described in the scenario?

The ministry then undertook several steps. The first was to determine the starting point: which scenario most closely resembled their current situation? The second step was to select empirical sources for research and here the four criteria we described earlier were used: the information from the sources had to be representative, significant, periodical and valid. The selected empirical sources where then applied to measure the developments and movements of the two key uncertainties. Next all the information of the earlier steps was combined to determine whether in reality elements were apparent which were mentioned in the scenarios (see Figure 8.2).

Figure 8.2   **The scenarios versus reality, based on the EWS in 2007 (after Botterhuis et al. 2009)**

---

10   Botterhuis et al. 2009.

Using the monitoring mechanism on a regular basis, a path between the present and the future emerges. It may be this path as described in one of the scenarios, but it may also represent a combination of developments from several scenarios. Using the unfolding path as a guide, the Ministry of Justice have been able to adjust their strategy, exercising call and put options, as appropriate.

The monitoring mechanism has another role too. It clearly shows when a scenario(s) has passed its 'best before' date and new scenarios should be developed. This is likely to be the case when significant new developments emerge which have not been described in the existing scenarios.

In 2010 the Ministry published a report: *Justice for Tomorrow. Signposts for Scenarios 2006–2010*, which described how they were continuing to monitor developments in the outside world following the design of the monitoring mechanism[11]. The ministry realized that they did not want to limit their intelligence to previously designated empirical sources, all of which showed only lagging indicators. They decided instead to try to monitor leading indicators by using an alternative monitoring mechanism: bringing in pictures and newspaper headlines of events or developments which were indicative for the scenarios (called *signposting*). The Ministry defined distinctive events which were specific to developments in a given scenario. They were careful to distinguish between events which indicate that changes have followed a certain development path (lagging indicators) and events which could precede a certain development path (leading indicators). The ministry then checked whether the selected news items contained lagging or leading indicators by looking at the years 2006 to 2009 using the popular 'year in review' books. The indicators they found were scored according to the strength of the signal. Signals in the yearbook such as more attention towards international topics rather than just national topics, and a shift away from social safety, were noted. In this way the ministry was able to get a clear sense of how accurately their scenarios matched what was unfolding and vice versa. And perhaps just as importantly, the exercise itself and particularly the well-designed publication *Justice for Tomorrow. Signposts for Scenarios 2006–2010* were an effective way of putting the future back on the agenda for the top civil servants in the Ministry.[12] In one sense, monitoring can simply be a neat technique for keeping the future and the external perspective on the agenda.

---

11   Ministerie van Justitie 2010.
12   Ministerie van Justitie 2010.

There are various criteria which you use as inputs for measuring progress and monitoring external developments. Information is most useful when it is representative, significant, periodical and valid. Periodicity refers to the frequency with which information is gathered, and validity to the degree in which the measured information and the monitored phenomenon match.[13, 14]

---

13   In Chapter 2 we already discussed the complications which can arise when monitoring the environment, like the difference between capta and data.
14   Botterhuis et al. 2009.

How an organization monitors trends depends amongst other things on the character of the organization, the information which is to be monitored, the available budget and the available manpower. You may choose to use some or all of the following: literature study, recording statistics, interaction with target groups and environment and new exercises with existing scenarios (refine, improving and checking). You can choose to monitor yourself, with or without a formal early warning system, but you can also use readily available information and data sets. However, it is important to think about the source which you will use. Much is monitored, but you need to be able to find and make sense of this information!

8.4   Incentive Structures and Information Systems

REWARDING: THE CONNECTION BETWEEN ACTION AND MONITORING

In some organizations employee bonuses are linked to the performance in a given year: short-term results are rewarded. The disadvantage of the link between a bonus and last year's performance is that employees are encouraged towards short-termism. Investing in R&D, for example, is at the expense of short-term profit but is essential for the long-term. However, when the incentive structure is based on short-term results, the incentive to perform over the long term disappears. Reducing R&D spending will reduce this year's costs, which will directly translate in higher profits. But at the expense of future turnover and profits!

The incentive structure plays an important role in staff policy when assessing whether employees are aiming for results in the short or long term. During the credit crisis the influence of the incentive structure became the subject of conversation again: bonuses for bankers were one of the factors considered to have encouraged them to take unrealistic risks.

Another problem with the incentive structure of some organizations is that it is rarely based on the actual performance of employees, rather it is closely correlated with external circumstances. For example, many bonuses are linked to net profit, which in turn can be highly dependent on external factors, such as interest rates, general economic growth or consumer confidence. When designing an incentive structure it is important to reflect whether you are rewarding something internal, which can be influenced, or something external which you cannot influence. In the introduction I described my experiences with a middle-sized financial conglomerate. In their medium-term plans they predicted their numbers with an accuracy of two decimal places, but every year their predictions turned out to be off by tens of per cents. The incentive structure of the company was linked to the profitability of the company as a whole. This profitability however depended heavily on the interest rate structure and the performance of the market: external factors which the company could not influence. In fact the bonus system meant that employees were rewarded for good financial weather and were punished for bad weather. The real performance of the people involved had very little to do with what they did themselves, in positive macroeconomic climates the company would do well anyway, and in bad conditions the company would automatically perform badly. In other words, it was like linking their bonuses to the prevailing weather; a bonus when it is sunny, and no bonus if it rains!

To guarantee that a bonus encourages employees not only run faster, but also in the right direction, three conditions are crucial: the arrangement should resolve an obvious problem, the process should be carefully designed (with real thought for cause and effect) and the performance should be measurable.[15] For starters it should be clear what you are measuring exactly and what you reward. Is it volume, turnover or margin? Do you reward market share or share of wallet? Is a police officer rewarded on the basis of the fall in crime statistics or on the basis of citizen satisfaction and perception of crime? Do you reward effort or result? And in management speak: is it input ('more boots on the ground'), output ('writing out x number of fines') or result ('increased security') that you want to reward? These are all questions which you need to consider when you measure and monitor.

My experience suggests that the role of staff policy in creating a future-oriented organization can be huge. When short-term results are rewarded, these can jeopardize continuity on the long term. Even worse: when people are only assessed on the basis of today's results, this may encourage unethical behaviour because some people may try to manipulate the outcome with little thought for the consequences of their actions in the long run. When I started working for Shell in 1992, they used staff policy in a strategic way. Every individual employee had a *current estimated potential* (CEP), which indicated what the highest possible level within Shell would be for this employee and which path the employee should follow to get there. Every year the CEP of the employee was evaluated and, where appropriate, adjusted. The policy was then replaced by a new evaluation method: employees were now evaluated on the basis of the past year results. This new method turned out to promote sloppiness and fraud and was seen as one of the causes behind the downward revision of the Shell oil and gas reserves in 2004.

MONITORING AND REPORTING: INFORMATION SYSTEMS

We have seen how important it is to translate the strategic conversations into monitoring systems and especially into reporting systems. In this respect, the governance, financial reporting, planning and control system and the information architecture of the organization plays a major role. Just measuring performance and monitoring external developments is not enough: the results should also be able to be used in a way which is useful to the organization. When you have good monitoring and reporting systems, it is much easier to use the results to guide the organization. The HR, finance and IT departments are crucial in creating a future-oriented organization. IT systems are becoming an increasingly important part of organizations and it is essential that they are designed to enable the mission, vision, roadmap and other strategic considerations of the organization.

Engineering company Arcadis previously measured turnover per product and per department. At one point they changed to measure their performance differently, that is per customer. This allowed them to be far clearer which customers were important to the company (and vice-versa, to which clients Arcadis was important). This is how the incentive system of the organization changed from being simply product-driven to customer-driven. This example shows how the design of the information system of

---

15   Van Uffelen 2008.

the organization should be absolutely in line with your mission, your vision and your strategy. And when guiding your organization the monitoring results are a crucial factor.

Before you start, you should think about what you want to monitor and why. In 2001 and 2002 The Netherlands Food and Consumer Product Safety Authority conducted a scenario project to check article 20 of the new Alcohol Law on enforceability (we discussed this project in Chapter 4). One of the questions which came up during this project was: how do you check when this law is observed or flouted? A monitoring organization is a condition for maintaining this law. So you need to design an organization which has the capability to undertake this monitoring. You need to build a system, hire people and above all link this information system to an incentive structure.

What you monitor is clearly important but it is also important when you monitor. The speed of monitoring has an impact on the response times and therefore on the applicability of the results. Data which is out of date can put you on the wrong track. Another important issue is how the results of a reporting system are used. In practice I often see a finance department which does not pass on information about unpaid bills to the sales department; which can lead to a continuous delivery of goods and services to a chronic non-paying customer.

An organization should put an information plan together which is about the information architecture and IT systems and which tells who in the organization should know what. Often this is where the moving starts, because the input of information guides your organization. How you guide/manage depends on how you monitor. The information household is therefore, in contradiction to what is often thought, strategically a very important part of the organization.

Systems thinking emphasizes the way in which activities and processes are interrelated in ways which may never have been originally intended by their designers. It puts attention on the way in which an information structure (the way of monitoring, the way of reporting and the use of information) characterizes an organization. An example of such an information structure is an *appreciative system*, which was described by system thinker Charles Geoffrey Vickers and further elaborated by Peter Checkland. Checkland posits that every organization monitors and interprets based on certain standards. In an appreciative system these standards are also continuously adjusted based on the monitored information: 'The very act of using the standards may itself modify them.'[16] Events and ideas are being monitored, interpreted and assessed in the organization. This evaluation or view again leads to action.

One of the most important pillars of this model is that standards are not based on normative or scientific standards, but that the source of these standards lies within the history of the system itself. The functioning of the system influences the used standards and the adjusted standards influence the functioning of the system in their turn: this is reflexivity as it was described in Chapter 5. Thus a learning organization arises and the 'planning as learning' proposed by Arie de Geus is shaped. The information which this organization is continually acquiring in relation to scenarios, options and the environment helps ensure that the organization keeps growing and keeps developing.[17]

This model of an appreciative information system gives rise to statements such as 'What gets measured gets done' and 'What you give attention to, grows'. After all, what

---

16   Checkland 1999b: A51.

17   Checkland 1999b: A51–2.

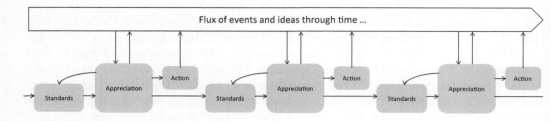

Figure 8.3   An appreciative system (after Checkland 1999b)

is monitored in an organization and thus is paid attention is considered important, and therefore is given even more attention. You can use this behavioural trait strategically: when you realize that things which are monitored are usually considered important, you can choose to monitor certain things just for this reason (see Figure 8.3 above).

At the beginning of this chapter I said that the annual figures are an important monitoring system, although they are the equivalent of the driver's rear-view mirror. Imagine that just as you have an 'accountant for yesterday' who registers your results of last year, you should employ an 'accountant for tomorrow'. After all, your annual report is an important platform to talk about the future. The Dutch corporate governance code (the Tabaksblat Code) which applies to listed companies requires that a risk paragraph is added to the annual report. Sensitivity analysis – for which scenarios and stress tests can be a concrete realization – explains how a company needs to show how sensitive it is to possible developments in the outside world; a great example of strategic risk management.

Of course it is impossible to give a correct prediction of the future based on the annual figures, but you can use them to acquire information about the progress along the roadmap and the sensitivities of the organization. Financiers, for example, use annual figures to generate assumptions about the future of an organization, which in turn will influence their decision to (further) invest in the company. Organizations themselves use annual figures for their forward-looking statements or profitability. Annual figures are an indicator by which you can check whether the organization is still on course and whether the vision is still within reach of the organization. Using your monitoring results you can adjust the roadmap and exercise other options. In short, annual figures not only provide information about the past, they can also be interpreted for the future.

CONCLUSIONS: MONITORING

1.   Constantly monitor developments in the world inside and outside the organization.
2.   Discuss the monitoring results and give them meaning with the help of the scenarios.
3.   Keep track of particular signs which you have identified as indicators of change
4.   Organize feedback by organizing a fit for purpose reporting system (an early warning system), IT structure and operating model. Use the results to know when to exercise call or put options.
5.   Reward, in whatever way, positive progress on the roadmap in the direction of the vision.

Epilogue: Welcome

Having read this book you are now a member of the 'club of strategic thinkers and leaders'. As a good strategic thinker and leader you will be curious both about your organization and the world outside it and you will continually explore them both. Because you realize that as soon as you can see the bigger picture, you can identify where and how you and your organization can intervene. And when you understand how and when you can influence your organization, you are able to improve the world – at least, in some part. Ultimately, knowledge of the outside world leads to better strategy. When you achieve that your organization will be working creatively and realizing its vision. At this point, the nautical metaphor is no longer adequate. For where the captain of a ship only navigates, the captain of an organization is able to adjust his or her organization, set sails and make waves.

The Bigger Picture

In the 1960s we had enough oil, in the 1970s we had enough money and in the first decennium of the twenty-first century we had enough personnel. The trend breaks: scarcity of oil in 1973, money in 2008 and personnel (which is still to come) came and will come as a surprise to many. But although these kinds of trend breaks are unpredictable, they can be foreseen as possible scenarios. To organizations which use scenarios, these trend breaks are not 'bad' scenarios but rather opportunities to prepare for.

In the 1950s and 1960s various countries had reasonable oil reserves at their disposal. The turning off of the oil tap by some producing countries did not have any real impact. The oil weapon was not a real threat.

But in the 1970s the world had changed. Daniel Yergin describes in his book *The Prize* how a combination of economic, political and military circumstances created a situation in which oil could be used as a weapon. And in 1973 exactly this happened. The balance between supply and demand was tense. The oil reserves represented only a few per cent of the total demand, so basically we had full supply. The US produced at the peaks of its capacity and the US became more and more dependent on import.

From Yergin's reconstruction of the first oil crisis we learn that, in the period prior to October 1973, few players were willing to see or correctly interpreted the signs which indicated that the oil weapon was about to be used. Their analysis of the threat of an oil crisis was based on analyses of the reserves of the oil market, of the security of supply, of the attitude of governments of OPEC countries and of countries outside OPEC. A change in those assumptions in one of the analyses would inevitably have consequences for the analysis of the possibility that the oil weapon could be used.[1]

---

1   Yergin 2003 [1991]: 585–99.

In the oil price scenarios and the analysis of possible strategies of oil-producing countries which Shell developed in 1971, the possibility that oil prices would rise was dominant.[2] In the oil price scenarios a price jump was postulated before 1976. An analysis of possible factors which could cause this was made and a military conflict was one of the factors. Thus Shell was prepared for a trend break and able to react quickly and successfully. To Shell, the oil crisis was an opportunity. It outperformed its competitors.

The credit crisis – scarcity of money – shows a similar profile to the first oil crisis in 1973, as does the Internet bubble of 2001: events which came as a surprise to many of the main characters, but which had been considered and prepared for by a small number of organizations. After the attacks of 9/11 people were anxious to do anything to prevent a financial disaster; monetary standards were enlarged and the money tap was turned on. But when the oil price rose because of the war in Iraq, the risk of inflation increased. To prevent inflation the money tap was turned off in 2005/2006 in the US. This caused rising interest rates and, as an effect with a small time delay, declining house prices, which was the forerunner for a worldwide crisis. To Rabobank, which had already mentally prepared for a credit crunch in 2003, the credit crisis of 2007 turned out to be an opportunity. Thanks to their state of readiness, where others faltered, 2008 resulted in a record profit.

The oil crisis and the credit crisis are two infamous examples. First of all, they prove that you can anticipate many things and that you can prepare for change if you just pay attention to the right signs and interpret the information correctly. Second, these examples show that you should not consider developments in different domains as unrelated. Your understanding will grow when you combine military, economic and political information. Both examples show how closely the oil price, the currency rate of the dollar, political decisions and military conflicts are connected.

The next potential trend breaks are announcing themselves. At this time we have sufficient people in the labour market; in most places in the world we still have enough water, and a large biodiversity in animals, plants and microorganisms. But in these fields, at some date in the future, the current abundance may switch to scarcity too. Can we prevent this? And if not, are we prepared for it and do we see the opportunities?

We could say that everything is connected to everything. Events on the world stage have large consequences; the connectivity means that even small events can have huge consequences.

For you as a strategic thinker the task is to map out how apparently very different things are related to each other. Of course this is a mission impossible. But you have travelled some distance when you realize that it is foolish to think narrow-mindedly. Reductionist thinking will only limit your view.

In Practice

With the task to see the bigger picture comes a big responsibility. Strategy is not just theory or science, it is something you should practise, a competence in which you should develop experience. But you are not alone and together we are a community. Contact with other strategic thinkers and leaders from different organizations is valuable: exchanging experiences enlarges our view – we can see energy, the currency rate of the dollar,

---

2   Non-external publications, written by Henk Alkema and Ted Newland.

demography, ecology and military interests in a bigger picture – and this can contribute to improvements in the strategy process. Thought leaders from banks, ministries, armed forces, multinationals, entrepreneurs and scientists regularly come together to exchange ideas. Now you have joined our club, I invite you to get in touch.

It All Starts with Asking Questions

In *The Hitchhiker's Guide to the Galaxy* by Douglas Adams computer Deep Thought is asked for the 'Answer to the Ultimate Question of Life, The Universe and Everything' and after seven-and-a-half million years of computing and checking, comes up with the answer: '42'. The answer is useless, because no one actually understands the question. It is at this stage that the search for the 'Ultimate Question of Life, The Universe and Everything' starts.

Strategy always starts with a question too. What will the oil price do in the future? Do we need 100 or 300 local banks in ten years' time? An organization can approach these problems in two ways. This first is problem-solving: you try to define the problem as accurately as possible, followed by undertaking empirical research and then, finally, you start acting. The second way is more strategic: you use the question as a basis to start an exploration which leads to new questions; new challenges suddenly appear and in the end you are able to generate more meaningful questions. These questions are not simply: 'Do we need 100 or 300 local banks?' but touch fundamental uncertainties such as the development of the macroeconomy and the social cohesion in society – all uncertainties which you avoid when you would try to answer only the original question. Just as in *The Hitchhiker's Guide to the Galaxy*, strategy is all about asking the right question.

It is important to keep thinking about which issues are important to the organization at any given moment. Sometimes it is helpful to raise questions about the mission and the formula for success. But then again, sometimes you need to look outside and wonder what is happening around the organization. Scenarios can help to create an awareness of possible future situations, but sometimes it is better to wonder where is it we want to go to: the vision. At certain moments the organization will want to generate options freely and it then asks itself: what might the organization do if it ends up in a certain situation? At other moments there is a need to formulate or adjust the roadmap which describes how the organization tries to realize its vision.

Developing Competences for Strategy

According to General Von Clausewitz several competences are indispensable for strategy:

Thus, then, in Strategy everything is very simple, but not on that account very easy. Once it is determined from the relations of the State what should and may be done by War, then the way to it is easy to find; but to follow that way straightforward, to carry out the plan without being obliged to deviate from it a thousand times by a thousand varying influences, requires, besides great strength of character, great clearness and steadiness of mind, and out of a thousand men who are remarkable, some for mind, others for penetration, others again for boldness or strength of will, perhaps not one will combine in himself all those qualities which are required to raise a man above mediocrity in the career of a general.

Carl von Clausewitz[3]

The most important question you ask yourself is why are you involved with strategy? Is it because you are a thinker and able to keep an eye on the long-term? Is it because you are a good listener and know very well what is going on in the organization? Or is it because you have no doubts and therefore are perfectly capable of taking the organization by the hand to execute the vision as planned in the roadmap?

There are some competences which are essential for strategy. You need critical thinking; you need courage to be the first to dare question sensitive assumptions – whether they relate to economic predictions or the disbelief in the future need of computers at home. At the same time you need to be able to articulate certainty and to guide the way, because it is difficult for an organization to follow someone 'who does not know'. Biologists carried out an experiment in which they removed a part of the brain of a randomly selected sardine. Then they put the test sardine back with its fellow sardines. This altered sardine turned out to be an excellent leader: the whole shoal followed it blindly, wherever it went. This experiment could suggest that a leader should not necessarily have an extra competence, but might lack one competence. A leader should lack the natural predilection to doubt or to hesitate.[4] The strategic leader however faces the challenge to combine a critical and questioning attitude with confidence in a certainty which invites others to follow!

Another important competence is that you have strong relationships with the people inside the organization. The bond of trust between the organization and yourself is required when you want to lead others in a certain direction. When an organization asks a short-term question, it is most likely that the response includes long-term uncertainties. Few people are not willing to share their doubts or fears with strangers. This means you should be an insider and an outsider at the same time; you have the trust of the organization while keeping an open mind and the ability to identify and see beyond the blind spots. You will need to accept that people are not really waiting for you with enthusiasm. It is never easy to embrace uncertainty and change.

Having read this book I have no doubt that there are things you do very well already, but there are also thing you still need to learn. In a *community of practice* we can learn from each other, by passing on knowledge and by exchanging experiences. This applies to both the process (and the capabilities which underpin it) and the insights which you generate during a strategic process. Whenever you find that it is difficult for you to doubt and to lead at the same time, or to be an insider and an outsider, you have several options. You can develop those competences yourself, but you can also ask others to help you.

In my view, thinking about strategy is not reserved to a few strategists or just the CEO. A strategic thinker is not one person or even one department, someone you can appoint or dismiss. On the contrary: strategy is a collective responsibility. Strategy should be found in each level of an organization and in each function. Whether you are a director of human resources or a researcher in R&D; whether you are a marketer or division manager,

---

3   Clausewitz (1832) 1997: 143.

4   Max Pam in television show *Buitenhof*, Nederland 2, 30 May 2010.

little of your time is spent on thinking about strategy, but you can give thought, now and then, to the changing circumstances in which you operate and look at the long term. Strategy is not something exclusive, on the contrary: in successful organizations we find strategy in all kinds of different places and in different shapes. An organization is not a machine which is run from the top. An organization is a community of people like you and me. We are in it together and only when we are collectively ready to change, can we change. Only by collectively looking at the long term and at the bigger picture can we aspire to create a better world!

Glossary

There are no fixed definitions for terms such as mission, strategy and success formula, and they are applied differently according to context. This glossary contains definitions of some of the most important terms used in this book.

- **Call option**   A call option provides the opportunity, but not the obligation, to start an activity. A call option is considered for new actions which score well and which are relevant, suitable and feasible in only one or a few of the scenarios. The call option helps the organization to be prepared and ready when needed. Starting an activity can also imply investigating, pre-investing, building up, extending, increasing and intensifying.
- **Contextual   environment** An   organization's   contextual   environment encompasses factors and actors which influence the organization, but which cannot be influenced by the organization. The contextual environment is outside of the sphere of influence of the organization.
- **Counter trend**   A counter trend is a development originating as a response and in the opposite direction to the original catalyzing development, e.g. globalization à anti-globalization.
- **DESTEP**   DESTEP is an acronym to indicate the developments in six domains which together provide an overall view of the dynamics in a relevant context. These are: Demography, Ecology, Society and Culture, Technology, Economy and Politics.
- **Distinctive competences**   Features and characteristics which distinguish your organization from competitors. The concept emerged from the combination of two management theories: Hamel and Prahalad's theory of core competences and Michael Porter's theory of competitive advantage.
- **Extrapolation**   A forecast based on the continuation of a historical trend.
- **Future proof option**   See **Robust option**.
- **Mission**   The mission is the 'greater cause' of an organization. The mission expresses the organization's purpose and added value. A mission is threefold and consists of the statutory purpose, a description of what the organization does and its core values.
- **Monitoring**   Monitoring involves measuring signals from both within and outside the organization. The purpose is to get a clear view on the direction in which the outside world is developing and to verify whether the organization is still on the right track.
- **Option**   An option is a possible action an organization can take and might exercise in the future, often to be prepared in advance and in the light of the scenarios.
- **Put option**   A put option provides the opportunity but not the obligation to stop an activity. A put option allows you to stop existing actions which do not score well and which are not relevant, suitable or feasible in one or more scenarios. New but highly uncertain activities can be accompanied by a put option which will enable you

to stop them if and when needed. Stopping an activity can also imply postponing, diminishing or reducing, or selling an activity.

- **Real option**   The term 'real option' is used to differentiate financial options, traded at the stock exchange, and options for real action which can be taken by organizations. Real options represent the opportunity – not the obligation – to carry out a certain action. We can distinguish between robust options, call options and put options.
- **Roadmap**   A roadmap is the plan describing a path of simultaneous and sequential actions which need to be taken to bridge the gap between the present and the desired future (the vision) of the organization. The roadmap is synonymous with strategy in the narrow sense. A business plan is a roadmap for one business.
- **Robust option**   A robust option is a real option which, when tested against all scenarios, proves a relevant, successful and feasible option in all scenarios. Such an option is also called a future proof option. Robust options may always be included in the roadmap, as they will be effective in any possible future scenario.
- **Scenario**   A scenario is a plausible and relevant image of the future which leads to new insights. It tells a story about the possible development of contextual factors in the future which the organization should take into account, but cannot influence. Scenarios enable the organization to anticipate changing circumstances.
- **Self-denying prophecy**   A self-denying prophecy creates an image which leads to actions which prevent the vision from becoming reality. This leads to a future other than that predicted.
- **Self-fulfilling prophecy**   A self-fulfilling prophecy creates an image which leads to actions which enable the image to become reality. In such a case the prophecy or vision is fulfilled directly or indirectly.
- **Strategy in the broad sense**   In this book the term strategy refers to the strategic planning process in which strategy is developed by discussing all strategic topics around mission, trends, scenarios, options, vision and roadmap. By acting and monitoring you connect the strategy with the current situation, or the operational with the tactical level of the organization.
- **Strategy in the narrow sense**   Strategy in a narrow sense refers to the roadmap: the plan for how to reach the vision, starting from where we are now.
- **Strategic thinking**   Strategic thinking is the opposite of reactive problem-solving: strategic thinking means looking ahead, embracing uncertainty and anticipating the future.
- **Success formula**   The success formula is also called the organization's business idea. It describes the distinctive features of the organization and answers questions such as 'What do we do?' and 'Who are we?'. The success formula is a self-reinforcing cycle in which both immediately visible specific activities and the organization's competences are important for the organization's success.
- **Transactional environment**   An organization's transactional environment encompasses actors and events in the direct environment of the organization which the organization can influence, such as customers, competitors and suppliers. Unlike the contextual environment, the organization and its transactional environment have a mutual dependency and direct interaction. Therefore the transactional environment contains the sphere of influence of the organization.

- **Trend** A trend is the historic development of a certain variable over time. In this book trend refers to the historic developments of variables in the contextual and transactional environment of the organization over time.
- **Vision** An organization's vision expresses its desired future and describes how the organization sees itself in that future. The organization attempts to realize the vision by using a roadmap. The mission expresses why the organization exists; the vision expresses what the organization wants to achieve.
- **Wind tunnelling** Wind tunnelling or stress testing means assessing planned activities, budgets and goals or new ideas in relation to a range of scenarios, to test them for their relevance and success in the future. The scenarios represent the wind conditions; the possible future contexts in which the current plan may unfurl.

Bibliography

Alkema, H.J. (2006) *Rethinking our Certainties*, presented at Oxford Futures Forum 2006.

Alkema, H.J. (2008) *Memories and Lessons from 30 Years in Strategic Planning*, presented at Oxford Futures Forum 2008.

Alphen, H.-J. van (2009) 'Centraal Planbureau zit er bijna altijd naast. Economische voorspellingen met cijfers achter de komma zijn ongeloofwaardig', *NRC Handelsblad*, 29 April, section 1, 7.

Aristotle, translated by J.A. Smith (1931) *On the Soul*, http://classics.mit.edu/Aristotle/soul.html

Bakas, A. (2009) *Microtrends Nederland*, Schiedam: Scriptum.

Bennis, W. and B. Namus (1985) *Leaders: The Strategies for Taking Charge*, New York: Harper & Row.

Bernard, A. (1980) 'World Oil and Cold Reality', *Harvard Business Review*, November–December, 91–101.

Botterhuis, L., P. van der Duin, P.A. de Ruijter and P. van Wijck (2009) 'Monitoring the Future. Building an Early Warning System for the Dutch Ministry of Justice', *Futures*, 22 November.

Brown, S.P.A., R. Virmani and R. Alm, 'Crude Awakening: Behind the Surge in Oil Prices', *Economic Letter – Insights from the Federal Reserve Bank of Dallas*, 3 (5), May (www.dallasfed.org).

Centraal Planbureau (2007) *Centraal Economisch Plan 2007*.

Checkland, P. and S. Holwell (1998) *Information, Systems and Information Systems: Making Sense of the Field*, Chichester, West Sussex: John Wiley & Sons.

Checkland, P. (1999a) *Soft Systems Methodology in Action*, Chichester, West Sussex: John Wiley & Sons.

Checkland, P. (1999b) *Systems Thinking, Systems Practice*, Chichester, West Sussex: John Wiley & Sons.

Clausewitz, C. von [1832] (2003) *On War*, Hertfordshire: Wordsworth Editions.

Collins, J. (1995) 'Building companies to last', *Inc. Special Issue – The State of Small Business*, www.jimcollins.com

Ellis, D. and P. Gray (1990) 'And Bomb The Anchovies', *Time*, 13 August.

Elsevier (2007) Cover, 31 March 2007.

Eramus, D. (2008) *The Future of ICT in Financial Services. The Rabobank ICT Scenarios*, Amsterdam: DTN Press.

European Commission (2003), *Leadership 2015, Defining the Future of the European Shipbuilding and Ship Repair Industry*, Brussels: Enterprise Directorate-General.

Hampden-Turner, C. and A. Trompenaar (1993) *Seven culture of capitalism*, New York: Currency Doubleday.

Het Financieele Dagblad (1993) 'Shell-topman: Energieverbruik derde wereld verdubbelt', 26 October.

Het Financieele Dagblad (1996) 'Shell: Olieverbruik stijgt tot 2021 66%', 22 November.

Het Financieele Dagblad (1998a) 'Shell-directeur: CO_2-emissie krijgt piek in eerste helft volgende eeuw', 11 February.

Het Financieele Dagblad (1998b) 'Shell belooft reductie van uitstoot broeikasgas', 21 October.

Het Financieele Dagblad (2008) 'Rabo dekt zich in tegen crisis', 1 February.

Fink, A., P. Hadridge and G. Ringland (2007) 'From Signals to Decisions', in B. Sharpe and K. van der Heijden (eds), *Scenarios for Success. Turning Insights into Action*, Chichester, West Sussex: John Wiley and Sons.

Fryer, B. (2003) 'Storytelling that Moves People: A Conversation with Screenwriting Coach Robert McKee', *Harvard Business Review*, June, 5–8.

Geus, A. de (1988) 'Planning as Learning', *Harvard Business Review*, March–April, 2–6.

Geus, A. de (1997) *The Living Company. Growth, Learning and Longevity in Business*, London and Sonoma, California: Nicholas Brealey Publishing.

Goold, M. and A. Campbell (1991) 'From Corporate Strategy to Parenting Advantage', *Long Range Planning*, 24 (1).

Gunsteren, H. van (2003) *Stoppen. U kunt het, u wilt het, u doet het niet*, Amsterdam: Van Gennep.

Halberstadt, G. (1998) 'Shell blijft in de verre toekomst kijken', *Het Financieele Dagblad*, 19 December.

Heijden, K. van der (1996) *Scenarios. The Art of Strategic Conversation*, Chichester, West Sussex: John Wiley and Sons.

Heijden, K. van der (1997) 'Scenarios, Strategies and the Strategy Process', *Nijenrode Research Papers Series, Centre for Organisational Learning and Change*, no. 1997–01.

Heijden, K. van der (2001) 'Back to Basics: Exploring the Business Idea', *Strategy & Leadership*, 29 (3), 13–18.

Hoeks, L. (2002) 'De professor die alles beter wist. De vrije val van Piet Vroon', *De Groene Amsterdammer*, 6 (9 February), .

Idenburg, Ph. J. i.s.m., E.J.C. Boerkamp, P.A. de Ruijter and S. Zuiderveld (2005) *Oog voor de toekomst. Over marketing en consumenten in een veranderende samenleving*, Schiedam: Scriptum.

Janssen, A.N.G. i.s.m., M.R. Gramberger, P.A. de Ruijter and J. van Heijningen (2007) *Regeren is vooruitzien! Scenario's maken en gebruiken voor beleidsontwikkeling, wetgeving en handhaving*, Den Haag: Expertisecentrum Rechtspleging en Rechtshandhaving, Ministerie van Justitie.

Kahane, A. and P. le Roux e.a. (1992) 'The Mont Fleur Scenarios: What Will be South Africa be Like in the Year 2002?' With a New Introduction by Mont Fleur facilitator Adam Kahane, *Deeper News, Global Business Network*, 7 (1).

Kahn, H. and A. Wiener (1967) *The Year 2000: A Framework for Speculation on the Next Thirty-Three Years*, New York: MacMillan.

King, M.L. (1963), 'I have a dream', http://www.archives.gov/press/exhibits/dream-speech.pdf

Khun, T. (1962) *The Structure of Scientific Revolutions*, Chigago: University of Chicago Press.

Leemhuis, J.P. (1985) 'Using Scenarios to Develop Strategies', *Long Range Planning*, 18 (2), 30–37.

Mak, G. (2002) *De eeuw van mijn vader*, Amsterdam: Atlas.

Merton, R.K. (1968) *Social Theory and Social Structure*, New York: Free Press.

Merton, R.K.(1995) 'The Thomas Theorem and The Matthew Effect' *Social Forces*, December 1995, 74(2):379–424.

Ministerie van Defensie (2010) *Eindrapport Verkenningen 2010. Houvast voor de krijgsmacht van de toekomst (Future Policy Survey, A new foundation for the Netherlands' Armed Forces)*, Ministry of Defence; translation available via www.deruijter.com.

Ministerie van Justitie (2010) *Justitie over morgen. Signposts voor scenario's 2006–2010*, Den Haag: Ministerie van Justitie, Directie Algemene Justitiële Strategie.

Mintzberg, H. (1994) 'The Fall and Rise of Strategic Planning', *Harvard Business Review*, January–February, 107–114.

Mintzberg, H., B. Ahlstrand and J. Lampel (1998) *Strategy Safari. A Guided Tour through the Wilds of Strategic Management*, New York: The Free Press.

Nichols, N.A. (1994) 'Scientific Management at Merck: An Interview with CFO Judy Lewent', *Harvard Business Review*, January–February, 89–99.

Noordik, A. and J. Blijsie (2008) *Hartelijk gefaciliteerd! Succesvol veranderen met de workshopaanpak. Praktijkboek voor het ontwerpen en faciliteren van workshops in organisaties*, Deventer: Kluwer.

Notten, P. van (2005) *Writing on the Wall. Scenario development in times of discontinuity*, Boca Raton, Florida: Dissertation.com.

NRC Handelsblad (2008) 'Bos verwacht stevige economische groei', *NRC Handelsblad*, 15 February 2008, www.nrc.nl.

Ogilvy, J.A. (2002) *Creating Better Futures. Scenario Planning as a Tool for a Better Tomorrow*, New York: Oxford University Press.

Porter, M.E. (1985) *Competitive Advantage. Creating and Sustaining Superior Performance*, New York: Free Press.

Prahalad, C.K. and G. Hamel (1990) 'The Core Competence of the Corporation', *Harvard Business Review*, May–June, 79–102.

Rabobank (2003) *Rentescenario's. De prijs van geld tot 2010*, Rabobank Nederland/Stafgroep Economisch Onderzoek (*Interest rate scenarios. The price of money up to 2010*) by Rabobank; translation available at www.deruijter.com.

Rabobank (2008) *Statuten*, www.rabobank.nl.

Rabobank (2009) *Themabericht 2009/13: Zoveel economen, zoveel meningen?*

Rietdijk, M. and M. van Winden (2003) *Slag om de toekomst. Bedrijfsstrategieën voor goede en slechte tijden*, Amsterdam: Balans.

Ruijter, P.A. de (2007) 'Viewing Futures Network: Collaborative Learning and Innovation at Rabobank', in: B. Sharpe, B. en and K. van der Heijden (eds.), (2007) *Scenarios for Success. Turning Insights into Action*, Chichester, West Sussex: John Wiley and Sons.

Ruijter, P.A. de and H.P. Lassche (2006) *Vereniging met toekomst. Scenario's en strategie voor branche- en beroepsorganisaties*, Beekbergen: VM Uitgevers.

Ruijter, P.A. de and N. Janssen (1996) '(Real) Option Thinking and Scenarios', www.deruijter.com.

Ruijter, P.A. de, H.J. Alkema, P. van Veen en and S. Stolk (2009) 'Chess or Go? Strategy and Scenarios: More Relevant than Ever', www. deruijter.com.

Ruijter, P.A. de, H.J. Alkema and S. Stolk (2012) 'How strategic planning can help us through the present world crisis', www.deruijter.com.

Scearce, D., K. Fulton and the Global Business Network community (2004) *What If? The Art of Scenario Thinking for Non-profits*, Global Business Network.

Scheepsbouw Nederland (2008) *5x Aanpakken*, Zoetermeer: Scheepsbouw Nederland (*5x Action*) Holland Shipbuilding Association; summary available at www.deruijter.com.

Schiffers, M. (2009) 'Shell zet investeren in windparken op laag pitje', *Het Financieele Dagblad*, 18 March 2009.

Schütte, P.M. (2008) *Scenario Thinking: Accelerating Strategic Learning*, Schuette & Company Management Consultants, www.schuette.nl.

Senge, P. (1992) *De vijfde discipline. De kunst en praktijk van de lerende organisatie*, Schiedam: Scriptum.

Shell *Memorandum of Association*, July 2005.

Shell (2005) *The Shell Global Scenarios to 2025. The Future Business Environment: Trends, Trade-offs and Choices*, www.shell.com/scenarios.

Soros, G. (2008) *De internationale kredietcrisis. De toekomst van de financiële markten*, Amsterdam/Antwerpen: Uitgeverij Contact.

Sull, D.N. (1999) 'Why Good Companies go Bad', *Harvard Business Review*, July–August, 42–52.

Trompenaars, F. and C. Hampden-Turner (1998) *Over de grenzen van cultuur en management,* Amsterdam: Business Contact.

Uffelen, X. van (2008) 'Bonus is de oorzaak van de kredietcrisis', *de Volkskrant,* 24 October.

Verbond Sectorwerkgevers Overheid, Samenwerkende Centrales Overheidspersoneel en Ministerie van Binnenlandse Zaken en Koninkrijksrelaties (2010) *De grote uittocht. Vier toekomstbeelden van de arbeidsmarkt van onderwijs- en overheidssectoren,* Den Haag: Ministerie van Binnenlandse Zaken en Koninkrijksrelaties.

VNSI (Vereniging Nederlandse Scheepsbouw Industrie) (2005) *Dutch LeaderSHIP 2015. The Power to Lead,* Zoetermeer: VNSI.

Wack, P. (1985a) 'Scenarios: Unchartered Waters Ahead', *Harvard Business Review,* September–October, 73–89.

Wack, P. (1985b) 'Scenarios: Shooting the Rapids', *Harvard Business Review,* November–December, 139–150.

Wetering, C. van de (2009) 'Kracht van verbeelding. Gewogen: masterclass retorica', *PM Magazine,* 25 September, 40–41.

Wilkinson, A. and R. Kupers (2013) 'Living in the futures', *Harvard Business Review,* May.

Wit, B. de and R. Meyer (1998) *Strategy. Process, Content, Context,* London: Thomson Learning.

World Business Council for Sustainable Development (2008) *Energy Efficiency in Buildings, Facts & Trends,* World Business Council for Sustainable Development (WBCSD).

World Business Council for Sustainable Development (2009) *Roadmap for a Transformation of Energy Use in Buildings,* World Business Council for Sustainable Development (WBCSD).

Yergin, D. (2003) [1991], *The Prize. The Epic Quest for Oil, Money & Power,* New York: Free Press.

Acknowledgements

This book started as a dream. Its realization was down to teamwork.

The original Dutch version was written with the help of Saskia Stolk, who used to work with me before she was offered her current job at the Council of the European Union. And it came about with the guidance and inspiration of Dr Henk Alkema, who wrote the 1971 Oil Price Scenarios for Shell which made scenario-based strategy famous.

My partner, Iris van Veen, created this English version based on the Dutch book. Not only did she create a first translation of the original text and illustrations, more importantly she kept everyone involved to the roadmap and managed the project very well, as she does with everything else in life. Together with Jonathan Norman, the editor at Gower who understood what we were trying to achieve and worked hard to help us realize it, she made sure that there is now a book which is accessible for all of those outside the Netherlands.

Finally, there are my colleagues and clients who offered their knowledge, practical help and allowed me to use their cases: Douwe Bekenkamp, Martin Bloem, Leo de Boer, Wim Boonstra, Lineke Botterhuis, Walter Brander, Ton Dassen, Henk van Essen, Henk Harmsen, Jolanda van Heijningen, Lydia van den Heuvel, Renate Kenter, Lucas Lombaers, Cees Onderwater, Ton van Oijen, Vincent Pijpers, Douwe van Rees, Sebastian Reyn, Bram Roelse, Martijn Schouten, Peter Schütte, Kees Turnhout, Peter van Wijck and many others.

I thank you all for making this vision become real!

About the Author

This is the story of Paul de Ruijter. Paul wrote his Master's thesis on 'Scenarios to Strategy' for the University of Twente based on his experience at Shell Group Planning in London. After that, he applied the scenario methodology to develop science and technology policy at the Royal Netherlands Academy of Arts and Sciences in Amsterdam.

Paul is managing director of De Ruijter Strategy, and he has been involved with scenario based strategy projects with clients ranging from cities, non-governmental organizations (NGOs), ministries, trade associations, multinationals and global institutions. Paul is Executive Lecturer at Nyenrode University, Delft University and the University of Amsterdam and is a renowned speaker at international congresses and seminars.

He is co-author of a book about business opportunities in South-Africa (1992), a book about Industrial Policy in the Netherlands (1999) and one on scenarios at Rabobank (2004). He has written a chapter in *Scenarios for Success* (2008) and was the lead author of a handbook on using scenarios in the public sector (2004) and another about scenarios and strategy for trade associations (2006).

Index